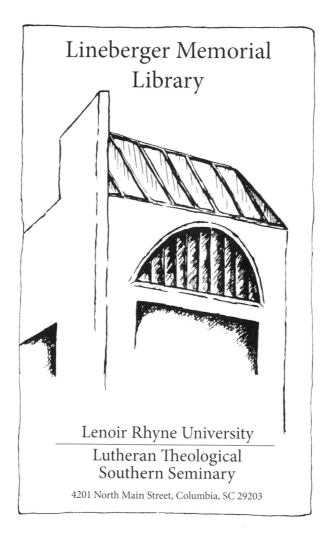

LIBRARY OF RELIGIOUS BIOGRAPHY

Edited by Mark A. Noll and Heath W. Carter

The LIBRARY OF RELIGIOUS BIOGRAPHY is a series of original biographies on important religious figures throughout American and British history.

The authors are well-known historians, each a recognized authority in the period of religious history in which his or her subject lived and worked. Grounded in solid research of both published and archival sources, these volumes link the lives of their subjects — not always thought of as "religious" persons — to the broader cultural contexts and religious issues that surrounded them. Each volume includes a bibliographical essay and an index to serve the needs of students, teachers, and researchers.

Marked by careful scholarship yet free of footnotes and academic jargon, the books in this series are well-written narratives meant to be *read* and *enjoyed* as well as studied.

LIBRARY OF RELIGIOUS BIOGRAPHY

William Ewart Gladstone: Faith and Politics in Victorian Britain
David Bebbington

Aimee Semple McPherson: Everybody's Sister • *Edith L. Blumhofer*

Her Heart Can See: The Life and Hymns of Fanny J. Crosby
Edith L. Blumhofer

Abraham Kuyper: Modern Calvinist, Christian Democrat • *James D. Bratt*

Orestes A. Brownson: American Religious Weathervane • *Patrick W. Carey*

Thomas Merton and the Monastic Vision • *Lawrence S. Cunningham*

Billy Sunday and the Redemption of Urban America • *Lyle W. Dorsett*

The Kingdom Is Always but Coming: A Life of Walter Rauschenbusch
Christopher H. Evans

Liberty of Conscience: Roger Williams in America • *Edwin S. Gaustad*

Sworn on the Altar of God: A Religious Biography of Thomas Jefferson
Edwin S. Gaustad

Abraham Lincoln: Redeemer President • *Allen C. Guelzo*

Charles G. Finney and the Spirit of American Evangelicalism
Charles E. Hambrick-Stowe

Francis Schaeffer and the Shaping of Evangelical America • *Barry Hankins*

Damning Words: The Life and Religious Times of H. L. Mencken
D. G. Hart

The First American Evangelical: A Short Life of Cotton Mather
Rick Kennedy

Harriet Beecher Stowe: A Spiritual Life • *Nancy Koester*

Emily Dickinson and the Art of Belief • *Roger Lundin*

A Short Life of Jonathan Edwards • *George M. Marsden*

The Puritan as Yankee: A Life of Horace Bushnell • *Robert Bruce Mullin*

Prophetess of Health: A Study of Ellen G. White • *Ronald L. Numbers*

Blaise Pascal: Reasons of the Heart • *Marvin R. O'Connell*

Occupy Until I Come: A. T. Pierson and the Evangelization of the World
Dana L. Robert

God's Strange Work: William Miller and the End of the World • *David L. Rowe*

The Divine Dramatist: George Whitefield and the
Rise of Modern Evangelicalism • *Harry S. Stout*

Assist Me to Proclaim: The Life and Hymns of Charles Wesley
John R. Tyson

Damning Words

The Life and Religious Times
of H. L. Mencken

D. G. Hart

WILLIAM B. EERDMANS PUBLISHING COMPANY

GRAND RAPIDS, MICHIGAN

Wm. B. Eerdmans Publishing Co.
2140 Oak Industrial Drive N.E., Grand Rapids, Michigan 49505
www.eerdmans.com

Published 2016
Printed in the United States of America

22 21 20 19 18 17 16   1 2 3 4 5 6 7

ISBN 978-0-8028-7344-6

Library of Congress Cataloging-in-Publication Data

Names: Hart, D. G. (Darryl G.), author.
Title: Damning words : the life and religious times of H. L. Mencken / D. G. Hart.
Description: Grand Rapids, Michigan : Wm. B. Eerdmans Publishing, Co., [2016] |
    Series: Library of religious biography | Includes bibliographical references and index.
Identifiers: LCCN 2016024767 | ISBN 9780802873446
Subjects: LCSH: Mencken, H. L. (Henry Louis), 1880–1956. | Mencken, H. L. (Henry
    Louis), 1880–1956—Religion. | Authors, American—20th century—Biography. |
    Journalists—United States—Biography. | Editors—United States—Biography.
Classification: LCC PS3525.E43 Z5823 2016 | DDC 818/.5209 [B]—dc23
    LC record available at https://lccn.loc.gov/2016024767

To Annie,
my Baltimore bambina

Contents

Foreword

Whatever in the world could lead the Wm. B. Eerdmans Publishing Company, a firm with a well-deserved reputation for its serious Christian books, to sponsor a volume on H. L. Mencken in a series of *religious* biographies? And whatever could have led Darryl Hart, himself the author of several worthy books patiently explaining the virtues of historical Calvinism, to think that any one at all could be interested in a *religious* biography of H. L. Mencken?

If a few knowledgeable academics might still remember Mencken as a major literary critic of the early twentieth century or a diligent student of the English language as spoken in North America, he is known to even more for his *assaults* on the Christian faith. My own history of engagement with Mencken might be representative. During the many occasions I taught courses on early-modern British history or early American history and paused in the effort to define "Puritanism," it would usually get at least a chuckle to quote something that H. L. Mencken published, as it happens, in 1917: "Puritanism is the haunting fear that someone, somewhere, may be happy." I'm pretty sure I also knew of his pithy put-down from 1949, though do not remember using it in class ("Show me a Puritan and I'll show you a son-of-a-bitch").

More commonly known is Mencken's evisceration of William Jennings Bryan and those who stood with Bryan in the evolution trial of John T. Scopes in 1925 at Dayton, Tennessee. The trial, which took place in the South--to Mencken "the Sahara of the Bozart"--allowed the journalist to depict the aging politician in the worst possible light: "a tinpot pope in the coca-cola belt and a brother to the forlorn pastors who belabor half-wits in galvanized iron tabernacles behind the railroad yards."

When Bryan died only a few days after the end of this trial, Mencken's column spread on the vitriol so thickly that it was censored by his usually indulgent editors at the Baltimore *Sun*.

Mencken, to be sure, remains eminently quotable, but also implacably antagonistic to anything that might reflect favorably on Christian faith.

As Darryl Hart is not afraid to document, the picture might seem only to get worse from finding out more about Mencken's opinions. Although renowned as a journalist, author, lexicographer, literary scholar, and master wordsmith, Mencken troubled some of his contemporaries with his enthusiasm for the pessimistic nihilism of Friedrich Nietzsche. He bothered even more with his belittling of democracy and his willingness to write critically about George Washington and Abraham Lincoln. After Mencken's private papers were published some years after his death, it turns out that he also shared the antisemitism that was then common among a certain set of sophisticated Anglo Americans, but that has become so widely condemned in our own.

A religious biography of this guy? Come on, Darryl! Come on, Eerdmans!

Attentive readers of this book will want to think again. Hart does not pretend that the Baltimore journalist-critic-writer with capacious intellectual curiosity was some kind of a crypto-Christian or saint-out-of-doors. Nor does he think that Mencken contributed directly or positively to strengthening Christian beliefs or practices.

He does, however, make a convincing case that close attention to this flamboyantly anti-religious figure pays significant dividends for those who do take the faith seriously. For one, Mencken had no time for the standard civil religion in which American ideals and Christian virtues are mushed together in a romantic longing for this-worldly social harmony. Mencken held that such visionary idealism blinded observers to the many serious flaws, injustices, and inanities that American civilization, like all civilizations, was rife. It is a sentiment that believers might also take to heart, especially because it comes close to the emphases of Christian realism in an Augustinian perspective.

Hart also makes a good case that Mencken's dyspeptic view of humanity led him to perceptive judgments about people, institutions, and events that could be similar to those made by believers who view humans as always in need of redemption (or sanctification). On the rare occasions when Mencken had positive things to say about Christianity or individual Christians, it was to point out how useful the faith was when it *opposed* conventional attitudes.

Hart shows as well that Mencken can be appropriated to underscore an uncomfortable biblical truth. Where believers in the United States have often been defensively protective of various rights or privileges or traditions, Jesus taught that his disciples would always face hostility or persecution or disdain in the world. This contrarian perspective, in Hart's judgment, deserves as much consideration as versions of the faith that, whether from the Left or the Right, seek to win over the larger culture.

Finally, Hart commends Mencken as an equal-opportunity critic. He finds ample proof that Mencken could blast away at utopian socialists and modernist theologians as vigorously as he did at traditional Christians. In passing Hart also notes how much richer (and much funnier) were Mencken's critiques of conventional religion than the shafts of the so-called New Atheists of our own day.

As this fine book shows, H. L. Mencken developed his acerbic stance over against an overwhelmingly Protestant culture. Those today who value the Christian elements in that culture, or who seek to reverse its mistakes, could find a surprising measure of guidance from this unexpected source. *That* is why this book makes an excellent contribution to a Library of Religious Biography.

MARK A. NOLL

Acknowledgments

Before 1983 I only knew Baltimore by its Harbor Tunnel, part of the Hart family route to relatives in North Carolina, or by trips with Christian summer camp staff to see the Orioles, back in the glory days of Earl Weaver and Brooks Robinson. But the accidents of graduate study transported my wife and me from Cambridge, Massachusetts to enroll at Johns Hopkins University, situated in a town that branded itself "Charm City." That attribute was not immediately obvious. But Baltimore's charms, subtle though they were, became evident during the six years we lived and worked there. It helped considerably that my dissertation subject, the Baltimore native, J. Gresham Machen, added historical depth to our experience (we lived in the same neighborhood where he played as a boy). Since then, the charms of Baltimore have been visible for consumers of Hollywood's chief export. Barry Levinson's four movies about Jewish life in Baltimore—*Diner*, *Tin Men*, *Avalon*, and *Liberty Heights*—reveal a city sufficiently vibrant to fuel his imagination. More recently, HBO's production of David Simon's *The Wire* shows a urban setting as much a character in the drama of cops and drug dealers as Bunk Moreland and Omar Little. Reading and writing about H. L. Mencken has been the icing on the cake. If Baltimore could produce the likes of Machen, Levinson, Simon, and Mencken, people from a small municipality very much in the shadow of the nation's capital and big urban siblings to the northeast, the city must have its charms. My wife's and my lives have been richer for Baltimore's contribution to national life. This book is a partial payment of our debt.

My first serious encounter with Baltimore's "bad boy" goes back to Johns Hopkins when James H. Smylie, then editor of *American Pres-*

byterians: Journal of Presbyterian History, asked my advisor, Timothy L. Smith, to recommend a graduate student to write about Mencken and Presbyterians in the United States. I had already encountered Mencken through Machen (as the introduction explains, Mencken wrote two pieces about his cross-town Calvinist). The article that Smylie eventually published included Mencken's reactions and critiques of Woodrow Wilson, Billy Sunday, William Jennings Bryan, and Machen. That inquiry was a foretaste of the delight I would experience while working on this book, a project fiddled with off and on for the last decade. Not every reader will find Mencken as appealing as this reader does. Some might regard him as cocky, overwrought, indulgent, vulgar, blasphemous, and just plain wrong. But given how well he was received in his own day and continues to be quoted by journalists and pundits, Mencken has more assets than liabilities. Joseph Epstein explained those advantages well when he wrote, "Mencken is one of that too-small company of modern writers who can make one laugh aloud." Epstein added, "Mencken's comedy—of phrase, of formulation, of perspective—partly explains his ability to lift the spirits." Mencken had no interest in uplift, to be sure. Yet, he has elevated my disposition for the last thirty years thanks in part to the unlikely search by a Presbyterian editor for a piece about a virulent and self-proclaimed anti-Calvinist.

As much as writers continue to invoke Mencken, serious investigation of him on the order of the attention given to Benjamin Franklin, William James, or Jonathan Edwards is scant. That is unfortunate but also the consequence of Mencken's refusal to endear himself to the world of professional scholarship where panels at academic conferences and university presses keep canonical authors alive. That is all the more reason why anyone who studies Mencken is indebted (as I am) to the labors of Fred Hobson, Terry Teachout, Vincent Fitzpatrick, and Marion Elizabeth Rodgers, biographers and editors who have without the subsidies and infrastructure of graduate programs and university libraries prevented Mencken from lapsing into antiquarian oblivion. This book may take religion more seriously than theirs, but without those biographers' strong shoulders this book would not be upright.

Two final words of thanks: the first to the administration of Hillsdale College where I have been teaching in the history department while writing this book. My colleagues and superiors have supported my labors in many ways but of special note, and deserving hearty thanks, is the college's funding for the images reproduced in this book. The second expression of gratitude goes to the officers and members of the Mencken Society, especially its president, Robert J. Brugger. This small organization promotes Mencken and his offbeat outlook. Attendance at its annual meeting has always stimulated fresh considerations of Mencken and his times. Those gatherings also afford my wife, Ann, to whom this book is dedicated, and me a welcome chance to return to the city that still possesses some of the charms that Mencken knew. Her capacity to enjoy with me the fun that Mencken poked at believers like us is one of those endearing attributes that make our marriage a delight.

Hillsdale, Michigan
June 3, 2016

Introduction

H. L. Mencken remains a man who needs no introduction to any American familiar with literary and social criticism during the first half of the twentieth century. A reporter for the *Baltimore Sun*, who covered most of the national political conventions for four decades, along with the Scopes trial, and prize boxing matches to boot, Mencken became a literary critic for the *Smart Set*, eventually took over that magazine, and then went on to found another literary publication, the *American Mercury*. As editor, Mencken published the early work of Sherwood Anderson, Willa Cather, William Faulkner, F. Scott Fitzgerald, James Joyce, Eugene O'Neill, and Ezra Pound. Many of those same authors revered Mencken. Even Ernest Hemingway, a novelist for whom Mencken had little regard, paid deference to the *American Mercury*'s editor in *The Sun Also Rises*. To explain Robert Cohn's inability to enjoy Paris, Hemingway blamed Mencken, who "hates Paris, I believe. So many young men get their likes and dislikes from Mencken."

The author of more than fifty books—the first to write in English on George Bernard Shaw and on Friedrich Nietzsche—Mencken wrote on topics that ranged as far afield as women and European night life. Mencken was also an amateur philologist whose *American Language* catalogued sometimes brilliantly the differences between British and American English. That overview hardly does justice to Mencken's output and influence. According to the literary critic Alfred Kazin, "If Mencken had never lived, it would have taken a whole army of assorted philosophers, monologists, editors, and patrons of the new writing to make up for him." According to Edmund Wilson, longtime critic for the *New Yorker* and the *New Republic*, Mencken was "without question, since Poe, our greatest practicing literary journalist." According to Terry Teachout, another critic and one of Mencken's biographers, Wilson's acknowledgment was "[i]f anything an understatement."

Aside from the sheer volume of his writing, Mencken was remarkable for a prose style rarely executed before or since. In a review of one of his books, Walter Lippmann acknowledged that Mencken's practice of calling average people "cockroaches and lice" lapsed into "unjust tirades." Even so, Mencken had attracted a large readership because "this Holy Terror from Baltimore is splendidly and exultantly and contagiously alive. He calls you a swine, and an imbecile, and he increases your will to live." Joseph Wood Krutch, a writer for the *Nation*, wrote soon after Mencken's death that the Baltimorean was the best prose writer in twentieth-century America, a man whose gift "was inimitable" and who used "as a genuine instrument of expression a vocabulary and a rhythm which in other hands stubbornly refused to yield anything but vulgarity." More recently, Joseph Epstein wrote that much of Mencken's appeal owed to his comedy and uplift. "Some writers . . . do lift one out of the gloom, and away from the valley of small and large woes," Epstein explained. Mencken was one of them, and one of the ways he did that, Epstein added, was by having "an appreciation for the reality of things." "His animus against the [idealists] of the world is that, with their concepts and notions, they flattened out reality—and, in the act of doing so, not only got things wrong but made them less interesting than they are." The collision of Mencken's candor and Americans' idealism was always riveting. To capture some of that amusement, this book violates rules learned in graduate school. This book includes many block quotations, the crutch of the young historian. The hope is that readers unfamiliar with Mencken will appreciate the appeal of his prose. Another reason for violating historical protocol is to stave off the boredom that afflicts authors when reading and proofing manuscripts. At least Mencken will keep this reader awake.

Even more remarkable than Mencken's felicity with the English language was the life responsible for this dent in the world of American letters. He was the son of a solidly middle-class cigar producer whose intention was for his son to inherit the business. Mencken received only a high school education, and a vocational one at that. Only after his father's unexpected death was Mencken free to pursue what had been his chief end as a high schooler—journalism. Covering a small city for a second-string newspaper was not the recipe for establishing national literary fame. In addition to distinguishing himself as a reporter who would tackle almost any assignment, in his spare time Mencken wrote reviews for magazines and also authored limited-print-run books on contemporary authors. His work ethic was unparalleled, but Mencken played as hard as he worked. Only in his early thirties, when he began to write popular op-ed columns that became syndicated and also edit literary magazines, did Mencken achieve a national reputation, one that lasted for the better part of three decades. By the time health forced him to stop writing at the age of sixty-eight, Mencken had written, by his own estimate, over 10 million words (at 250 words per page, that is 2.5 million manuscript pages), and that does not include correspondence. Mencken remains one of the most frequently quoted authors.

What does any of this have to do with religion? Why should Mencken qualify for entry in a series of religious biographies of prominent Americans? To say that Christianity framed Mencken may sound like an overstatement or an expression of pious, wishful thinking. At a basic level, Mencken represents a later iteration of the Enlightenment outlook—the capacity of reason to arrive at truth, the need for freedom of inquiry and speech, the danger of privileging family, wealth, and creed. If so, then the Christian religion framed Mencken's attitude in a manner comparable to the way that Christianity functioned as the backdrop to the Enlightenment. The incomparable intellectual historian Henry F. May wrote that Protestantism framed the Enlightenment in America and was responsible for the interplay, contest, and mingling of religious and secular conceptions of "the nature of the universe and man's place in it, and about human nature itself." May added that "Protestantism [was] always in the background, the matrix, rival, ally, and enemy" of the Enlightenment. If Protestant Christianity functioned this way for a variety of free and heterodox thinkers in the late eighteenth century, it continued to do so in Mencken's era, even if not at the same level of philosophical reflection. Everywhere he turned, Mencken could not help running into Christian assumptions and expressions. If Mencken went to the national convention for the Progressive Party in 1912, he heard the delegates sing "Onward, Christian Soldiers." If he tried to publish or promote literature that was the slightest bit frank about the less virtuous aspects of sex, he faced obscenity laws. If he covered the deliberations of state governments, he encountered laws that prohibited teaching about human origins that contradicted Genesis. And if he wanted to have a drink between 1918 and 1933, he had to do so illegally. Everywhere Mencken went, he ran into Christian expressions and influences that most Americans considered to be normal, routine, unobjectionable, like the way that American shoppers in the month of December continue to take references to Christ's birth or crooning about it for granted.

As a skeptic and a nonbeliever, Mencken had to find a way to clear space for all his words and ideas, and for many of his amusements. How he did that was important. Unlike today's "new atheists," Mencken did not rant, and he did not engage in ridicule, at least not without some real knowledge of Christianity and its adherents.

The point is not that Christianity defined Mencken and that he ironically owed a debt to the believers who bemused him. Instead, taking account of his life makes little sense without noticing how his literary battles with Puritanism, his columns against Prohibition, his pointed coverage of the Scopes trial, his protracted legal contest with Boston's Watch and Ward Society, or the book he considered his most important, *Treatise on the Gods*, set Mencken apart from his contemporaries and gave him a lot to say along with a large readership that wanted to listen. Christianity and its dominant position in American society was not responsible for producing Mencken. But it was a sufficiently large part of his experience and thought to justify a religious biography.

Two different audiences could benefit from reading the pages that follow. The first is Mencken aficionados and students of twentieth-century American literary life before World War II. For many of these readers, Mencken represents a rabble-rouser and iconoclast who took aim at Christianity because he perceived it as a genuine threat to literary accomplishment everywhere in a Protestant-saturated United States. What may surprise those familiar with Mencken is how much he wrote about Christianity and the manner in which he wrote. A standard account of Mencken and religion is that he mainly ridiculed belief in hopes of removing it from its privileged position in American life. S. T. Joshi, for instance, writes in the introduction to a collection of essays on religion, that Mencken "was one of the last American intellectuals to speak out forcefully, pungently, and satirically against the follies of religion." Joshi adds, Mencken relentlessly "exposed the multitudinous absurdities presented to his gaze by a country in which Fundamentalists, Christian Scientists, theosophists, and religionists of every other creed and sect cavorted before a populace too foolish and credulous to detect the logical fallacies and contradictions to known fact that every religion offers in such abundance." Mencken's most recent biographer, Marion Elizabeth Rodgers, may not share Joshi's animus toward religious belief, but she too frames Mencken as first and foremost a defender of liberty, someone who sought to remove every barrier to the "sacred documents" of the Constitution and Bill of Rights. For Rodgers, chief components of that libertarian project were Mencken's efforts to rally Clarence Darrow to defend John T. Scopes's teaching of evolution in a Dayton, Tennessee, public school, and to remove the stifling influence of "Victorian Puritanism" in American literature. Yet, what people who share Mencken's scorn for religion do not notice is that he devoted far more time to religious beliefs, practices, and institutions than someone who was simply antagonistic might reasonably spend. Mencken was also much more conversant with Christian theology and the niceties of church polity and liturgy than someone might expect of a person only interested in stripping the altars bare. To be sure, Mencken remained throughout his life unmoved by the claims of Christianity. But he also recognized that its concerns, writings, and institutions were significant aspects of human existence that could no more be dismissed than death, ambition, friendship, taxes, and the veneration of Abraham Lincoln.

The other group of readers who may benefit from an acquaintance with Mencken comprises those interested in the history of Christianity in the United States. In writing about the 1920s, for instance, Sydney Ahlstrom said Mencken "piped the tune and provided the laughs" for young intellectuals when the Baltimorean wrote, "Every day a new Catholic church goes up; every day another Methodist or Presbyterian church is turned into a garage." George Marsden also appealed to Mencken in his book on fundamentalism to provide a sense of how contemporaries described conservative Protestantism and to offer Mencken's choice vernacular: "Heave an egg out a Pullman window and you will hit a Fundamentalist almost anywhere in the United States today." Mencken also makes for good copy in the biographies of his religious contemporaries, such as Edith Blumhofer's account of the Los Angeles evangelist Aimee Semple McPherson. There she refers to a column that Mencken wrote in 1926 during Sister Aimee's trial for perjury in fabricating her kidnapping. Mencken could not resist the irony: "no self-respecting judge in the Maryland Free State, drunk or sober," would entertain charges for "perjury uttered in defense of her honor." Aside from the flair that Mencken's quotations add, his lifetime of reflections about and reactions to Christianity in the United States provides a remarkably handy source for understanding how non-Christians perceived Christians. Historians of religion are good at exploring believers and their own self-understanding, or even the squabbles that often divided Christians. But what does Christian ministry and endeavor look like from the outside? Might the matters that believers considered so momentous take on a different hue when seen through the eyes of someone who was knowledgeable but had no stake in the controversy? Might Mencken's observations render molehills out of the mountains on which Christians sometimes died? And most importantly, might Mencken's reflections about American Christianity reveal a naïveté among believers who regarded their nation Christian even when populated by writers like Mencken and his fans? What if Christians had to legislate, formulate policy, support academic institutions, patronize museums, and run for office knowing that folks like Mencken were as much a part of the citizenry as were the faithful?

To demonstrate the rewards paid by a consideration of Mencken's attitude toward Christianity, consider his commentary on J. Gresham Machen. For people who know the history of Christianity in the United States, Machen is a relatively familiar figure, the scholarly Presbyterian fundamentalist who taught at Princeton Seminary, combated liberalism in the Presbyterian Church USA, and formed a renegade seminary (Westminster) and denomination (Orthodox Presbyterian). He was relatively popular in the 1920s, though not nearly as famous as William Jennings Bryan, Aimee Semple McPherson, or Billy Sunday, and his hometown was Mencken's, though Machen and Mencken came from different sides of the Jones Falls. To Mencken devotees, Machen is just one more obscure figure from the past, no more familiar than Sylvanius Stall, another clergyman, whose views on sex hygiene attracted Mencken's attention. But Mencken not only knew about Machen and wrote two short pieces about him. Mencken also revealed a level of discernment about the fundamentalist controversy that may surprise religious historians as much as Mencken's followers.

Mencken first wrote about Machen in 1931 for the *American Mercury* in a piece called "The Impregnable Rock." He began by noting Machen's relative obscurity compared to the "clowns" Aimee Semple McPherson, Billy Sunday, and John Roach Straton. In comparison, Machen "was no mere soap-boxer of God, alarming bucolic sinners for a percentage of the plate." Mencken may have been giving Machen the Baltimore ben-

6

efit of the doubt. It did not hurt that Machen's defense of the "inspired integrity of Holy Writ" wound up exposing the hypocrisy of Prohibition. That Machen was a "wet," Mencken explained, was "remarkable in a Presbyterian." But Mencken assumed Machen was a wet because "the Yahweh of the Old Testament and the Jesus of the New are both wet— because the whole Bible is, in fact, wet." Beyond Mencken's irreverent dig at the Word of God, he understood the importance of scriptural authority to Protestants and saw through modernist and evangelical appeals to anything else:

> The instant [modernists] admit that only part of the Bible may be rejected, if it be only the most trifling fly-speck in the Pauline Epistles, they admit that any other part may be rejected. The divine authority of the whole disappears, and there is no more evidence that Christianity is a revealed religion than there is that Mohammedanism is. . . . They thus reduce theology to the humble level of a debate over probabilities. . . . The Catholics get rid of the difficulty by setting up an infallible Pope, and consenting formally to accept his verdicts, but the Protestants simply chase their own tails. By depriving revelation of all force and authority, they rob their so-called religion of every dignity.

Of course, lots of Protestants disagreed with Mencken's "impregnable" logic. He was, however, capable of entertaining a basic contention of Protestant Christianity and following its implications even after writing a book, *Treatise on the Gods*, that argued that religion was little more than the construction of human weakness.

In January of 1937, Mencken again turned to Machen. The occasion this time was the latter's sudden death on the first of the year after a brief bout with pneumonia. Once again, Mencken could not resist taking a swipe at William Jennings Bryan, and used Machen to wind up:

> The fantastic William Jennings Bryan, in his day the country's most distinguished Presbyterian layman, was against Dr. Machen on the issue of Prohibition but with him on the issue of Modernism. But Bryan's support, of course, was of little value or consolation to so intelligent a man. Bryan was a Fundamentalist of the Tennessee or barnyard school. His theological ideas were those of a somewhat backward child of 8, and his defense of Holy Writ at Dayton during the Scopes trial was so ignorant and stupid that it must have given Dr.

Machen a great deal of pain. Dr. Machen himself was to Bryan as the Matterhorn is to a wart. His Biblical studies had been wide and deep, and he was familiar with the almost interminable literature of the subject. Moreover, he was an adept theologian, and had a wealth of professional knowledge to support his ideas. Bryan could only bawl.

Despite the cheap shot, Mencken once again displayed an ability, sometimes lacking both in students of American Christianity and among his devotees, to see a difference among Bible believers, even Presbyterian ones. Furthermore, Mencken also recognized, despite his own disbelief, that as much as supernatural faiths might look fantastic in the modern world, the adherents of those faiths could be admirable in maintaining apparently laughable convictions. Thus, Mencken could not resist noting the folly of the progressive, respectable, and intelligent Protestants who dominated the mainline churches:

> [Modernists] have tried to get rid of all the logical difficulties of religion, and yet preserve a generally pious cast of mind. It is a vain enterprise. What they have left, once they have achieved their imprudent scavenging, is hardly more than a row of hollow platitudes, as empty [of] psychological force and effect as so many nursery rhymes. They may be good people and they may even be contented and happy, but they are no more religious than Dr. Einstein. Religion is something else again—in Henrik Ibsen's phrase, something far more deep-down-diving and mudupbringing. Dr. Machen tried to impress that obvious fact upon his fellow adherents of the Geneva Mohammed. He failed—but he was undoubtedly right.

Mencken seemed to be able to tell the difference, again in ways remarkably better than students or deriders of American Christianity, between the serious and the ephemeral forms of belief. For that ability, at least, he deserves sustained attention.

To be clear, the aim is not to encourage readers to regard Mencken as a thinker with incomparable insight into the meaning of life, the mechanics of language or logic, or the nature of society and politics. Mencken was a man of definite opinions but without a desire to create a school of thought or a movement. He was merely one writer among many who trusted his own judgments, who sought and enjoyed notoriety, but who also liked being a dissenter from all the political, literary, or philosophical parties. "I am my own party," Mencken wrote. The mistake is to read Mencken as anything more than an uncannily witty, gifted, and prolific author and editor who stirred up as much trouble in America's established institutions as any American ever did. As Fred Hobson concluded after writing his own version of Mencken's life, he "was a remarkable man who led a life that was rich, full, complex, historically significant—above all, fascinating." The contention here is that religion was not merely a bystander in Mencken's experience and career but a significant part of his reflection and output. Few who have studied Mencken attach much significance to his writing about faith. What needs to be seen is that his observations of and reactions to religion were as much a part of his writing as were his complaints about urban politics or the American novel.

In addition to identifying an understudied part of Mencken's life, this book may even have relevance for the vexatious nature of religion in the nation's public life. How Mencken handled a subject that had so little appeal to him personally and produced so much mischief may be instructive both to believers and to skeptics at a time when the United States is even more prone to religion-inspired hysteria than in an earlier era when liquor, dirty novels, and contraceptives were illegal. Mencken will not put an end to the so-called culture wars. His attitude as an unbelieving minority in a majority Christian society, however, might show a way to demilitarize the combat.

CHAPTER ONE

Lamentable Heresies

H. L. Mencken was baptized in the fall of 1880, a few months after his birth on September 12, into the Protestant Episcopal Church. His baptized name was Henry Louis. The initials came later when, in his first business venture as a nine-year-old printer of business cards and a neighborhood newspaper, Mencken's choice of movable type prevented spelling out his whole Christian name. With the *r*'s in his printing kit either broken or defective, he resorted to "H. L."

Previous biographers have generally avoided attributing any significance to Mencken's baptism. When mentioned, the Christian initiation rite is simply rendered a convention of nineteenth-century American culture in which Mencken's parents obligingly participated. This interpretation makes sense since, along with his extended family, Mencken was never a churchgoer or claimed to be a Christian. But something in those baptismal waters hooked Mencken because the Christian religion would never be far from his observations of the world or how he understood himself in contrast to the rest of his fellow Americans. Even though Mencken would eventually be received into communion in the Lutheran church, his dissent from American pieties contributed to his emergence as one of the most astute observers of American Christianity whose mocking might have done more good for the body of Christ if his devout readers had not been so shocked by his irreverence. His experiences as a boy, which included large doses of Christian influence, helped him become a major critic of the American version of Christian civilization along with its inconsistencies and blemishes. His baptism was simply his initiation into a world with which he would have to reckon (even if many of his interpreters have not).

Questionable Characters

Later in life, Mencken wrote that his ancestors "for three hundred years back were all bad citizens." He explained that they "weren't moral—in the conventional sense" and were "always against what the rest were for." As much as Mencken used this genealogy to explain his own iconoclastic temper, his baptism as an Episcopalian points to a different side of his family. The Christian rite by no means indicated a family of churchgoers or even Godfearers. But it did very much reveal Christian morality "in the conventional sense."

The Menckens of the Old World hailed from the vicinity of Bremen and achieved no distinction until the first half of the seventeenth century. Then Eilard Menke (the original family name) became the arch-presbyter at the cathedral of Marienwerder (now Kwidzyn). But Mencken's family traced their lineage to one of Eilard's cousins, Helmrich. A merchant in Oldenburg, Helmrich produced a son, Lueder, who refused to continue in the family business and went out on his own by completing in 1682 a PhD at Leipzig University. Lueder taught law at the university for most of his career—in addition to serving as rector. His brother, Johann, was also an academic, who stood at the front of a line of professors in the Mencken family who taught at Leipzig, Wittenberg, and Halle. The family member with whom Mencken most identified was Johann Burkard Mencke, another PhD, who completed his degree in 1694 and four years later, at the age of twenty-four, was elected a member of the Royal Society. A year later he became the editor of what many consider the first scholarly journal to be published in Germany (*Acta Eruditorum*). The reason for the American Mencken's identification with Johann Burkard was not so much his scholarly accomplishments as his capacity for mocking such achievements. A 1715 work, *The Charlatanry of the Learned*, exposed satirically the pretensions of scholars and pedants. "It gave me a great shock," Mencken reported to a friend. "All my stock in trade was there—loud assertions, heavy buffooneries, slashing attacks on the professors."

This discovery, however, did not come until Mencken was in his thirties, and it gave him a way to chart the history of the West. The eighteenth century of Johann Burkard Mencke represented the high point of Mencken family cultural fortunes and of European civilization more generally. It was a time, according to Mencken, when life was "pleasanter and more spacious than ever before." It "got rid of religion," "lifted music to first place among the arts," "took eating and drinking out of the stable and put them into the parlor," and "invented the first really comfortable human habitations ever seen on earth." It was also the time when Mencken's forebears made their mark in Leipzig with a street named Menckestrasse and a memorial window in the city's Thomaskirche.

But the Mencken clan declined and fell after ancestors moved to Wittenberg and endured the Napoleonic Wars and the subsequent French occupation of the city. Mencken's great-grandfather, Johann Christian August (1797–1867), was the first family member for almost 150 years not to have attended university. He also lacked a profession and made his way by working on farms and eventually operating an inn. His son (Mencken's grandfather), Burkardt Ludwig (1828–1891), apprenticed as a cigar maker in Saxony, the trade that sustained the family through the 1890s and that Henry Louis would be expected to inherit and maintain. The grandfather took his trade to the United States in 1848, after the democratic revolutions in Europe that made the democracy in North America look orderly had occurred. Burkardt Ludwig quickly established himself, and his business as a cigar maker and shopkeeper, in Baltimore. Despite the heavy influx of German immigrants to the United States during the 1840s, Mencken's grandfather remained aloof from German American immigrant culture and institutions. An indication of such ethnic independence was his marriage to Harriet McLelland, a woman of English and Scottish stock. Burkardt's independence was also responsible for the American line of Menckens being baptized not as Lutherans but as Episcopalians.

Mencken's mother's side of the family, the Abhaus, was much less accomplished than the Menckens. His mother's line was also much more German. They came to America from Hesse, though they had originally been French Protestants who sought refuge in Germany during the troubles of church reform in France. In 1852 Mencken's grandfather, Carl Heinrich Abhau, settled in Baltimore and tried to make a life as a cabinetmaker. Unlike the Menckens, who were aloof from the German community in Baltimore and only went to church (Episcopal) for the baptism of a baby, the Abhaus throughout the 1860s and 1870s entered fully into German American life, which included attending services at the Lutheran church. Mencken later expressed gratitude for the peasant stock of his Abhau ancestors. "If it were not for my peasant blood, the Mencken element would have made a professor out of me."

Whatever the influence of distant ancestors, Mencken's parents, August and Anna, met at festivities sponsored by Baltimore's German Americans, and in 1879 were married. August had excelled in math during his brief education in a private school but left the halls of learning to work odd jobs in Pennsylvania before returning to Baltimore to establish his own (with his brother) cigar manufacturing firm (somewhat against the designs of his father). August's marriage to Anna also escaped the designs of the Mencken *paterfamilias*—whom Henry later described as the "undisputed head of the American branch of the Menckenii" with "jurisdiction over all its thirty members." Whenever Burkardt arrived in August's home, "he deposited his hat on the floor beside his chair, mopped his dome meditatively, and let it be known that he was ready for the business of the day"—which included everything from "infant feeding and the choice of wallpaper at one extreme to marriage settlements and the intricacies of dogmatic theology at the other." Although August's choice of a bride had escaped the elder Mencken's rule, Burkardt did require the son to be married in Baltimore's Saint John the Baptist Episcopal Church.

Later in life, Mencken would reveal opinions about Germany during the United States' intervention in European wars that would cost him professionally and personally, but those notions he hardly inherited from his father, who continued in Burkardt's isolation from Baltimore's German American community. Unlike the grandfather who celebrated the glories of Old World Mencken success even while looking down on German American commoners, the father disregarded even family accomplishments. A successful merchant of cigars, with shops in Baltimore and Washington, DC, August supported a Mencken brood that began with Henry's birth on September 12, 1880. It was a conventional middle-class home in which the baby was "encapsulated in affection, and kept fat, saucy, and contented." By the time he turned three, the family had moved from renting to home ownership. The location chosen on Baltimore's west side was definitely "not a German neighborhood."

The Mencken household was also a religion-free zone. August was, like his father, a skeptic and likely submitted his children for baptism to please a wife who regarded christening as a rite of passage in civilized society. But Burkardt, the grandfather, enjoyed a good argument about Christian theology and indirectly catechized his grandson in an awareness of church teachings that would extend throughout the boy's life. Henry would later tell the story of accompanying his father and grandfather on business trips, one of which included a stop at Saint Mary's Industrial School just outside Baltimore (where Babe Ruth, between 1902 and 1914, received a modest education). The Xaverian Brothers tried to teach "problem boys" a trade, including cigar making. The school acquired tobacco from Burkardt and August tried to market the cigars, but to no effect, since "the cheroots that the boys made were as hard as so many railroad spikes." After conducting business, Burkardt's custom was to sit down with the Xaverians and "debate theology." "These discussions," Mencken recalled,

> seemed to last for hours, and while they were going on I had to sit in a gloomy hallway hung with gory religious paintings—saints being burned, broken on the wheel and disemboweled, the Flood drowning scores of cows, horses, camels and sheep, the Crucifixion against a background of hair-raising lightnings. . . . I was too young, of course, to follow the argument; moreover, it was often carried on in German. Nevertheless, I gathered that it neither resulted in agreement nor left any hard feelings. The Xaverians must have put in two or three years trying to rescue my grandfather from his lamentable heresies, but they made no more impression upon him than if they had addressed a clothing-store dummy, though it was plain that he respected and enjoyed their effort. On his part, he failed just as dismally to seduce them from their oaths of chastity, poverty and obedience. I met some of them years afterward, and found that they still remembered him with affection, though he had turned their pastoral teeth.

Such good-natured opposition to Christianity left a lasting impression on the grandson whose readers (whether Christian or infidel) took note of the antagonism but often missed (and still do) the respect that accompanied disbelief. Whether he inherited this trait directly from Burkardt is one of those nurture-nature questions that evade the expertise of average mortals. But Burkardt did manage to balance the chip on his shoulder about divine matters. He was both a Mason *and* a "Christian of the Protestant sub-species" who had "lost his confidence in Jahveh" before Henry's birth. This "outright infidel" permitted his three daughters "to commune freely with the Protestant Episcopal Church" and also required that his sons subscribe, as he had, "toward the Baltimore crematorium."

August may not have enjoyed debate as much as his father, Burkardt, but he too was responsible—in this case, directly—for schooling the young Henry in the basic pieties of American Protestantism. Sunday school was an invention of Anglo-American Protestantism that caught more spiritual fish than the churches. An institution first established during the run-up to the Second Great Awakening when Protestants in the United States fanned out across the countryside to perform good works and build a righteous society, Sunday school was designed to provide basic literacy for working-class children. Since these kids could not go to school during the week but had to work instead, and since most Americans rested each Sunday to observe the Sabbath, Sunday school became a device for extending the blessings of civilization to members of those families unable to attend common or private schools. It did not hurt that the curriculum used to teach reading, writing, and arithmetic was overtly religious and moral; this was simply another way to reinforce the ties between revealed religion and civilizational advance. In the 1870s when public schooling became more common and in some cases required, Sunday schools needed to find a different mission since local school districts had made their efforts redundant. At this point, the program of Sunday school shifted from secular subjects to explicitly religious ones, especially mastering the contents of Scripture.

The devotional character of Sunday school by the time of Mencken's boyhood makes ironic his "infidel" father's decision to send the Mencken boys to the local Methodist church for Sunday school. Even more remarkable is how much Henry apparently learned:

> I can't remember the time when I did not know that Moses wrote the Ten Commandments with a chisel and wore a long beard; that Noah built an ark like one we had in our Christmas garden, and filled it with animals which, to this day, I always think of as wooden, with a leg or two missing; that Lot's wife was turned into a pillar (I heard it as *cellar*) of table salt; that the Tower of Babel was twice as high as the Baltimore shot tower; that Abraham greatly pleased Jahveh by the strange device of offering to butcher and roast his own son, and that Leviticus was the father of Deuteronomy.

Mencken did not remember "any formal teaching" or any particular instructor, but he did gain the sort of biblical literacy that was typical for most Americans drawn into the reach of the Protestant churches and their related agencies.

What stood out in Mencken's memory of Sunday school was the "heartiness of the singing." His favorite song was "Are You Ready for the Judgment Day?"—"a gay and even rollicking tune with a saving hint of brimstone."

> We grouped it, in fact, with such *dolce* but unexhilarating things as "In the Sweet By-and-By" and "God Be With You Till We Meet Again"—pretty stuff, to be sure, but sadly lacking in bite and zowie. The runner up for "Are You Ready?" was "I Went Down the Rock to Hide My Face," another hymn with a very lively swing to it, and after "the Rock" came "Stand Up, Stand Up for Jesus," "Throw Out the Lifeline," "At the Cross," "Draw Me Nearer, Nearer, Nearer, Blessed Lord," "What A Friend We Have in Jesus," "Where Shall We Spend in Eternity?" . . . and "Hallelujah, Hallelujah, Revive Us Again." . . . It was not until I transferred to another Sunday-school that I came to know such lugubrious horrors as "There Is A Fountain Filled with Blood." The Methodists avoided everything of that kind. They surely did not neglect Hell in their preaching, but when they lifted up their voices in song they liked to pretend that they were booked to escape it.

The idea that the boy who grew up to be known as America's chief infidel learned these classic songs of born-again Protestantism and even relished singing many of them is one of those jaw-dropping aspects of Americana. But such was the conventional nature of Protestantism in American society, that infidels and believers alike shared a common biblical vocabulary and repertoire of pious song.

Mencken himself was surprised that his father, being "what Christendom abhors as an infidel," would send him to Sunday school and expose him to "Wesleyan divinity." The reason was simple. August wanted a peaceful house for a Sunday afternoon nap:

> This had been feasible so long as my brother and I were puling infants and could be packed off for naps ourselves, but as we increased in years and malicious animal magnetism and began to prefer leaping and howling up and down stairs, it became impossible for [August] to get any sleep.

Whether or not August knew the program of Sunday school, it was a marvelous tonic for his rambunctious boys. As Mencken observed, singing was the aspect of Sunday school that children most enjoyed; "there they are urged to whoop their loudest in praise of God," he recalled, "and that license is an immense relief from the shushing they are always hearing at home." Still, the father never worried that his sons would succumb to local Protestant pieties. "The risk," August explained to Henry, "was much less than you think," since the Methodists "had you less than two hours a week, and I had you all the rest of the time." "I'd have been a hell of a theologian to let them nail you."

The Making of a Bookworm

Terry Teachout makes the astute observation that Mencken the man revealed the limitations of an autodidact—someone who settles into intellectual ruts because he is self-taught. This feature of Mencken's intellectual development was likely the result of what Mencken the boy experienced in his formal education. He began at a private school, Knapp's Institute, an institution of predominantly German American demographics. When Mencken turned twelve, August sent him to the Baltimore Manual Training School (later Baltimore Polytechnic), a high school that trained students for manual labor. Since Mencken's brothers, Charlie and August, both went to the Polytechnic and became engineers, August may have had similar hopes for his oldest son. Either way, Mencken's formal education was hardly the sort of training someone would have chosen for a man who became one of the most prolific authors and influential editors in the world of American letters.

Mencken's recollections of Knapp's Institute, named for the headmaster, Friedrich Knapp, are likely the best source for what a private school in 1880s Baltimore was like. The student's memories have more to do with the people than academics. The student body was mainly German American. It included a large enough group of Jewish American boys to offer classes in Hebrew. The multicultural academy also attracted Latin Americans, "chiefly Cubans and Demerarans," whose handkerchiefs always smelled of perfume. Like the students, Mencken remembered the teachers less for their ethnic heritage than for their smells or political convictions. One instructor in particular left "a powerful aroma" that served "admirably as a disinfectant." When this teacher advocated an eight-hour workday during class and Mencken relayed the radical idea to his father, the sweet smell of perfume could not inoculate the elder Mencken, a liberal in the classical model of free markets and small governments, from worrying that the school harbored political nihilism. Knapp himself was a Swabian who in 1850 had migrated to Baltimore, about the same time as Mencken's grandfather, Burkardt. He wore "the classical uniform of a German schoolmaster—a long-tailed coat of black alpaca, a boiled shirt with somewhat fringey cuffs, and a white lawn necktie." His coat and hands were covered with chalk dust, some of which must have accompanied Knapp's regular doses of snuff. What impressed students more than Knapp's attire was the rattan he carried to keep wayward students in line with a swat to the backside. The routine of caning was always the same:

> The condemned would be beckoned politely to the place of execution beside the teacher's desk, and at the word *Eins* from the professor he would hold up his hands. At *Zwei* he would lower them until they stuck out straight from his shoulders, and at *Drei* he would bend over until his finger-tips touched his ankles.

Depending on the infraction, a student may have received as many as four swats, but usually received only one. Student etiquette required the "condemned to make an outcry" and then to "massage his *gluteus maximus* violently as he pranced back to his bench." The response from the teacher was also predictable: "You can't rub it out." This was the sort of discipline that allowed Knapp to boast about the superiority of private schools over the public ones that were beginning to compete for children: "No authentic graduate of F. Knapp's Institute . . . had ever finished on the gallows."

At school festivities, when Mencken, always a trencherman, indulged in hot dogs, he earned them by performing mathematical tricks. At one of the annual picnics Mencken ate six *wecken*—at the time he thought *weckers* was the plural for *wecke*, the German name for the crisply baked wheat-flour bread on which the dog was served. The ensuing bellyache was so painful that five bottles of sarsaparilla could not cure it. Ample quantities of food and drink did not relieve students from having to demonstrate the intellectual feats accomplished under Knapp's instruction. Mencken recalled having to divide complex fractions or multiply long numbers with decimals and admitted that he had "no interest whatever in figures." Mencken's father was keen that his boys learn math, and consequently "it gave him a great kick if I came out with an error of no more than plus-or-minus ten per cent." The boy's reward was a nickel, sufficiently valuable to purchase a "grab-bag containing at least half a pound of broken taffy and a ring or stickpin set with a large ruby."

What Mencken may have failed to learn formally under Knapp's guidance, he acquired innately, especially his affinity for language, a love that came to him as naturally as his appetite for hot dogs. The man who would grow up to compile in his spare time a comprehensive index of the American usage of the English language, the three-volume *American Language*, as a boy was a remarkably keen observer of the idiosyncrasies surrounding verbal communication. As a student Mencken sat in on the Hebrew language class that Knapp provided for the dozen or so Jewish Americans enrolled—"long enough to learn the Hebrew alphabet." He also acquired knowledge of German, including an ability to read Gothic type and recite from memory the conjugation of "*haben* down to *Sie wuerden gehabt haben*." His knowledge of German verbs was the result of teachers ramming "it into their pupils as they rammed in the multiplication table."

Mencken's interest in language was insatiable, and he learned more outside school in the polyglot neighborhood of his family than he ever did in formal instruction. His understanding of German came largely from the "hired girls who traipsed through the Hollins Street kitchen during the 1880s" before being snatched away by "some amorous ice-man, beer-man or ash-man." His maternal grandfather also spoke German on his visits to Hollins Street, but his mother would respond to her father's German in English. "Such bilingual dialogues sometimes went on for hours, to the fascination of my brother and me." It also prompted Mencken to ask his grandfather, in what would become a favorite family anecdote, that if the German word for kiss was *kuss*, should not the German for fish be *fush?* Still, the idiosyncrasy of German was not the only linguistic oddity to catch Mencken's fancy. He was an avid reader from an early age and would persist even when warned by his mother about the dangers of reading in poor light. During one summer evening when he was seven, a story called "The Moose Hunters" left a lasting impression while he read in the gloaming on the front porch. Mencken already had "discovered a new realm of being and a new and powerful enchantment" in reading, but then he made the discovery that the word "moose" had no plural "but remained unchanged *ad infinitum*."

19

Such discoveries give a boy a considerable thrill, and augment his sense of dignity. It is no light matter, at eight, to penetrate suddenly to the difference between *to*, *two* and *too*, or to that between *run* in baseball and *run* in topographical science, or *cats* and *Katz*. The effect is massive and profound, and at least comparable to that which flows, in later life, out of filling a royal flush or debauching the wife of a major-general of cavalry.

Even if Mencken's proclivities pointed him in the direction of reading, writing, and editing, words were not his first love. A series of Christmas gifts elicited dreams briefly of becoming an artist, a chemist, and a photographer. His career as a watercolorist "was brief and not glorious." His glance at vinegar through a microscope revealed a "revolting mass of worms" that kept him away from vinegar for a year. His passion for photography also faded. It was music that was his abiding love as a boy and throughout his life. When he was eight years old, his father purchased a piano for the Hollins Street home. He took lessons from a string of teachers that included a "series of lady teachers" who proceeded to "wreck" his technique and "debauch" his taste. Even so, Mencken became proficient enough to be of use to his father. Whenever August wanted to drive unwelcome guests from the home, he would ask Henry to perform. His program consisted of "marches and gallops, all of them executed with the loud pedal held down." Eventually, the "dreadful din" forced the guests to leave. These performances as "bouncer" made Mencken a "slave to the *forte* pedal," a thrall that continued to afflict his piano playing with the Saturday Night Club.[1]

Despite Mencken's deficiencies as a pianist, music connected with his soul and became the lost love of his life. He recalled trying to compose music as a boy, and that desire would continue throughout his career. "When I think of anything properly describable as a beautiful idea," he confessed, "it is always in the form of music." In fact, he would later describe his inability to fulfill his musical desires as tragic:

[M]y lifelong libido that has never come to anything [makes me] aware of the eternal tragedy of man. He is born for things that are

1. The Saturday Night Club was an informal gathering of professional and amateur musicians for which Mencken played piano. The group first met in 1904 and would continue to gather weekly for almost fifty years. See chapter 9 below.

beyond him, as flight through the air is beyond a poor goldfish in a globe, and stardom in Hollywood must remain forever outside the experience . . . of all save a few hundred of the girls in the ten-cent stores. . . . I have written and printed probably 10,000,000 words of English, and continue to this day to pour out more and more. . . . [M]y booth has been set up on a favorable pitch, and I have never lacked hearers for my bally-hoo. But all the same I shall die an inarticulate man, for my best ideas have beset me in a language I know only vaguely and speak only like a child.

If the piano proved to be lovable irritant, the printing press became Mencken's alternative vehicle for self-expression. When he was eight years old and just figuring out the wonderful world of words, Mencken received for Christmas a Baltimore No. 10 Self-Inker Printing Press, with a font of No. 214 type. The details, preserved in the receipt August Mencken had kept, were inconsequential to the general mass of humanity, except for those who actively read Mencken. For him the specific printing press and font added a "degree of concern bordering on the super-colossal" because the press "determined the whole course" of his life:

> If it had been a stethoscope or a copy of Dr. Ayer's Almanac I might have gone in for medicine; if it had been a Greek New Testament or a set of baptismal grappling-irons I might have pursued divinity. As it was, I got the smell of printer's ink up my nose at the tender age of eight, and it has been swirling through my sinuses ever since.

This was the same press that forced Mencken to use his initials, H. L., rather than Henry or Harry, once his father had accidentally broken all the lowercase *r*'s on the very morning when Mencken had lifted the device from its holiday wrappings. He proceeded to start a business of printing business cards and soon moved on to a four-page newspaper printed on sheets filched from the hired girls' piles of wrapping paper. Instead of covering local news like the local cops hauling away neighborhood ruffians, children getting lost, or car horses falling dead in the street, Mencken lifted stories from his competitor, the *Baltimore Sunpaper*. The most important item he ever printed was the news that William I, the German kaiser, had died at the age of ninety-one in Berlin. Otherwise, the paper was a failure. It suffered from all the afflictions that would kill other newspapers—"insufficiency of capital, incomplete news service, an incompetent staff, no advertising, and a press that couldn't print."

Still, the activity of writing, editing, and printing stuck and soon received vigorous reinforcement from Mencken's emerging reading habits. After he finished reading his first story at age seven, "The Moose Hunters," an adventure of four boys in the woods of Maine, Mencken returned to the streets of West Baltimore, played leapfrog, became sick by chewing tobacco, and learned to spin tops. But soon he began to feel "the powerful suction of beautiful letters—so strange, so thrilling, and so curiously suggestive of the later suction of amour." By then he was eight and had turned to *Grimm's Fairy Tales*, a copy of which he had received as an award at Knapp's Institute. He recalled that his difficulties with the tales fanned into flame his first sense of literary criticism. Grimm was much more difficult than "The Moose Hunters," and Mencken never finished it. Only when "Snow White" came out as a movie did he retry the *Fairy Tales*, "and gagged at it again." He blamed the experience on Grimm and the translator. He also confessed that his artistic instincts ran opposite the direction of the mysterious and fanciful. "I was born, in truth, without any natural taste for fairy tales, or, indeed, for any other writing of a fanciful and unearthly character." This explained his "lifelong distrust of poetry," which he considered nonsense—"sometimes, to be sure, very jingly and juicy nonsense, but still only nonsense." Additionally, this was likely the basis for Mencken's aversion to all uplift and didactic literature so common in the juvenile stories of the day, such as those of Horatio Alger. "Some of the boys I knew admired it vastly, but I always ran aground on it."

Mencken himself chalked up this distaste for conventional boys' books to his own very literal mind, something he likely inherited from his father. Such literalism prompted him to be "very ill adapted to engulfing the pearls of the imagination." "All such pearls tend to get entangled in my mental *vibrissae*," he explained, "and the effort to engulf them is as disagreeable to me as listening to a sermon or reading an editorial in a second-rate (or even first-rate) newspaper." From *Alice in Wonderland* to *Twenty Thousand Leagues under the Sea*, Mencken could only laugh, that is, if he even finished the story.

Even so, he had discovered the power of words and was hungry for more. Mencken was still an eight-year-old and found himself at home in need of something to read. He tried the Baltimore newspapers, but they had too many "political diatribes," and he knew "no more about politics than a chimpanzee." Ladies magazines were another option, but *Godey's Lady's Book* and *Ladies' Home Journal* were worse than the papers because "they dealt gloomily with cooking, etiquette, the policing of children, and the design and construction of millinery." Nor was the reading fare of the hired girls satisfactory, complete with "ghastly woodcuts of English milkmaids in bustles skedaddling from concupiscent baronets in frock-coats and cork-screw mustaches." In despair, Mencken resorted to the row of books atop the secretary, "dismal volumes in the black cloth and gilt stamping of the era." His father had collected these but seldom read them since the elder Mencken was given to news stories on the condition of the country and the world, both of which he thought were "going to Hell." Sometimes August read a book, but usually it turned out to be a pamphlet "on the insoluble issue of the hour," such as *Looking Backward*, *If Christ Came to Chicago*, or *Female Life among the Mormons*. Nevertheless, in the collection of books in the Mencken family parlor were Shakespeare, Dickens, George Eliot, an encyclopedia, and such titles as *Uncle Remus*, *Ben-Hur*, and *The Adventures of Baron Munchausen*.

Mencken the boy had entered "paradise," especially when he encountered Mark Twain. He had heard his father mention the author, but Twain could have been, for all Mencken knew, "a bartender, a baseball-player, or one of the boozy politicoes my father was always meeting in Washington." The Twain volumes lacked pictures of "the usual funereal character" but included images that were "light, loose and lively." Mencken hustled one of the books, "a green quarto," up to his bedroom and stretched out on his bed with *Huckleberry Finn*.

> If I undertook to tell you the effect it had upon me my talk would sound frantic, and even delirious. Its impact was genuinely terrific. I had not gone further than the first incomparable chapter before I realized, child though I was, that I had entered a domain of new and gorgeous wonders, and thereafter I pressed on steadily to the last word. My gait, of course, was still slow, but it became steadily faster as I proceeded. As the blurbs on the slip-covers of murder mysteries say, I simply couldn't put the book down.

Later, when August spied Mencken reading the book in the family sitting room and recognized the author, he blurted, "Well, I'll be durned."

Mencken learned that his father had read Twain appreciatively before "children, labor troubles and Grover Cleveland" had begun to annoy, but the son proceeded to take the entire Twain canon "at a gulp." He was still only a boy and easily related to Huck Finn, while passages from *A Tramp Abroad*, *The Innocents Abroad*, and *The Gilded Age* produced bewilderment. One woodcut of barefoot German girls, with a caption that read "Generations of Bare Feet," created confusion because at the time Mencken associated the word "generation" with a word his father then bandied about in frustration over the rise of organized labor—"federation." It left him wondering "idiotically what possible relation there could be between a band of little girls in pigtails and the Haymarket anarchists." Even so, that woodcut was responsible for instilling in Mencken an interest in things German along with "a vast contempt for the German language."

> It was "A Tramp Abroad" that made me German-conscious, and I still believe that it is the best guide-book to Germany ever written. Today, of course, it is archaic, but it was still reliable down to 1910, when I made my own first trip. The uproarious essay on "The Awful German Language," which appears at the end of it as an appendix, worked the other way. . . . [I]t confirmed my growing feeling, born of my struggles with the conjugations and declensions taught at F. Knapp's Institute, that German was an irrational and even insane tongue, and not worth the sufferings of a freeborn American.

But Huck Finn stood out as the best, and Mencken would return to it every year for most of his adult life. "Only one other book, down to the beginning of my teens," Mencken confessed, "ever beset me with a force even remotely comparable to its smash."

Twain was the hinge of Mencken's literary education. From Huck Finn he proceeded to the rest of the books on his father's shelf of dusty books. He read most of Dickens but did not make sense of the English novel until he tackled Thackeray six years later. George Eliot "floored" him "as effectively as a text in Hittite," and he kept away from the Eliot oeuvre for the rest of his life. Adam Bede and Daniel Deronda became as "hollow and insignificant as the names of Gog and Magog." Once he had read through most of the contents of the family library, he headed down the street to the local branch of the Enoch Pratt Free Library. By the time he was nine he had borrowing privileges and "began an almost daily harrying of the virgins at the delivery desk." Mencken's fondness for books took a toll on his frame (and his disposition), as he spent two-thirds of his time with books and only one-third with "trees, fields, streets, and people." "I acquired round shoulders, spindly shanks, and a despondent view of humanity." Such "madness" lasted until his adolescence, when he "began to distinguish between one necktie and another, and to notice the curiously divergent shapes, dispositions and aromas of girls." Even so, the damage was done, and Mencken entered at a very early age the world of language and literary arts.

The Man in the Boy

Did Mencken know at the time that by identifying with Mark Twain over fairy tales he was doing something subversive? Was he also foreshadowing the kind of literature that he would later champion as an editor, works that ran against the grain and that challenged the moral universe that Victorian writers and educators hoped to promote through art that was uplifting and didactic? Of course, as an eight-year-old, Mencken had no knowledge that he was reading books that in other parts of the country were banned. (In fact, *The Adventures of Huckleberry Finn* would continue to generate controversy well after Mencken's death; between 1996 and 2000, according to Herbert N. Forstel, the only books banned more than Twain's novel in the United States were the novels of J. K. Rowling's Harry Potter series.)[2] Also likely was Mencken's own lack of self-awareness of the meaning of such reading habits. Were his literary preferences as a boy evidence of the sort of harm that bad books could do to the children who read them? Or did Mencken's own dispositions (the egg) produce interest in literary works (the chicken) that ran against the grain of American's Protestant culture?

In March of 1885 the *New York Herald* reported on the decision of the library directors of Concord, Massachusetts, to place *Huckleberry Finn* on its *Index Expurgatorius*. The reasons for banning Twain's book from the public library of a town that boasted a "summer school of philosophy" varied, but its questionable morality headed the list. One director described *Huckleberry Finn* as "absolutely immoral in its tone."

---

2. *Banned in the U.S.A.: A Reference Guide to Book Censorship in Schools and Public Libraries* (Westport, CT: Greenwood Publishing, 2002).

Another complained that it contained "but very little humor." Still another faulted Twain for telling the story in "the language of a rough, ignorant dialect," and for employing a "systematic use of bad grammar and an employment of inelegant expressions." *Huckleberry Finn*, accordingly, was "trash of the veriest sort" and failed to elevate readers. In fact, the directors had little trouble dispensing with the novel since they were already familiar with Twain's style, philosophy, and morality. The staff responsible for the Pratt Free Library in Baltimore did not object to Twain or Huck, but that was inconsequential for Mencken since his father owned a copy of the book.

Concord's actions touched off a debate that would reignite a century later among Americans concerned less about Huck's sense of duty and loyalty than about his views on race. Again, Mencken and his family were oblivious to debates held in Boston's suburbs, but from the perspective of the nation's literary world, the Mencken bookshelf was on one side in a budding culture war that involved the reputation of Twain himself. According to the *Springfield Republican*, "Mr. Clemens is a genuine and powerful humorist, with a bitter vein of satire on the weaknesses of humanity which is sometimes wholesome, sometimes only grotesque, but in certain of his works degenerates into a gross trifling with every fine feeling." For that reason, the stories about Huck Finn and Tom Sawyer were "no better in tone than the dime novels which flood the blood-and-thunder reading population," their "moral level" was "low," and their perusal could not be "anything less than harmful." The *Saturday Review* countered with a different estimate of Twain. "He has, when he likes, tenderness and melancholy, and an extraordinary sense of human limitations and contradictions." As such, Huck's moral struggles blended "poetry and pathos" humorously. "In Mark Twain the world has a humorist at once wild and tender, a humorist who is yearly ripening and mellowing."

Although recent efforts to ban *Huckleberry Finn* have had less to do with Huck's conflicted conscience than with Twain's racism (or racist language), editors and authors continue to worry about the harmful effects of certain stories and characters from children's literature on the moral development of young readers. William Bennett, for instance, started a cottage industry of children's books with his anthology *Book of Virtues: A Treasury of Great Moral Stories* (1993). The collection's aim is to help "the time-honored task of the moral education of the young." In addition to needing good moral examples in parents and other adults, children require moral literacy—that is, stories, poems, and essays that show what virtue looks like. "Children must have at their disposal a stock of examples illustrating what we see to be right and wrong, good and bad—examples illustrating that, in many instances, what is morally right and wrong can indeed be known and promoted." The problem, however, according to Bennett, is that children are not born with the virtues that Americans generally esteem—"honesty, compassion, courage, and perseverance." Providing wholesome literature is one way to acquaint children with these virtues.

One writer whom Bennett included in his anthology was C. S. Lewis, a contemporary of Mencken, who wrote a variety of popular children's stories and reflected on the importance of such literature in the formation of a moral disposition. The excerpt from Lewis's *Abolition of Man* that Bennett reprinted highlights how important character formation is for youth to grow up to be virtuous adults. Lewis quoted Plato, who wrote, "the little human" must be made to feel "pleasure, liking, disgust, and hatred at those things which really are pleasant, likeable, disgusting, and hateful." But when Lewis wrote about his own fairy tales, such as the Narnia series, he spoke much less about morality than about the need to say something. In this case, Lewis conceived of fairy tales as an alternative to the sort of "stained-glass and Sunday school" obligations on which he had been reared. "Why did one find it so hard to feel as one was told one ought to feel about God or about the sufferings of Christ?" The answer was duty. "An obligation to feel can freeze feelings." Casting reverence for the divine in hushed tones made Christianity seem "almost medical." So Lewis attempted an imaginary world that might capture the "real potency" of religion. And since he thought that children's literature was necessarily distinct from the sort of story that could arouse an adult's imagination, his stories might even enrapture all ages.

Of course, Lewis would go on to become one of the most popular and widely read defenders of Christianity while Mencken would grow up to be one of the most famous skeptics in the United States, sometimes mistaken as a forerunner of the "new atheism." Since Lewis had an affinity for fairy tales and Mencken was tone-deaf to them, the temptation is to link each author's verdict on Christianity to his literary formation. Since Lewis rarely wrote about American literature and apparently never read Mark Twain, the contrast between Mencken's boyhood hero and Lewis's childhood reading fancy is impossible to draw. Still, the contrast is worth exploring. The literary interests of two important twentieth-century writers who came down on different sides of Christian faith were markedly different and yield at least one way of trying to explain Lewis's faith and Mencken's disbelief.

As Mencken did while playing with his brother August (with whom he would live throughout most of his adult life), Lewis created an imaginary world where schoolboys accomplished great deeds of heroism and might. He would later use this world as the basis for his Narnia stories. But in addition to these fantasies, Lewis was also fond of the Beatrix Potter tales, and especially their illustrations. They were, he confessed, "the delight of my childhood." "The idea of humanised animals," he added, "fascinated me perhaps even more than it fascinates most children." When Lewis went to school and sat under formal instruction, he left behind the world of fantasy and discovered the potency of verse, first through Matthew Arnold's *Sohrab and Rustum* and then through the standard literary canon of Homer, Virgil, Dante, Milton, and Shakespeare. The idea that the novel was the major literary form was itself novel in Lewis's education. The epic reigned in the classroom, and novels were frivolous literary forms. Yet the power of stories and imagination would not let Lewis go. And when as a young man he tried on the philosophies of George Bernard Shaw and Friedrich Nietzsche and found them ill-fitting, Lewis found stories to be the great appeal of Christianity (especially as explained by G. K. Chesterton). For instance, Lewis thought the materialism of Enlightenment thinkers was "small beer" compared to poets like George Herbert who conveyed the nature of human existence through the prism of "Christian mythology."

Of course, to compare Mencken to Lewis is unfair since their experiences were so different. Mencken would only receive a high school education on route to becoming a leading literary critic in the United States and an important figure in the rise of literary modernism. Lewis, by contrast, attended England's best universities and became acquainted with the literary canon before becoming a professor of literature, popular essayist, and author of children's books. Terry Teachout observes that one of Mencken's greatest defects as a man of letters was his status as a literary loner. For instance, Mencken would eventually conclude that Henry James wrote nothing but "hot air," a verdict that for Teachout indicates the "limits" of Mencken's education. Perhaps, Teachout adds, Mencken "was right to assume he would have gotten nothing out of college but 'balderdash' of 'chalky pedagogues.'" But when Mencken began to swim in deeper literary waters as a young man, he was "over his head" in part because he lacked the sort of training available to the likes of a C. S. Lewis.

This is not to suggest that had Mencken gone on to attend Baltimore's own contribution to the renaissance of American higher learning, Johns Hopkins University, founded in 1876, he would have rendered a different verdict on Christianity. A better British comparison to Mencken is G. K. Chesterton, a man six years older, who was also a journalist and humorist, and who, like Mencken, highly regarded contemporary authors such as George Bernard Shaw. Chesterton's education before becoming a journalist, art critic, author of detective novels, and Roman Catholic apologist was better than Mencken's—he attended a tony and historic Anglican school, followed by training at a college for art. But unlike Mencken, Chesterton grew up with a taste for imaginary worlds and didactic narratives. He recalled that his very first memory was of a prince crossing a bridge on the way to rescue a princess, an image that came from a toy theater that Chesterton's father had constructed for the child. He later conceded that he liked "romantic things like toy-theaters" because his father had introduced him to toy theaters. Chesterton also admitted that he had an affinity as a boy for moralizing tales because a child "knows nothing about cunning or perversion" but sees only "the moral ideals themselves" and that "they are true." In contrast to Chesterton (and to Lewis), who also became an apologist for Christianity, Mencken, the lifelong and outspoken agnostic, never had a taste for the kinds of stories that enraptured those who would later liken the virtues of children's literature to the Christian story. If British schooling polished Chesterton's or Lewis's imaginative instincts, Mencken's own formal education stopped at a vocational high school. For the rest of his ideas about the world, religion, and the arts, Mencken was on his own.

These comparisons should not, however, render Mencken the boy merely a materialist or agnostic in the making. If his reflections as a man were at all indicative of his experience as a boy, he did possess a genuine wonder about his surroundings in Baltimore and beyond. His description of Baltimore, for instance, may have lacked the enchantment of Lewis's Narnia, but Mencken's hometown packed a sufficiently gritty punch to ignite his imagination. To the notion that Baltimore was a "swell" town, Mencken affirmed that he could not recall "ever hearing anyone complain of the fact that there was a great epidemic of typhoid fever every Summer, and a wave of malaria every Autumn, and more than a scattering of smallpox, especially among the colored folk in the alleys, every Winter," which left spring as "the only season free from serious pestilence." During the hot months, "every public place in Baltimore was so furiously beset by bugs of all sorts that communal gatherings were impossible," a feature of urban living that gave Mencken and his brother Charlie "a pleasant source of recreation." Baltimore also possessed a variety of smells that fortified the fainthearted. Because the city's sewers emptied into the Back Basin, it "began to acquire a powerful aroma every Spring, and by August smelled like a billion polecats." The occupants of Mencken's own neighborhood in West Baltimore had to endure "mephitic blasts" from a nearby glue factory. But local wisdom had it that the "bouquet of the Back basin" accounted for the long life of office workers near the wharves who lived to be one hundred years old, and for the strength and tenacity of the African American stevedores who "were the strongest, toughest, drunkenest, and most thieving in the whole port."

The sounds of Baltimore were almost as powerful in stimulating Mencken's imagination as were the smells. Children "were not incarcerated in playgrounds," and so roved the streets and were constantly yelling or singing. The week before Christmas they blew horns, and around July 4 they set off firecrackers. Almost every home had a dog that "barked more or less continuously from 4 a.m. until after midnight." Many homeowners still kept chickens; this resulted in a percussion of hens clucking and the sirens of roosters crowing. During business hours, "the impact of iron wagon tires on hard cobblestone was almost like that of a hammer on an anvil."

But the city's best feature was its proximity to what Mencken called "the factory" of Chesapeake Bay and its menu of treats. The hard-shell crabs of his youth, "at least eight inches in length" and with "snow-white meat almost as firm as soap," seemed limitless in supply. "Any poor man could go down to the banks of the river (Patapsco), armed with no more than a length of stout cord, a home-made net on a pole, and a chunk of cat's meat, and come home in a couple of hours with enough crabs to feed his family for two days." Soft-shell crabs were next in the list of delicacies, along with shad roe. In fact, Mencken remembered vividly the day his mother came home from Hollins Market with word that the fishmongers were selling roe. She was indignant because roe had previously been included with the purchase of shad. Terrapin was an acquired taste, Mencken admitted, because "its consumption involved a considerable lavage with fortified wines," a circumstance that put most of the women off. Still, his mother bought "pint jars of the picked meat . . . with plenty of rich, golden eggs scattered through it, for a dollar a jar." Two ducks also cost only a dollar during a hunting season that ran "gloriously from the instant the first birds wandered in from Labrador to the time the last stragglers set sail for Brazil." Oysters were much less popular, and the combination of raw oysters and a shot of rye whiskey was considered the equivalent of being kicked by a mule. Even so, one of the city's better hotels served an oyster stew and an oyster potpie that were "magnificent."

The attention Mencken gave to food as a boy would later catch up with the man who began to lose his lanky physique in his late twenties when during business trips he frequented New York City's restaurants and beer halls. He never subscribed to his father's regimen of hoisting a hooker of rye before every meal, allegedly "the best medicine he had ever found for toning up his stomach." Of course, as a boy the treatment was unavailable. But father and sons together consumed the meals that followed this alcoholic appetizer. His favorite lunch included "a huge platter of Norfolk spots or other pan-fish, and a Himalaya of corn-cakes." On the side were "succotash, buttered beets, baked potatoes, string beans, and other such hearty vegetables." For dessert the Mencken boys ate oranges and bananas when available, served "with a heavy dressing of grated coconut." This repast likely ran to three thousand calories, Mencken estimated, and left its eaters "somewhat subdued."

Although Mencken likely committed the sin of gluttony, he took delight from pleasures beyond the dining room table as well. Since August was presiding over a successful cigar business, with manufacturing in Baltimore and stores in both his hometown and Washington, DC, the family could afford a summer house in Ellicott City. The town was a mere ten miles from the Hollins Street house, but accessible in the 1880s primarily by train. August Mencken would commute back and forth to the city to maintain the business while Henry explored the wilds of Howard County:

> The impact of such lovely country upon a city boy barely eight years old was really stupendous. Nothing in this life has ever given me a more thrilling series of surprises and felicities. Everything was new to me, and not only new but romantic, for the most I had learned of

31

green things was what was to be discovered in our backyard in Hollins street, and here was everything from wide and smiling fields to deep, dense woods of ancient trees, and from the turbulent and exciting life of the barnyard to the hidden peace of woodland brooks. . . . When a thunder-storm rolled over the hills it was incomparably grander and more violent than any city storm. The clouds were blacker and towered higher, the thunder was louder, and the lightning was ten times as blinding. I made acquaintance with cows, pigs and all the fowl of the barnyard. . . . There was something new every minute, and that something was always amazing and beautiful.

Mencken did not need imaginative literature to create a world that was entirely other when his visits to the country were his "Wild West," "Darkest Africa," "Ultima Thule." The surrounding region even had its own anthropophagus, "a half-grown yahoo who was supposed to hunt little boys over the countryside, and to inflict mysterious indignities." The Menckens only went to Ellicott City for two summers before finding a summer cottage closer to Baltimore in Mount Washington. But the country made such a "powerful impression" that Mencken claimed he remembered every detail—"the wonderful adventures in the woods and along the brook, the fascinating life of beasts and birds, the daily miracles of the farm."

Of course, readers may chalk up Mencken's memories of boyhood wonder and adventure to his own admiration for if not emulation of one of his favorite authors—Mark Twain. Mencken's memoirs present him as urban Huck Finn. Still, the rest of his life and his writings did not contradict the awe that pervaded Mencken's childhood memories. He became a keen observer of the affairs and follies of the human race—particularly the human beings with whom he shared the United States—because people and their causes and activities fascinated him as much as the countryside had bedazzled him as an eight-year-old. He was also a penetrating critic of human affairs at the very least because he was skeptical about the myths and romances that people concocted to justify even the loftiest of their schemes. Perhaps he was as hard on moralizing politicians as he was indifferent to children's fantasy stories because he did not believe what he observed could be correlated to an unseen world of fairies, goblins, talking goats, angels, or gods.

Still, some of Mencken's apathy toward myth and mystery is attributable to the almost infinite variety of matters he observed in the world around him. It was as if he could not contemplate unseen things because he had so many sights, sounds, tastes, and smells to observe, catalogue, and interpret. Had Mencken grown up in a home where older generations welcomed mythmaking, he might have warmed to the fantastic and uplifting stories that many American children loved. He may also have been predisposed to entertain the miraculous claims of the Christian religion that most of his neighbors took for granted. As it was, his very conventional baptism in the Episcopal Church received practically no support or encouragement amid the Mencken family's surroundings. If ever the line attributed to Ignatius of Loyola, "Give me a child until he is seven and I will show you the man," correctly described a person's youth, that man was H. L. Mencken.

CHAPTER TWO

The Maddest, Gladdest, Damnedest Existence Ever

On Palm Sunday 1895, Mencken was one of forty-three adolescents to be confirmed (received as a member) at Baltimore's Second English Lutheran Church. This rite of initiation followed a period of catechetical instruction in which, according to Mencken's brother, Henry never looked at the catechism until arriving at church and even then generally failed to answer the pastor's questions. If the Lutheran minister thought Mencken was simply going through the motions, he was correct. What he may not have known was that instead of studying the Lutheran catechism, young Mencken was beginning to read T. H. Huxley, the English scientist who promoted Darwinism and whom Mencken credited with giving "order and coherence to my own doubts" and converting "me into a violent agnosticism." (Atheism for Mencken was silly, as he would explain later in life.) Still, despite Mencken's intellectual adventure, the custom of the Mencken household, no matter how skeptical its head or its wards, was for children to join the church. As long as August Mencken Sr. was alive, Henry complied with his father's will.

By 1899 August Mencken was dead, and his eldest son finally had the clearance to pursue what he really wanted—not to run his father's cigar business but to report the news. His very first story took him back to church, the Otterbein Memorial United Brethren congregation at Fifth and Rowland Avenues, to be specific. There, as Mencken reported, "Charles H. Stanley and J. Albert Loose entertained a large audience last night with an exhibition of war scenes by the cineograph." Here was material that the mature Mencken would have skewered with his acute sense of human folly—Protestants of pacifist background viewing scenes from a war (the Spanish-American) that underscored the hubris of United States foreign policy. But Mencken played it straight because he was trying out for full-time reporting with the *Baltimore Morning Herald*. So excited was Mencken with the prospect of seeing his writing in print that he "was up with the milkman the next morning" to inspect the paper. When he found his copy, "exactly as written," "there ran such thrills through my system as a barrel of brandy and 100,000 volts of electricity could not have matched."

Even when Mencken started as a reporter, he could not escape Christianity. He was officially a church member and lived in a society dominated by Protestant expectations. But work as a journalist would increase his skepticism about ideals even as it opened worlds of intrigue that captured Mencken's wonder. He confessed that the life of young newspaper reporters was "the maddest, gladdest, damnedest existence ever enjoyed by mortal youth." The reason was:

> At a time when the respectable bourgeois youngsters of my generation were college freshmen, oppressed by simian sophomores and affronted with balderdash daily and hourly by chalky pedagogues, I was at large in a wicked seaport of half a million people, with a front seat at every public show, as free of the night as of the day, and getting earfuls of instruction in a hundred giddy arcana, none of them taught in schools.

Born Again

Mencken admitted that his childhood and home life were utterly conventional. He was "a larva of the comfortable and complacent bourgeoisie," "encapsulated in affection," and "kept fat, saucy and contented." The only psychological significance of his upbringing was that his entry into and acquaintance with the world was "placid, secure, uneventful and happy." According to those circumstances, Mencken's future was fixed; he would work for his father in the cigar business and then inherit the enterprise. The problem was that Mencken's capacity for the manufacture and selling of cigars was far from placid, uneventful, or happy. At the age of sixteen, after graduating from the Baltimore Polytechnic Institute, he started as a bookkeeper's assistant in his father's office. "When I was sent to the bank with checks to deposit I made mistakes; when I had bills to make out, I made worse ones." He failed in that aspect of the business and moved to the actual construction of cigars. Again, Mencken failed. His father then tried him as a salesman. He missed again. "I detested approaching customers." But these three strikes could not put the son "out" of the business. As long as the father lived, the son could not leave the game. "My father had his heart set," Mencken later wrote. "There was no apparent way of escape."

Whether Mencken put himself into the work was another matter. The family had spoken occasionally of sending him to Johns Hopkins University, where August hoped his son might study for a law degree. At one time, the family back in Germany had made funds available to Mencken descendants to attend university. But they had also determined that American members of the family need not apply. So if Mencken were to pursue an education, it would be on his own. And he did. In off hours, the junior partner in the cigar firm continued to read. He read Stephen Crane's *Red Badge of Courage* and works of the iconoclast literary critic James Huneker, a man who also bucked family expectations and left a career in law; he became a writer Mencken emulated and later befriended. He not only read but wrote. Rudyard Kipling inspired him to try poetry, and Mencken's very first published piece was an "ode" to baseball. He also dabbled in short stories, and even took a correspondence course in creative writing.

What Mencken truly wanted to do was become a reporter, but his father insisted on the family business. At first, when Mencken approached his father about another line of work, August admitted that he too had not wanted to run a business as a young man. Even so, August was "so plainly dashed" by Henry's desire to leave the business that the son decided to go along, even though he felt like an inmate with suicide as the only escape. Mencken would later write about his reasons as a middle-aged man for not taking his life even while believing that human existence was fundamentally without purpose or meaning. As an older adolescent, suffering from "the green sickness of youth," however, he was so unhappy as to find "death . . . preferable to life." He had been a star student in high school but was now "deflated" because "it quickly appeared that I knew nothing." Still, he went along and did nothing rash. For two years before turning eighteen, in addition to doing some writing, he went to the theater and burlesque houses, and lived at home with a mother who understood his frustration but could do nothing to change his circumstances. His only hope was another conversation with his father about the business during the summer of 1899.

That conversation never came. Instead a plot device that only an inferior fiction writer could imagine intervened to liberate Mencken from his captivity. On December 31, 1898, August Mencken experienced an acute kidney infection from which he never recovered. Various remedies, including the application of leeches, only bought the patient another two weeks of painful and sometimes unconscious and at other times raving life at the family home. August Mencken died five months short of his forty-fifth birthday. Mencken's reaction to his "deliverance" was mixed. He later wrote that it was a "tremendous relief to me." Later in life he explained to Edgar Lee Masters, the author of *Spoon River Anthology*, that if August had lived, "I'd have stuck on in the tobacco business for at least a few years longer, probably to my permanent damage." But with relief also came grief and even anxiety over his reaction. "His death was the luckiest thing that ever happened to me," Mencken confessed. Then he added that "we were on good terms and I missed him sorely after he was gone." The grief Mencken expressed was arguably real since he was in many respects the spitting image of his father on business, politics, race relations, religion, and education. Where they differed was ambition. As Fred Hobson notes, Mencken would go on to compare his father to Abraham Cahan's fictional hero David Levinsky, "a man 'who fail[ed] to achieve the goal of his life,' who succeed[ed] in winning headway in all other fields save the one which was secreted in the innermost chambers of his heart and mind." In August Mencken's case, those fields were mathematics and engineering. He had to settle for "practical activities" and so could "never remain contented." Mencken wrote, "My father was a 'David Levinsky,' though of a different race, of a different mould, and different circumstances." Ironically, by succeeding in those practical realities, August gave Henry the comforts of a middle-class life from which the son could pursue his goals—once providence intervened to remove the chief obstacle to Mencken's pursuit.

Once set free, Mencken was soon seeking work at the *Baltimore Morning Herald*. (August died on a Friday, and Henry visited the *Herald*'s offices the following Monday.) Terry Teachout opines that Mencken's initial encounter with the *Herald*'s editor should have been the subject of Norman Rockwell. "I was eighteen years, four months and four days old," Mencken wrote, "wore my hair longish and parted in the middle, had on a high stiff collar and an Ascot cravat, and weighed something on the minus side of 120 pounds." Max Ways, the paper's editor, proceeded to put the freshly scrubbed and primped applicant through the paces. He asked Mencken about his education, writing experience, and reasons for wanting to work on a newspaper. All the West Sider could say in response was that "it seemed to me a sort of celestial call: I was bursting with literary ardors and had been writing furiously for what, at eighteen, was almost an age—maybe four, or even five years." Ways was unimpressed but polite. He informed Mencken that he had no openings at the time and told him to come back another night. Ways may have thought that ended the encounter, but Mencken was driven. The aspiring writer returned to the *Herald*'s offices the next day, and every day for four straight weeks. (Another source says he waited two weeks before returning.) Finally, by February 23, less than six weeks after August's death, Henry had his first assignment—covering a lecture at a United Brethren church and writing about an instance of horse stealing. Aside from giving in to Mencken's persistent pleas, Ways had also heard from one of Mencken's classmates who was working at the paper that the would-be cub reporter was "a worthy fellow with some talent for writing." Between his father's death and his first stories as a journalist—cut out and preserved on the first page of Mencken's scrapbook—the aspiring writer had had a conversion experience; he had gone from the agony of feeling trapped in a thoroughly predictable business enterprise to the elation of being set free to explore the city, people, ideas, and customs on his own terms.

Vocational freedom had severe restrictions for Mencken, a person who as a man would seldom take a vacation or rest from writing or editing. Although he no longer needed his father's approval to work for a newspaper, he still needed an editor's approval to be hired. Because so much of the newspaper business—writing, editing, laying out the paper—happened at night, Mencken could continue with the family business and show up at the *Herald*'s editorial offices after hours in hopes of securing assignments. Max Ways gave him a few, like the one at the church, but not enough for Mencken to leave his day job. Every morning for several weeks after August's death, the dutiful son showed up at Aug. Mencken & Bro. at 8:00 a.m. and worked until 5:30 p.m. Because August's estate was still not settled, Mencken would often discuss legal matters with his uncle, Henry, for another half hour. Over the next hour, he recalled, "I had to get home, change my clothes, bolt my dinner, and return downtown to the *Herald* office."

When Ways gave assignments to Mencken, they were the least desirable ones and took him to Baltimore's suburbs, to places the regular reporters were loath to go. One night Mencken needed to range between Catonsville on the western side of the city and Back River on the east, and from Tuxedo Park on the north side to Mount Winans in the south. He spent sixty cents on trolley fares, half his daily wages at the cigar business. Mencken was too timid to ask about an expense account. When he did inquire how far his beat—Mencken called it his "diocese"—extended, Ways gave the line that gave reporters both a long leash and a firm sense of who held it: "You are supposed to keep on out the road until you meet the Philadelphia reporters coming in." That definition did not please the overworked Mencken, though it was a line he would use on journalistic cherubs when he was on the other side of the city editor's desk. Part of the reason for Mencken's displeasure with Ways's response was that the aspiring journalist was not only working nonstop between getting up and going to bed, but had also been enduring this schedule for almost six months. Not until July 2, 1899, did Ways hire Mencken as a regular writer for the modest salary of seven dollars a week.

Michael Schudson observes that in the 1890s journalism in the United States entered a period characterized by professionalism and objectivity. The old reporter was generally a "hack" who wrote solely for a paycheck. "He was uneducated and proud of his ignorance; he was regularly drunk and proud of his alcoholism." The new journalists of Mencken's generation were better educated—many were college graduates, "younger, more naive, more energetic and ambitious," and "usually sober." Many of them were more interested in writing than in simply being reporters. The ability to communicate clearly and without cant was important to the editors who hired the new journalists. The alleged innocence of the new class of reporter dictated his commitment to realism or "just the facts." The mood of the period, shared by the press and progressive reformers, was, as Clarence Darrow phrased it, "tired of preachers and sermons" and "ask[ed] for facts." The world had "grown tired of fairies and angels," and asked for "flesh and blood." Observation was key to the new journalism—not fitting circumstances into preconceived ideologies (such as those of a political party or economic class), but looking at reality. This journalistic realism used the natural sciences as a model and located truth in the external phenomena that could be seen by someone free from prejudice. Schudson writes that the world "was disenchanted as never before."

One of the reporters who embodied the new journalism was Theodore Dreiser, an aspiring writer who started as a reporter in 1892 in Chicago and later held a complicated literary relationship with Mencken. When he moved to the *New York World*, he saw pasted on office walls a sign that read: "Accuracy, Accuracy, Accuracy! Who? What? Where? When? How? The Facts—The Color—The Facts!" Dreiser added:

> While the editorial office might be preparing the most flowery moralistic or religionistic editorials regarding the worth of man, the value of progress, character, religion, morality, the sanctity of the home, charity and the like, the business office and news rooms were concerned with no such fine theories. The business office was all business. . . . "Get the news! Get the news!"—that was the great cry in the city editorial room. "Don't worry much over how you get it, but get it, and don't come back without it! Don't fall down! Don't let the other newspapers skin us—that is, if you value your job! And write—and write well. If any other paper writes it better than you do you're beaten and might as well resign."

Mencken was well aware of the quest for objective journalism defined by factual reporting, but that was the editorial policy more of the *Herald*'s competitor, the *Sun*. Ways preferred "a more imaginative and colorful" style; as a reporter, he himself had a knack for humor as well as a "trick of pathos." For this reason, reporters for the *Herald* wrote "rather briskly" compared to those of the *Sun* or the *Congressional Record*. One indication of Ways's editorial standards was the first story that Mencken knew to have pleased the editor. It was about the death of an African American street preacher who died street-side while singing a hymn. Mencken acknowledged that he was not "present at ringside" but had to "rely on the cops for the facts." But "I must have got a touch of drama into my report, for Max was much pleased" and rewarded his reporter with tickets to a show.

Once he had won Ways's approval, Mencken moved from scattered assignments around the suburbs to regular stints in the city's police districts—first the southern neighborhoods, then the central district, the "premier" responsibility for the city's journalists since it had the courts, the jail, the hospital, and the morgue. Here the eighteen-year-old witnessed the aftermath of life's "harsher matters."

I well recall my first suicide, for the victim was a lovely young gal who had trusted a preacher's son too far, and then swallowed poison: she looked almost angelic lying on her parlor floor, with a couple of cops badgering her distracted mother. I remember, too, my first autopsy at the morgue—a most trying recreation for a hot Summer day—, and my first palaver with a burglar, and my first ride with the cops in a patrol-wagon, but for some reason or other my first murder has got itself forgotten. . . . In those days carbolic acid was the favorite drug among persons who yearned for the grave, just as bichloride of mercury was to be the favorite of a decade later, and I saw many of its customers brought in—their lips swollen horribly, and their eyes full of astonishment that they were still alive. Also, I saw people with their legs cut off, their arms torn off, their throats cut, their eyes gouged out. It was shocking for a little while, but then no more.

Mencken was by no means an innocent. His observations of the Hollins Street neighborhood, recorded in his memoir *Happy Days*, indicate that his parents hardly protected him. He ranged widely through a sordid world as freely as twenty-first-century children surf the Internet. Even so, Mencken had to adjust quickly to a side of human existence that was even darker than he had been led to believe.

His description of his first execution—a hanging on July 28, 1899— suggests the way he coped—with indifference shrouded by hardness of mind and soul:

When I was assigned to it as legman for one of the older reporters I naturally suffered certain unpleasant forebodings, but the performance itself did not shake me, though one of the condemned lost his black cap in going through the trap, and the contortions of his face made a dreadful spectacle. The affair was staged in the yard of the city jail, and there was a large gathering of journalists, some of them from other cities, for quadruple hangings, then as now, were fancy goods. I went through the big iron gate at 5 a.m., and found that at least a dozen colleagues had been on watch all night. Some of them had sustained themselves with drafts from a bottle, and were already wobbling. When, after hours of howling by relays of colored evangelists, the four candidates were taken out and hanged, two of these bibbers and six or eight other spectators fell in swoons, and had to be evacuated by the cops. The sheriff of Baltimore was required by law to spring the trap, and he had prepared himself for that office by resorting to a bottle of his own. When it was performed he was assisted out of the jail yard by his deputies, and departed at once for Atlantic City, where he dug in for a week of nightmare.

Mencken himself may have been one of the few reporters without a bottle, but within a year he was on a voyage to Jamaica in hopes of beating a chronic cough—a fear of tuberculosis was his explanation for the voyage. There he took up smoking and drinking with a vengeance. During this same time, Mencken likely contracted gonorrhea through his nighttime adventures. The proper medication quickly cured Mencken. But the young reporter was not above the torments that his duties required him to observe and ponder (and sometimes endure).

Mencken quickly ascended through the ranks of newspaper reporters, partly owing to real talent and partly to a work ethic that kept him sober and eager. He went from following the police blotter and city morgue to covering city hall within his first year, and increasingly received Ways's trust. For the 1899 elections, Ways gave Mencken, then only nineteen, three columns on the front page. This was a story of significance since Baltimore's elections usually were accompanied by at least one murder. "But the tide was now flowing toward peace and decorum, and though I roved the town all day, looking for dead and wounded," Mencken explained, "I had to base my lead on the surprising fact that no one had been killed, and only a few poor bums hurt."

Even if the drama of city life was becoming less dramatic, Mencken found his routine as a newspaperman eminently agreeable. He arrived home after work about three in the morning, and with a quiet house engaged in reading before going to bed and "sleeping like a top." He rose generally around ten and spent several hours in "literary enterprises" before going to work late in the afternoon. The worst part of the job was that it was so strenuous—"it worked me too hard." But even this circumstance did not deter Mencken because he was "still full of the eagerness of youth, and hot to see the whole show." The best part of the job was "the show": "a newspaperman always saw that show from a reserved seat in the first row. The rest of humanity had to wait in line and struggle for places but not a reporter." The performances that Mencken chronicled as a young journalist provided precisely the sort of perspective that other writers of his generation only found by going into exile in Europe. Some biographers would later complain that "the smell of the city room" lingered in everything that Mencken wrote. But Terry Teachout turns this lament on its head: "It was the discipline of daily journalism that freed [Mencken] from the clutches of the genteel tradition." The city room of the *Herald* was to Mencken what "Europe was for Henry James: the great good place where he became himself," as Jonathan Yardley phrased it. Fred Hobson made the same point: the streets of Baltimore became Mencken's "equivalent of the Mississippi riverboats on which Samuel Clemens had served his apprenticeship."

As much as the city of Baltimore shaped Mencken's sensibilities, the young man himself exhibited an extraordinary work ethic that would characterize not only his green years as a cub reporter but also his entire career as editor, literary critic, and essayist. By the time he had turned twenty, he was picking up out-of-town assignments.

Mencken's first "really juicy" one was in May 1901 in Jacksonville, Florida, covering the largest recorded fire in US history at the time. When he arrived, "all set to load the wires with graphic prose, there seemed to be nothing left save a fringe of houses around the municipal periphery, like the hair on a friar's head." His presence in Jacksonville coincided with the delivery of relief donations from the citizens of Baltimore, gifts that alerted Mencken to the "imbecility of the public effort to aid . . . victims." The boys at Pimlico race track had collected one hundred used horse blankets, and the saloon keepers of Maryland had donated one hundred cases of Maryland rye whiskey. When the mayor of Jacksonville heard about the generosity of Baltimoreans while in Mencken's presence, he could only laugh. With temperatures in the eighties, the residents of Jacksonville hardly needed to be kept warm. The rye only presented the problem of how to keep it out of the wrong people's stomachs, which added the wrinkle of how to use a police force already overworked. The donations turned out to be a challenge for Mencken as well, since his editor wanted to run a statement of gratitude from the mayor of Jacksonville to the city of Baltimore. Rather than covering the fire's destruction, Mencken wound up hectoring the mayor for a statement.

Another prime assignment that proved disappointing was Mencken's first admission to the Senate press gallery. There he encountered "the peculiar smell that radiates" from legislators—"that sickening mixture of stale beer and free lunch, contributed by the city members, and cow and sweat, contributed by the locals." The best of all out-of-town assignments was the 1902 eruption of the Martinique volcano. The second blast, which did not occur until reporters had sailed within viewing distance, was ten times more powerful than the first; Mencken called it "the most stupendous spectacle ever staged on earth." As it turned out, Mencken's knowledge of the volcano had to come from other reporters' accounts. He could not make the trip because he had to be in court to help with continuing contests over his father's estate. He had still not escaped August's long shadow.

The Jacksonville fire proved to be a practice run for Baltimore's own historic blaze, which on February 7, 1904, broke out in the city's business district. Mencken had climbed the rungs of the *Herald* to become, in 1901, the Sunday editor, and two years later, the city editor. To say that his life revolved around the paper is an understatement, since his existence for the better part of three days during the infamous "great Baltimore fire" was all-encompassing. Mencken had unknowingly fortified himself for this marathon by staying out after a Saturday's work at one of the drinking clubs until 3:30 a.m. He had planned to sleep in, but a phone call interrupted his slumbers, and eight hours after retiring for the evening a reporter escorted him to the office for what "promised [to be] swell pickings for a dull Winter Sunday." Not until Wednesday, February 10, did his "pants and shoes, or even [his] collar, [come] off again." Not until the following Sunday did Mencken have a chance to bathe. For the first three days, he worked sixty-four hours straight. He paused for six hours of "nightmare sleep," before embarking on a "working schedule of from twelve to fourteen hours a day, with no days off and no time for meals until work was over." Even for a twenty-three-year-old man, the work was "brain-fagging and back-breaking; but it was grand beyond compare—an adventure of the first chop, a razzle-dazzle superb and elegant, a circus in forty rings."

As indifferent to Baltimore's citizens as Mencken's reaction may sound, the exhilaration he felt owed less to the fire's destructive power than to the challenge of producing a newspaper in an office building that itself had caught fire. The *Herald*'s editors and staff first assembled at a nearby hotel and decided to seek assistance from the *Washington Post* in producing a paper. Mencken went by train with several colleagues to the command center for the *Herald*'s first edition of fire news. They produced only four pages, but that was as much as any Baltimore paper could manage since all the major dailies had succumbed to the fire. To the streamer head that read "Heart of Baltimore Wrecked by Greatest Fire in City's History," Mencken later rewarded the copy he composed from the nation's capital with his stamp of approval: "It was simple; it was direct; there was no fustian in it; and yet it told the story perfectly." But the *Post* would not accommodate the *Herald* for long since it had working relations with Baltimore's *Evening News*.

Mencken and his crew regrouped for a second edition by enlisting the aid of a small paper, Baltimore's *World*. That paper was too small, however, for ongoing production and coverage of so great a story. So Mencken went with his editorial team to Philadelphia, where the afternoon paper, the *Evening Telegraph*, could accommodate the production of a morning publication. This remote production also required Mencken to secure a special arrangement with the Baltimore & Ohio Railroad that gave the *Herald* access to a train dedicated to its editorial and printing work. The first paper out of Philadelphia was "a gorgeous thing of fourteen pages, with twenty columns of advertising." It knocked "the eyes out of the *Sun* and *Evening News*," and Mencken and his colleagues "rejoiced and flapped [their] wings accordingly." Mencken would remain in Philadelphia for the next five weeks. "We were printing a daily newspaper 100 miles from base—a feat that remains unparalleled in American journalism." After he returned home, it took Mencken months to recover from the initial week of effort. It also confirmed his observation about the effects of alcohol on literary endeavor. Those who refused to drink until work was over "needed only brief holidays to be substantially as good as new." Those who drank moderately while working "showed considerable fraying, and some of them had spells of sickness." Those who drank "in the classical manner" were useless by the second week in Philadelphia and were later "floored by serious illness."

A Man of Letters Trapped in the Body of a Journalist

Mencken wrote whatever his editors at the *Herald* asked him to. One estimate puts his volume as a cub reporter at five thousand to six thousand words a day. One of his early assignments was to cover a performance by John Philip Sousa's concert band, an event that played to Mencken's lifelong interest in and performance of serious music. This concert fell to the most recent hire by Mays mainly because no one else wanted to attend it. In 1901 Mencken took on the job of drama critic for the paper and received a piece of advice that he would apply to most of his work as a literary critic and editor—the critic's first task was to write something that readers enjoyed, whether or not the reviewer was correct or his aesthetics sound. Mencken even found outlets for his creativity within the newspaper itself. In 1901 he started to contribute to the editorial page with columns carrying his own byline. The pieces were semi-regular and appeared under different names—from Knocks and Jollies to Baltimore and the Rest of the World. The newspaper column was in its infancy; Mencken experimented with the genre and eventually left his own stamp on the editorial page. Sometimes he published his own efforts at poetry, the sort of schoolboy imitations of Kipling or Swinburne in which he had dabbled since high school. When he switched to prose, he tried aphorisms, a form that he would arguably perfect; comments on literature; and sarcastic observations about city hall's politicians and the people who followed them.

Although the newspaper offered Mencken a creative outlet, he was not content with the medium's range of ideas. While doing basically all the editors asked, Mencken expanded his repertoire on the side. His poems appeared as early as 1899 in the *Bookman*. He also wrote short stories and sent them to editors. *Short Stories* published several of them and paid Mencken fifteen dollars. From *Frank Leslie's Popular Monthly*, a respectable Victorian New England magazine, Mencken received over three times that sum for additional short stories. Considering the verbosity that now greets anyone with a computer and Internet service, a world where editors of small magazines and journals (like websites) were looking for text to fill their publications and sell to the public is not hard to imagine even if it is foreign to the twenty-first-century reader. Even so, few were the journalists who aspired to write beyond the newspaper. Even fewer were the ones who succeeded. As a twenty-something reporter, Mencken was beginning to make his way as a man of letters.

That awareness led to his first published book, a collection of his poetry, *Ventures in Verse*, published in 1903 by Marshall, Beek & Gordon (a publisher that Mencken later admitted had used this book to showcase its skills in book production). Even before this assemblage of forty poems in a hand-set edition with a print run of one hundred copies, Mencken had started a novel, based on the life of Shakespeare, but abandoned it after fifty pages when his ignorance of the Bard had sunk in. His poems, however, had all previously been published, and their appearance between two covers, no matter the publisher's designs, gave Mencken a higher profile both among the *Herald*'s staff and with readers of newspapers near and far. He later admitted, "as incredible as it may seem, it got a number of friendly notices," which Mencken collected through a clipping service and began to paste in a scrapbook. A reviewer for the *Chicago Record-Herald* called the poems "salable rather than sincere," nowhere evoking "any abiding and profound sense" of the "call of the spirit." Although the reviewer hoped Mencken would tap his "higher capabilities," he feared the poet was firmly one of those "cursed with the fear of being thought serious." A reviewer for the *Cleveland Leader* took notice of the book if only because he had come to trust Mencken as a drama critic for his "capacity and honesty." Mencken's own reaction to the book was a resolution to give up verse. But he did credit poetry with being "the best of all preparations for writing prose" because it "improves that sense of rhythm and tone-color—in brief, that sense of music—which is at bottom of all sound prose."

Mencken's writing outside the *Herald* and his widening reputation led to his second book, a short (just over one hundred pages) guide to George Bernard Shaw's plays. The idea for the volume came from Mencken's own interest in Shaw—an appeal that failed to abide once the Baltimorean recognized that the playwright was an "Ulster Polonius" who sermonized more than dramatized. He approached the American publisher of Shaw, Brentano, but was unsuccessful. Then Mencken proposed the book to Harrison Hale Schaff, the director of the Boston publishing house John W. Luce, who agreed to publish it. When the volume came out in 1905, it was the first book devoted to the playwright, but even before its publication the thrill (not released by the retread of previously published poems in *Ventures in Verse*) was more than Mencken could handle alone:

> I was so enchanted that I could not resist taking the prints to the office and showing them to Meekins [Lynn Roby Meekins, a managing editor at the *Herald*]—on the pretense, as I recall, of consulting him about a doubtful passage. He seemed almost as happy about it as I was. "If you live to be two hundred years old," he said, "you will never forget this day. It is one of the great days of your life, and maybe the greatest. . . . Go to your office, lock the door, sit down to read your proofs. . . . Take the whole day off, and enjoy yourself." . . . So I locked myself in as he commanded, and had a shining day indeed.

For understanding Shaw, Mencken's book largely flopped, but for gaining a sense of the young journalist's outlook, *George Bernard Shaw* reveals more than Mencken likely knew. Terry Teachout concludes that most of the book "is given over to stilted plot summaries," a reason for most subsequent critics of Shaw to pay little heed to Mencken as anything other than "a curiosity." Teachout adds plausibly that Mencken was still young, appropriately intimidated by the world of literary criticism, and not yet aware that "his homemade prose style was as well-suited to serious criticism as it was to yellow journalism." But Mencken felt sufficiently secure to render Shaw on the infidel side of the great intellectual division between the forces of orthodoxy and those of heterodoxy. In fact, Mencken introduced Shaw to readers by setting the playwright in the context of Charles Darwin's epoch-making takedown of Christendom. Before Darwin, "the fight against orthodoxy" had to contend with "ignorance, antiquity, piety, organization, and respectability," and did so with the ineffective weapons of either "impious doubt" or "the bludgeon of sacrilege." With Darwin came the artillery of scientific facts. "For six thousand years it had been necessary," Mencken summarized, "in defending a doctrine, to show only that it was respectable or sacred. Since 1859, it has been needful to prove its truth." What made Shaw notable was his embodiment of this revolutionary insight. His plays cast doubt upon virtue by showing its vicious side, or by demonstrating the virtuous aspects of vice. "In this fact lies the excuse for considering [Shaw] a world-figure," Mencken opined. Shaw was the "embodiment of the *welt-geist*."

In recommending Shaw, Mencken could not resist contrasting the playwright with ecclesiastical figures. Though simplistic, the difference was that between the ideal and the real. "The function of the dramatist is not that of the village pastor," Mencken wrote. "He has no need to exhort, to call upon his hearers to come to the mourner's bench." Instead, "the world" expects the playwright to yield impressions. Mencken was overly optimistic about the world's audience since he was writing in the heyday of Victorian aesthetics, which expected art to teach what was good, true, and beautiful. But that did not prevent him from venturing his own aesthetic, in which the artist "concerns himself . . . with things as he sees them." The effect of such artistic expression was iconoclastic. Before "the world became engaged in its crusade against sham and error," the conflicts depicted, for instance, in the works of Shakespeare, were internal or civilizational. But in modern drama the opposition was between "new schemes of human happiness and old rules of conduct." For that reason, when audiences saw *Mrs. Warren's Profession*, a play in part about the social hypocrisies surrounding prostitution, they would fail to question "the legal and ecclesiastical maxim that the Magdalen was a sinner, whom mercy might save from her punishment but not from her sin." After seeing the play, instead of "being unthinking endorsers of a doctrine they have never even examined," they would become "original thinkers" who, if they still condemn the Magdalen, do so "not because a hundred popes did so before them, but because on hearing her defense, they found it unconvincing."

Terry Teachout classifies Mencken's book on Shaw as a punctuation mark in the Baltimorean's career. After his first venture in literary criticism between two covers, Mencken wrote no more fiction or poetry himself. He had found a genre that suited his interests and abilities, though reactions to the book would have hardly confirmed this observation. Mencken sent a copy of the book to Shaw, who never responded. Only in 1920 would Mencken learn that Shaw was impressed, even if the Ulsterman had found the tone "flippant," as reported by Fred Hobson. But even as Mencken was emerging as a critic with sensibilities that would propel him as an editor, not to be missed was his understanding of the times in which he lived. As a skeptic (shaped largely by his father's skepticism), Mencken saw a world dominated by Christianity in which iconoclasts like himself needed to rally together to create space for their own original ideas. Given the freedoms that Mencken enjoyed professionally (to write almost whatever he wanted and have it published) and personally (not many pleasures were denied a young bachelor in a medium-sized city), his sense of combat looks overblown. Then again, anyone who has noticed the oddity of Christmas music performed by everyone from the Mormon Tabernacle Choir to Dean Martin accompanying shoppers in the United States during the month of December might gain a glimmer of Mencken's predicament.

Critic of Ideas (and Everything Else)

Mencken may not have exhibited in his book on Shaw the confidence of his later writing, but such self-assurance was not far off. In fact, his second book, *The Philosophy of Friedrich Nietzsche*, published in 1908, exhibited the qualities that gave Mencken's writing vigor while adding intellectual heft to his outlook. The idea for the book came from Harrison Hale Schaff, his editor at Luce, who had actually wanted Mencken's volume on Shaw to show connections to Nietzsche's iconoclastic ideas. Although Mencken would acquire a reputation as America's Nietzsche, he was initially unenthusiastic about the project. Schaff wanted an introductory volume, similar to the book on Shaw, that would acquaint American audiences with the German philosopher. As it turned out, Mencken's was the first book in English on Nietzsche at a time when little of the philosopher's oeuvre had been translated. Mencken also faced the challenge of having little background in philosophy, German or otherwise. His most advanced degree, after all, was a high school diploma from a vocational institution. And it was a somewhat green journalist with little formal education on which Nietzsche's initial reception in North America would rest. For nine months, while maintaining his duties as a journalist (in 1906 he had moved from the *Herald* to the *Sun*), Mencken read up on German philosophy—"dull . . . not to say repulsive"—before turning to all of Nietzsche's published writings in the original. He found the works first at the Enoch Pratt Free Library in Baltimore but also needed to use the Library of Congress in Washington. If Mencken had gone to college and then to graduate school, this would have been his dissertation. As it was, his writing of *The Philosophy of Friedrich Nietzsche* was akin to CBS news anchor Dan Rather, while earning his stripes as a reporter in Dallas during the 1960s, writing a book on Jürgen Habermas.

The book came in three sections: one part was biographical, another arranged Nietzsche's ideas according to topics, and the last explored the philosopher's critics. Less important than whether Mencken presented Nietzsche correctly—he was, after all, on virgin terrain—was what the writer saw in the philosopher. The chapter on Christianity was the longest and began with Mencken's judgment that Nietzsche's "fearless criticism of Christianity has probably sent forth more ripples than any other stone he ever heaved into the pool of philistine contentment." The philosopher's complaints against the religion were two: first, that it was untrue, and second, that it was degrading. The first point was hardly controversial by the late nineteenth century, since "a literal faith in the gospel narrative is confined to ecclesiastical reactionaries, pious old ladies and men about to be hanged." But Nietzsche's second contention, that Christianity had made the world worse—or even more daring, that Christianity was "cruel and degrading"—was the German's original feature.

The Nietzschean point that Christianity introduced into the world a slave morality was easy to describe but required Mencken to find scientific support. For Nietzsche, Christianity "waged a deadly war against the highest type of man. . . . It has taught men to regard their highest impulses as sinful—as temptations." Although Mencken would later use this claim against cultural and intellectual rubes—whether the snake handlers of Dayton, Tennessee, or the moralists of Boston—as a young man he linked Nietzsche's point, as he had with Shaw, directly to Darwin. Instead of using the German philosopher to support artistic achievements that were not beholden to Christian morals, Mencken saw Nietzsche as essentially confirming Darwin's conclusion about the survival of the fittest. Rather than pointing to men who could rise above the mediocre and create superior artistic expressions or build advanced cultures, Mencken interpreted Nietzsche as validating Darwin's account of how people survived the spread of disease. "The man who is able to get all of the food he wants, and so can nourish his body until it becomes strong enough to combat germs of disease," Mencken wrote, "such a man, it is obvious, is far better fitted to live than a man who has none of these things." In other words, Nietzsche was the philosophical icing to Darwin's cake:

> [M]an might defy the law of natural selection as much as he pleased, but he could never hope to set it aside. Soon or late, he would awaken to the fact that he remained a mere animal, like the rabbit and the worm, and that, if he permitted his body to degenerate into a thing entirely lacking in strength and virility, not all the intelligence conceivable could save him. Nietzsche saw all this clearly as early as 1877. He saw that what passed for civilization, as represented by Christianity, was making such an effort to defy and counteract the law of natural selection, and he came to the conclusion that the result would be disaster. . . . Self-sacrifice, he said, was an open defiance of nature, and so were all the other Christian virtues.

Philosophers and historians have written at length on the relationship between Darwin and Nietzsche, in part to account for the "anti-Darwin" claims in the latter's writing. That Mencken did not weigh in on these complicated matters of intellectual development and the relationship among Darwin, Darwinians, Nietzsche, the struggle for existence, the will to power, and theories of morality is no blemish upon his otherwise youthful achievement. If Mencken missed many of the subtleties that played out in the last two decades of the nineteenth century among schools of German and English philosophy, he was astute in picking up on one of the important tensions between Nietzsche and Darwinism (at least)—an optimistic reading of natural selection. While social Darwinists and progressive Protestants turned Darwin into a consoling scientific vindication of Western civilization's advance over the barbarity of those peoples and societies outside the West's influence, Mencken would have none of it. He quoted his favorite Darwinian apologist disapprovingly: "The ethical progress of society depends, not on imitating the cosmic process and still less on running away from it, but in combating it." To this Mencken responded with a plea for bravery: "We must either believe with the scholastics that intelligence rules, or we must believe, with Haeckel, that all things happen in obedience to invariable natural laws. We cannot believe both. . . ." Why Mencken (or Nietzsche) believed this telling point was more an indictment of Christianity than of, say, the ideas of John Locke or of Aristotle, or even the conventions of a newspaper editor, is a mystery. But it did show that Mencken had no interest in turning Darwin into reassuring truths about his readers' comfortable place in the cosmic order. He was apparently willing to acknowledge at least some of the disquieting consequences of evolution's assault upon orthodoxy.

The qualification "some" is important because when Mencken turned to Nietzsche's account of the so-called "higher range" of humanity's endeavors, such as philosophy and education, he resisted the conclusion that such reflection was a distraction from a person's animalistic struggle for existence. He heartily approved of the German philosopher's argument that philosophers should be forced to fend for themselves rather than be dependent on state subsidies. Mencken quoted Nietzsche: "Let philosophers spring up naturally, deny them every prospect of appointment, tickle them with salaries—yea, persecute them! Then you will see marvels." The lesson was clear. Truth could only come from an independent outlook. Salaries and administrations prevented a philosopher's quest for the true state of things. At the same time, Mencken recognized that philosophy of any kind could be a distraction from simply eating, gaining strength, escaping disease, procreating, and nurturing offspring. He acknowledged that critics of Nietzsche complained that an education had practically nothing to do with visibly increasing "a man's chest expansion or his capacity for lifting heavy weights." Mencken's response on behalf of Nietzsche was the "obvious" point that "a man who sees things as they are, and properly estimates the world about him, is far better fitted to achieve some measure of mastery over his environment than the man who is a slave to delusions." In other words, between the man who believed that smallpox was curable by denying its existence and the man who held no such superstition, "it is plain that the latter is more apt to live long and acquire power."

If Mencken's effort to hold out a place for philosophy and education within Nietzsche's notion of struggle for existence was strained, the philosopher's views on marriage were much easier to square with achieving mastery over the physical environment. The simple function of marriage was procreative—to produce a race of supermen. This arrangement left a basic inequality between men and women since the latter were the ones who bore children, thus leaving women in a weakened condition in the struggle for existence. As Mencken summarized, "the exercise of the will to exist is divided between . . . the man seeking the welfare of the race as he actually sees it and the woman seeking the welfare of generations yet unborn." This basic nature of marriage left little room for the sort of romantic ideals and religious virtues that surrounded Victorian notions of marriage. In fact, the sentimentality of romantic love left marriage partners without the wisdom necessary to evaluate a prospective mate. For this reason, Mencken approved of Nietzsche's recommendation of arranged marriages or "putting the selection of mates into the hands of third persons likely to be dispassionate and far-seeing." He also believed that Nietzsche's provision for unhappy spouses to escape their marriages readily was a sound one. When the German philosopher's understanding of women included a suspicion that their efforts to secure a mate were "deceptive, insincere, and pernicious," Mencken did not flinch. In fact, Nietzsche's opposition to women's suffrage made sense since it would bring the "contamination of the masculine ideals of justice, honor, and truth by the feminine ideals of dissimulation, equivocation, and intrigue." The irony of this understanding of the sexes was that Nietzsche, with Mencken's help anyway, produced a conventional— even Christian—understanding of women. A single woman could not be trusted, but a mother was "more sublime" than a father because maternity "produced a more keen sense of race responsibility." Because Nietzsche had not written about the future of marriage, Mencken weighed in on his own. He believed its days were numbered. "So soon as women are capable of making a living for themselves and their children without the aid of the fathers of the latter, the old cornerstone of the family—the masculine defender and breadwinner—will find his occupation gone, and it will be ridiculous to force him, by law or custom, to discharge duties for which there is no longer need." Meanwhile, as soon as women "became capable of doing men's work and of thus earning a living for themselves and their children without the aid of men," the assault on marriage will have achieved the status of full-blown war. What the decline of marriage would mean either for the survival of the race or for the breeding of superman Mencken failed to answer.

Even so, Nietzsche's appeal to Mencken was formidable and would last well beyond any of the surface connections that had emerged in his acquaintance with Shaw. The reason for the attraction came in one of the book's concluding paragraphs. "[Nietzsche] believed that superior men, by which he meant the alert and restless men, were held in chains by the illusions and inertia of the mass," Mencken explained, "that their impulse to move forward and upward, at whatever cost to those below, was restrained by false notions of duty and responsibility." Had Mencken still been a cub reporter whose editor constantly overlooked his work or refused to print his stories, this account of the superior man might have made sense as a way to vent frustration with office politics that kept writers of talent down. Or had Mencken had a self-understanding that he was the next writing genius to emerge in American letters and so resented the hacks whose prose so readily surfaced in magazines and books, Nietzsche's aristocratic air might have provided a release for such frustrations. But this was not Mencken's experience. He worked hard, gained the attention of his superiors, was grateful and even amazed at his success, advanced up the ranks, and even had a sense of his own limitations as a poet and fiction writer. Fred Hobson explains what Nietzsche did for Mencken well:

> Most of [Mencken's] ideas were in place before he ever encountered Nietzsche. But what Nietzsche offered him was *certification* of those ideas, a philosophical framework into which to place them. . . . [H]e also offered a manner, an extravagant, hyperbolic style, unleashing a torrent of metaphors and similes. He was the iconoclast telling the truth magnified by ten diameters.

Terry Teachout described the Nietzsche effect as Mencken having caught the first glimpse of the role the journalist would play—"the journalist with a hammer for whom Judeo-Christian morality was 'something to wield his sword upon.'"

Becoming H. L. Mencken

The book on Nietzsche received a wider circulation than the one on Shaw. For instance, the reviewer for the *New York Times* complimented Mencken for his style, intellect, and humor (and the writer had not likely seen any of the journalist's opinions on the editorial page). Meanwhile, the president of Columbia University, Nicholas Murray Butler, said Mencken "has written one of the most interesting and instructive books that has come from the American press in many a long day." "Mr. Mencken can write," Butler added, and "has something to write about." This was heady company for a young man with only a high school education and whose jackets still smelled of the city room's stale cigar smoke. But with a little bit of luck and a lot of perseverance, Mencken was beginning to perform on a national stage. More important, he had found the material for his act. The standard creative outlets of poetry and fiction were out. Criticism—of books, ideas, manners, you name it—would be his bailiwick.

Crucial, of course, to discovering both his style and his method of attack was finding an audience. Not many Americans read Mencken's book on Nietzsche. For the Baltimorean to reach a wider public, he would need to continue to use the megaphone that newspapers provided. Journalism was hardly averse to criticism, and with the op-ed page Mencken could begin to register his idiosyncratic perspective on a seemingly infinite variety of topics. One indication of the use to which Mencken could put the editorial page and the breadth of its canvas was a column he wrote about Henry James, who had given a widely publicized 1905 speech at Bryn Mawr College on the English language. The expatriate novelist conceded that English itself was an "unrescued Andromeda," but his most controversial point—reported throughout the nation—concerned the way Americans used English. The effects of schooling and journalism on American speech rendered the nation's usage "below the mark." Mencken's editorial in response was a foretaste of an inimitable style that rivaled James's not only for dexterity but also for sheer vitality:

> The average newspaper reporter writes better English than Henry, if good English means clear, comprehensible English. . . . Take any considerable sentence from any of his novels and examine its architecture. Isn't it wobbly with qualifying clauses and subassistant

phrases? Doesn't it wriggle and stumble and stagger and flounder? Isn't it "crude, untidy, careless," bedraggled, loose, frowsy, disorderly, unkempt, uncombed, uncurried, unbrushed, unscrubbed? Doesn't it begin in the middle and work away from both ends? Doesn't it often bounce along for a while, and then, of a sudden, roll up its eyes and go out of business entirely?

Such a riposte, as outrageous as it might be to professional critics, was indicative not only of Mencken's facility with English but also of the confidence that would establish him as one of the leading literary operators of the first half of the twentieth century. As Teachout observed, this kind of self-assurance was "impressive in so young a man," and it would "serve him well in his battles against the cultural establishment."

At the same time, even while establishing Mencken's reputation as an iconoclast, such forays into literary criticism had all the fingerprints of his Baltimore, middle-class home. As Teachout observes, Mencken's outburst against James would have been even more impressive had it not been so "wrong-headed." It "smacked of the philistinism of his father, the bourgeois burgher from Southwest Baltimore who knew what he liked and liked what he knew." For Fred Hobson, Mencken's early performances were a testimony to another generation of Menckens. In the particular case of Mencken's admiration for Nietzsche and the German self-consciousness that the project had awakened in the journalist, he was assuming the role of his grandfather, Burkardt, "a sort of *German* grandee among American shopkeepers, one of high birth who dwelled among Philistines." However parochial and prejudicial those instincts were, that Mencken could turn them into assets that the rest of the country would listen to and laugh about was truly remarkable.

CHAPTER THREE

Civilized Adults in Their Lighter Moods

By 1908 Mencken was a man of the world. He was also still a son in the Mencken family home on Hollins Street. Whether the tension between the cosmopolitanism of his professional interests and the Victorian norms at home reflected (or masked) a deeper psychological or spiritual wound is anyone's guess (and so far no biographer has cracked the code, despite the mounds of evidence that Mencken left behind). These two sides of Mencken's life prompted Terry Teachout to wonder: "Had Harry Mencken been more deeply scarred by his father's early death than he realized—or cared to admit? Did the relief that swept through him when August died, and the shame that surely followed it, make him cleave too closely to his mother out of a sense of guilt? Or was there some other trauma in his young life . . . ?" Mencken apparently did not sense an urgency to choose. He simply went on with his conventional life in Baltimore and his iconoclastic voice in print.

To celebrate the publication of his Nietzsche book and new responsibilities at the *Sun*, in 1908 Mencken took his first trip to Europe. He was by this point writing editorials (unsigned) and doubling as the paper's drama critic. He had also found his own idiom: "Any literate boy of nineteen can write passable lyrics, but I doubt that any man ever had a sound prose style before thirty," Mencken recalled. "I had written sound journalese," but "in 1906 I suddenly developed a style of my own and it was in full flower by the end of that year." Between writing for the *Sun* and outside assignments, he had doubled his salary and could afford a cruise. He sailed to Liverpool, spent several days in London, and then used Mark Twain's *A Tramp Abroad* as a guidebook to Germany, with a stop in Leipzig to find the street—Menckestrasse—named for his ancestor, the seventeenth-century philosopher Lueder. Despite a budding German self-consciousness that came with his immersion in Nietzsche's original language, London was the highlight of the trip. Visits to the graves of favorite English authors like Oliver Goldsmith and William Makepeace Thackeray still had the capacity to move him.

After his return to the States, Mencken's responsibilities continued to increase. In 1910, when Charles Henry Grasty acquired the *Sun*, Mencken became second in command of an afternoon daily, the *Evening Sun*. He was responsible for writing editorials and an initialed column, reviewing plays, and overseeing letters to the editor. Mencken's work on the Nietzsche book also paid dividends by showing off his talents outside Baltimore. In 1908 he received an offer to review books for the magazine the *Smart Set*. At the time, Mencken did not consider himself to be a book reviewer. But after a train ride to New York where he met the magazine's editor, Fred Splint, Mencken returned to Baltimore with a contract (for fifty dollars a month) and a satchel full of books. The place to which he took those books was the family home on Hollins Street. Had he been willing to move to New York City, as Terry Teachout speculates, Mencken could have tripled his salary. But as he would later explain, New York City was a place to make money while Baltimore was a city to enjoy the money made. And as much as Mencken enjoyed Baltimore's eating and drinking establishments, he was remarkably content to come home each night after a shift at the newspaper "to a plate of his mother's sandwiches."

The Free Lance

Lots of people still quote Mencken in columns and editorials because he is so quotable. What people quote are his opinions, and the reason is that people remember Mencken not for his books on Nietzsche or Shaw, or for his reporting on Baltimore's "Great" fire, but for his verdicts on human folly. In his preface to the second volume of his memoirs, *Newspaper Days*, Mencken clarified this point when he declared that he had a "close, confidential view of the manner in which opinion is formulated." "More than once," he added, he had "staggered out of editorial conferences dripping cold sweat, and wondering dizzily how God got along for so many years without the *New Republic* and the Manchester *Guardian*." Upon further reflection, he also marveled that the

human race had not revolted "against the imposture, [dug] up the car-
cass of Johann Gutenberg, and heave[d] it to the buzzards and hyenas
in some convenient zoo." Mencken must have thought along the same
lines some thirty years earlier when he was writing editorials for the
Evening Sun. On one side of his opinion-making brain, he had to tow the
party line of the owner and his progressive outlook. There his editorials
showed support for reforms and reformers, such as voting rights, regu-
lation of industrial behemoths, and opposition to capital punishment,
along with backing for William Jennings Bryan and Woodrow Wilson
(whom Grasty had wanted to edit the *Sunpapers*).

On the other side, Mencken spouted the edgy opinions that created
a national following. In the pieces that carried his initials, he used the
rhetorical flourishes and wit that were his trademark. In one editorial
that celebrated alcohol—a topic that did not fit the progressive play-
book—Mencken praised the effects of adult beverages:

> What would become of the romance if there were no alcohol? Imag-
> ine a teetotaler writing *Much Ado About Nothing*, or the Fifth Sym-
> phony, or *Le Malade Imaginaire*, or *Peer Gynt*, or the Zend Avesta, or
> the Declaration of Independence or any other great work of feeling
> and fancy! Imagine Wagner, bursting with ginger-pop, at work upon
> *Tristan and Isolde*. Imagine Leonardo, soaked in health drinks from
> Battle Creek, fashioning the unfathomable smile of Mona Lisa.

As Fred Hobson observed, here are the telltale signs of Mencken's
opinion writing—"the sense of the outrageous, the catalogues, the cadences." Even if you took the opposite side, could withstand the shock,
and stay with Mencken's sprint through the catalogue of geniuses, you
could not suppress a grin.

Mencken found relief from the conflict between the newspaper's official voice and his own commentary on the world when one of the *Sun*'s
owners, Harry Black, recommended that Mencken take a freer hand
as editorialist. This suggestion led to the creation of the Free Lance, a
daily column that began in 1911 and continued until 1915. Mencken
had the liberty to train his critical eye on any subject except for Baltimore's clergy, though if they took issue with him he had permission to
respond. In his own words, a "private editorial column devoted wholly
to my personal opinions and prejudices" "launched me as a general
assassin." Obviously, Mencken's idea of "stirring up the animals" was

not what all readers wanted from their newspaper. But the arrival of "Baltimore's bad boy" did ensure readers who were either thrilled or horrified. It also brought an end to Mencken's outside writing. At the same time, the column gave him a chance to try out ideas in a public forum before cautious editors. Teachout is correct when he writes that the "trumpet-blowing troublemaker" of the Jazz Age was the creation of a much longer process of editorial page writing that went on "out of sight of the rest of America." Part of the excitement that Mencken created in his columns owed to the pious diction he regularly mixed into his observations, such as:

> The lesson for the day is from the twentieth chapter of Exodus, the sixteenth verse.

> The lesson for the day is from the thirteenth chapter of the Gospel according to St. Luke, the fourteenth, fifteenth, sixteenth and seventeenth verses.

> Texts for excellent sermons upon the observance of the Sabbath: Matthew, xii, 2 and 3. Mark, ii, 27. Mark, iii, 3. John, v, 16.

At the time, the newspaper column was still in its infancy—Mencken was one of the first journalists in the United States to write a signed editorial page column that opined about contemporary affairs. Other writers had space in which to assemble poems, observations from readers, or light, humorous asides about odd occurrences. Mencken's column stood out, not only because it was signed or because it was provocative, but also because the rest of the editorial page was so dull. He went out of his way to be controversial. The trick was to expose frauds, which fit in with progressive reformers and muckrakers. But Mencken's knack was to bring to light all shams—even those of do-gooders. Demonstrating hypocrisy was too easy for Mencken. His outlook highlighted the gap between human idealism and execution, especially among the uplifters and moralizers who thought they could actually improve people, society, or governments. Meanwhile, the column allowed him to write on almost anything. The only reason the Free Lance was not more significant was that it remained a local phenomenon. Only Baltimoreans read Mencken, even if he was the forerunner of nationally syndicated columnists like Heywood Broun and Walter Lippmann. Even so, for

Mencken the column was decisive for his own writing and editing: "Before it had gone on a year," he later recalled, "I knew precisely what I was about and where I was heading." In the column, "I worked out much of the material that was later to enter into my books, and to color the editorial policy of the *American Mercury*."

Book Critic

If Mencken desired a reputation beyond Baltimore's newspaper readers, writing for the *Smart Set* was his quickest access to it. His path to the magazine was a circuitous one, but with all the writing projects that Mencken had during his midtwenties, the chance of his writing literary criticism for a publication that had rejected several of his poems was hardly surprising. The connection came through Theodore Dreiser, another German American, who had already written *Sister Carrie* (1902) but was still working as an editor for Butterick Publications, the publisher of a variety of magazines. In 1907—at the suggestion of one of Mencken's Baltimore friends (George Bronson Howard)—Dreiser asked Mencken about following up his books on Shaw and Nietzsche with another on the German philosopher Arthur Schopenhauer. Mencken declined, but he did persuade Dreiser to print—of all things— articles on baby care for one of Butterick's magazines, the *Delineator*. One of Mencken's Baltimore acquaintances through an eating and literary club, the Vagabonds, Leonard K. Hirshberg, was a physician who needed a writer to put his ideas on babies before a wider audience. The articles that Dreiser published became yet another book that Mencken authored, *What You Ought to Know about Your Baby*, published in 1910 by Butterick. (The book begins with a mother, holding a crying baby, entering a train car, and trying to quiet the child by bouncing the baby in her arms. "Crime number one! Babies should *not* be bounced up and down; it nauseates them; it strains them; it makes them unhappy.")

When Mencken and Dreiser met in the latter's office in 1908, Dreiser described the former as a "taut, ruddy, blue-eyed, snub-nosed youth . . . whose brisk gait and ingratiating smile proved to me at once enormously intriguing and amusing," reminiscent of a "spoiled and petted and possibly over-financed brewer's or wholesale grocer's son who was out for a lark." This was the beginning a difficult friendship. The more each man grew to know the other, the more he disapproved. But each saw in the other enough of the same sensibilities to embark on a codependent professional relationship that drew sustenance from a small circle of friends. Mencken discovered that he needed an author to champion as a book critic, and Dreiser knew he required a reviewer to laud his novels. That both men were German American was icing on this literary cake. For the time being, Mencken wrote pieces for a number of the magazines in which Dreiser had a hand. When Mencken traveled to New York City for business, he regularly dined with Dreiser and caroused at beer halls. The Baltimorean returned the favor and invited Dreiser to the Mencken home for Thanksgiving. In 1909 Dreiser rewarded Mencken with an offer to be a staff writer for the *Delineator* at the rate of fifty dollars per week. Nothing could pry Mencken out of Baltimore, not even the desire for fame. He declined, but Dreiser passed along Mencken's name to the editor of the *Smart Set*, and from that point on the Mencken name crept into the annals of the nation's literary history.

The *Smart Set* was an odd platform from which to create a splash in literary circles, but it was within Mencken's reach. The magazine started as a literary supplement to *Town Topics*, a publication run by Civil War veteran Colonel William D'Alton Mann that covered New York society. The *Smart Set* regularly printed fiction, poetry, epigrams, and French essays. Some of the authors who contributed were James Branch Cabell, O. Henry, Jack London, and Frank Norris. Mann paid all his writers poorly and so profited nicely from the magazine. But when the colonel became entangled in a lawsuit over a story in *Town Topics* that besmirched the reputation of Theodore Roosevelt's daughter, Alice, Mann determined to beef up the *Smart Set*'s reputation by making it more serious. He did so by hiring George Jean Nathan and Mencken to write for the magazine. Although Mencken and Nathan would stand out in the world of publishing for their work first at the *Smart Set* and then at the *American Mercury*, they also stood apart. Although born in Fort Wayne, Indiana, Nathan was from a wealthy, cosmopolitan family that owned a vineyard in France and a coffee plantation in Brazil. While Mencken had received his advanced degrees on the streets of Baltimore, Nathan had studied at universities in Bologna, Paris, Heidelberg, and even at Cornell. Between them, the *Smart Set* provided readers with a critical perspective on literature (Mencken) and theater (Nathan). Nathan recalled meeting Mencken in 1909: "The stranger thrust out his hand to me and exclaimed, 'I'm H. L. Mencken from Baltimore and

I'm the biggest damned fool in Christendom and I don't want to hear any boastful reply that you claim the honor.'" Even if Nathan had the better pedigree, Mencken was the one that made both Nathan and the *Smart Set* memorable. As Terry Teachout observed, without Mencken the *Smart Set* and Nathan would both be "footnotes" to the history of American literature.

One of Mencken's earliest contributions was a brief notice about a book by Henry S. Williams on drinking, *Alcohol: How It Affects the Community, the Individual, and the Race* (1909). The author was a widely published scientist who regularly wrote for *Harper's* on scientific and historical topics, such as the Greek origins of modern science and the beginnings of the alphabet. Mencken paid respects to Williams by observing that he was no "blowzy evangelist, howling in a gospel tent, but a pathologist of learning and intelligence." At the same time, if not for Mencken's notice, Williams would have passed into obscurity after his death during World War II. (A Google search for Williams retrieves Mencken's review before anything else.) The book in question was one of the many written in support of the temperance movement and the eventual prohibition of the sale and distribution of alcohol in the United States. Politicians, Christians, and scientists all had their objections to alcohol. Williams was not concerned with "whether a wine-bibber can ever hope to go to Heaven." Instead, he marshaled scientific evidence to show that alcohol "attacks the vital organs, interferes with the mental processes and promotes the growth of the germs of disease." Apparently, Williams also provided statistics that demonstrated alcohol's direct contribution to crime. Mencken was underwhelmed by the alarming rate—50 percent—of criminals who consumed alcohol. The same reasoning could prove that it was responsible for "50 percent of all poetry, 60 percent of all philosophy, 70 percent of all prose fiction, and 99 percent of all music."

Aside from questions about the science and statistics of alcohol, Mencken took greatest exception to a relatively materialist conception of the good life, one that measured it by length of years rather than by quality of existence. The Christian supporters of temperance would not have agreed with Mencken's understanding of quality, but some believers might have found agreeable his notion that a well-lived life may have more significance than one that is simply long had they not been so eager for any reason—even the kind supplied by Dr. Williams—to shut down the local saloon and corporate brewery. Mencken was entirely underwhelmed by Williams's connection between total abstinence and "extreme longevity." To accept Williams's conclusion, Mencken asserted, readers first needed to "accept the theory that the usefulness and agreeableness of life are to be measured by its duration, and by its duration only." This did not make sense since the ordinary way of estimating a life was to look not at its length but at its breadth. The proof: "Fifty years of Shakespeare were worth more to the world than the innumerable hundreds of all the centenarians that ever lived." It was a savvy point that actually lined Mencken up more with people who believed in "higher" things—as Christians may well have—than with moralists whose ethical standards became merely a way to prolong physical life without reference to the spirit. Mencken saw it as his duty to remind them of "the art of life." Reading a book shortens life because it strains the eyes and atrophies muscles that could well use exercise. But "the man of thirty who has read many books is more creditable to the race, all other things being equal, than the man of ninety who has merely lived ninety years." This point did not relieve alcohol of its many crimes that cried "aloud to heaven." Still, even if alcohol makes life shorter, "by dulling the tragedies of existence and heightening its joys, it also makes life more bearable."

Another of Mencken's early targets was G. K. Chesterton, a British journalist who after his conversion to Roman Catholicism in 1922 would become for English-speaking Roman Catholics what C. S. Lewis was for the Anglo-American Protestant world. In 1909, when Mencken first took notice of Chesterton, the Englishman was still an Anglican, though more traditional than his Unitarian parents. Chesterton's book *What's Wrong with the World* (1910) was a series of roughly fifty shortish essays of social criticism in which the thirty-something writer assessed economics, human nature, feminism, and politics, and raised serious doubts about modern society's progress. Mencken objected not so much to Chesterton's thesis—that to "create anything good" we need to know what good is—but to his wordiness. Chesterton's platitude was worthy of President William Howard Taft, a Republican "milch-cow of optimism." If its truth was so obvious, why "rage and roar over it—to the extent of nearly four hundred pages"? "Suppose it to be a fact that our 174 warring sects," Mencken continued, "are getting precious few of us into heaven—who cares?" "Isn't it a fact that nine-tenths of us, like the melancholy shades in *Man and Superman*, prefer Hell?" Mencken's calculation of Nietzsche's popularity compared to Chesterton's may have made sense if he had only readers of the *Smart Set* in mind, though even here the idea that 90 percent of the magazine's readers had by 1910 abandoned all worries about an ultimate reckoning in the deity's moral accounting books is hard to fathom. At the same time, Mencken likely soothed readers who thought too long about the loss of ultimate significance with his depiction of how the average civilized man lived:

> As a matter of fact, we blunder along, barking our shins at every step and walking straight into every tree, not because we need quinine, but because that is the happy-go-lucky human way. If it were not for the fun of watching the other fellow gouge out his eyes and break his neck, we might stop to lament our own lacerations. As it is, we hail life as the greatest of adventures and accept without protest the trivial fact that it is meaningless.

Chesterton's outlook squeezed all the fun and anxiety out of life. If human existence were the "orderly and tedious march" that he proposed, "with all the hands trooping up the celestial gangplank in a lockstep . . . and clubbed into line by ecclesiastics on muleback," what man "worthy of the name would care to live"?

Chesterton provided another chance for Mencken to hone his skills as a book critic when the Englishman produced a book on a subject close to Mencken's own literary endeavors—a study of George Bernard Shaw. The 1909 book was the beginning of a periodic exchange between Chesterton and Shaw that Mencken refused to follow—it featured a 1928 debate between Shaw and Chesterton, moderated by Hilaire Belloc. What attracted Mencken's eye was Chesterton's rendering of Shaw as a Puritan, in addition to being an Irishman and a Progressive. By Puritan, Chesterton meant the Calvinist trait of contemplating God only through the mind or by ideas. Puritanism also stood for "savage negation" or a "philosophy of taboos." This was the consequence of abandoning sublime affirmations about God for a series of restrictions the purpose of which was to cultivate holiness or even perfection. Chesterton detected this negative spirit in Shaw and attributed it to his schooling with Irish Methodists. But Mencken was unconvinced. Shaw was no "economic Carrie Nation," no "Irish Luther." Shaw was not even much of a philosopher, even though Chesterton complimented the Irishman for making philosophy accessible. "At one moment, he seems to subscribe to a sort of rationalism," Mencken complained, "and at the next moment he is a thoroughgoing empiricist." He did agree with Chesterton that Shaw was a writer who excelled at "stirring up the animals." For Mencken this was a benefit, for Chesterton a liability.

The reason for the difference was theological. Mencken faulted Chesterton for losing Shaw and maintaining the Englishman's familiar themes: "that the only real truths in the world are to be found in the Nicene Creed, that science is a snare and human reason a delusion, that Hans Christian Anderson was a greater man than Copernicus, that sentiment is more genuine than hydrochloric acid, that all race progress is an empty appearance." That sequence of assertions, from exaggeration to the ridiculous, did not prevent Mencken from complimenting Chesterton. Indeed, as much as the nonbelievers among Mencken's readers could (and still do) thrill to see the iconoclast mock the unbelievable truths that believers affirmed, they seldom picked up on (and still don't) Mencken's praise for Christians when they deserved it. He admitted to enjoying Chesterton's "dialectical manner" even if not being convinced. The Englishman had become "the world's foremost virtuoso of sophistry and paralogy." "Not since St. Augustine have the gods sent us a man who could make the incredible so fascinatingly probable."

Chesterton's book on Shaw was closer to the sort of literary criticism on which Mencken made his name, but his duties at the *Smart Set* and his reading interests throughout his life extended as much to the Dr. Williamses of the book world as to the novelists who might enter the American or Western literary canon. In a book notice on John D. Rockefeller's autobiography, *Random Recollections of Men and Events*, Mencken had occasion to mock the industrialist's contention that Standard Oil Company was a "law-abiding and patriotic corporation." "You may know that he is wrong," Mencken wrote, "as certain as you know that virtue is its own punishment, and yet, when he . . . looks up into your eyes with that pious smile of his, you are literally forced to believe him, no matter how piteously your tortured intelligence shrieks." Rockefeller's only equals in "the higher chicanery of the dialectic" were Augustine, Tertullian, Origen, Philo Judaeus, and Hilary of Poitiers, since he was a "money grubber and a theologian," and skilled in the "casuistry of the jury lawyer, the ballyhoo evangelist and the politician." Mencken kept a finger on the pulse of all American religion, as evidenced in his review of Leon C. Prince's *The Sense and Nonsense of Christian Science*. Once again, Mencken mixed ridicule with playfulness in the face of religious idealism:

A *streptococcus* and the first reader of the Mother Church may be equally ideal and apparitional and yet their mutual reaction is real enough—to them. Let the *streptococcus* invade the first reader and the latter will inevitably fall ill, and though it may ease his mind to deny that the *streptococcus* is there, and even help him to get well, the *streptococcus* will be there all the same.

Mencken admitted that he had gone round with Christian Scientists about the chicken-and-egg nature of their metaphysics—"they have an answer to my answer to their answer, and I have an answer to their answer to my answer to their answer." For that reason, he made a habit of retiring after the first round of answers, "with my wind still in me, my eyes unblacked and all of my teeth in my gums." Just the same, Mencken recommended Prince's book—"short enough to be read at one sitting, and good enough to be reread at some other sitting."

Nevertheless, while Mencken entertained readers with his observations about the books that tumbled across his desk from American publishers, he was earning his stripes as a critic whose judgments signaled a shift in American literature. With Willa Cather's first novel, *Alexander's Bridge* (1912), Mencken did not detect a new direction in American fiction. He did observe that Cather was imitating Edith Wharton—a feature that Cather herself conceded and that lowered his estimate of her novel. Still, Mencken was not simply looking for novelty. Beginning writers, he argued, can choose either to study in "the School of Plot" or "the school of Piffle." Cather deserved credit for aiming higher, the result of which was "a very promising piece of writing." The book's weakness was Cather's resolution of the love triangle through death—"not a working out of the problem" but a "mere evasion" of it. Still, Mencken credited Cather with creating believable dialogue, descriptions "full of feeling and color," and "well drawn" characters. At the same time, Mencken used *Alexander's Bridge* to educate his readers on the pitfalls and achievements of good writing; this technique allowed him to enter the larger conversation about national letters. He recognized that Cather confronted a problem that all writers face—how to explain genius in a character. "It is easy to explain how William Jones fought and died for his country," Mencken explained, "but it would be impossible to explain (or, at any rate, to convince by explaining) how Beethoven wrote the Fifth Symphony, or how Pasteur reasoned out the hydrophobia vaccine, or how Stonewall Jackson arrived at his miracles of strategy." Shakespeare solved the conundrum; he made "Hamlet a comprehensible and convincing man by diluting that half of him which was Shakespeare by a half which was a college sophomore." Or Shaw did it by "drawing a composite portrait of two or three London actor-managers and half a dozen English politicians." Wisecracks like those were sufficiently literary to keep readers on their toes, but their comic effect made a Mencken review a literary achievement in its own right.

When it came to Joseph Conrad, Mencken again attempted to explain how good literature worked, this time by distinguishing drama from melodrama. His 1912 essay for the *Smart Set* was not a review of a specific Conrad title but a general recommendation that concluded with advice on the novelist's best efforts—the short stories "Youth" and "Falk," and the novels *Typhoon* and *Heart of Darkness*. Aside from a grab bag of positive comments about Conrad's characters, Mencken took the opportunity to instruct readers about differences between melodrama and realistic fiction. His "real objection" to melodrama was that "its effects are too staggering" in comparison to its "too puny" causes. For instance, why does "the tall, saturnine gentleman in the elegant dress suit" tie the youthful and vivacious woman to the railroad tracks, "with the Cannon Ball Express bearing down at ninety miles per hour"? The melodramatist's explanation is to render the gentleman as equal parts Satan and Don Juan who is retaliating for the woman's refusal of his advances. Mencken found such stories amusing, not because men did not sometimes really tie women up in front of approaching locomotives, but because life teaches that the melodramatist's reasons are silly. The reason why men bind women to train tracks, "when it is forthcoming at all, is always much more complex than the melodramatist's answer"—"so enormously complex" that it transcends "all the normal laws of cause and effect." This is what distinguishes melodrama from good writing, or Joseph Conrad from Richard Harding Davis, the journalist and popular fiction writer whom Mencken had read as a boy and whose stories inspired teenage boys with hopes for fame, courage, and conquest. On the surface, a novel like Conrad's *Nostromo* was similar to Davis's *Soldiers of Fortune*. But while the latter merely showed the surface of "South American turmoil," the former explored the motives behind the turmoil. Mencken conceded that he did not know if Conrad was accurate in his study of human motivation. But he was "wholly convincing" in rendering a portrait of human psychology that revealed much more than the standard American literary contrasts between virtue and vice, civilization and barbarism, piety and infidelity.

Even so, Conrad was no match for Theodore Dreiser, the American novelist with whom Mencken had a love-hate relationship. In 1902 when *Sister Carrie* was published, Mencken was just starting as a newspaperman and had little time for extracurricular reading. But by the time his second novel came out, *Jennie Gerhardt* (1911), Mencken was writing reviews for the *Smart Set* and could use his new platform to assign grades. The one he gave to Dreiser was A plus: "If you miss reading *Jennie Gerhardt* . . . you will miss the best American novel, all things considered, that has reached the book counters in a dozen years." Mencken went on to qualify that and enlarged the time frame to include all American literature. With the "Himalayan exception of *Huckleberry Finn*"—Mencken often invoked mountainous metaphors in his evaluations—"I am firmly convinced that *Jennie Gerhardt* is the best American novel I have ever read." He assured readers that he had read a lot, from Nathaniel Hawthorne and Harriet Beecher Stowe to Edith Wharton and William Dean Howells. He reassured them that he had "read and survived them and in many cases enjoyed them." Even so, Dreiser's second novel stood apart and "a bit above" them all. Mencken conceded that *Jennie Gerhardt* lacked "the grace of this one, the humor of that one, the perfect form of some other one." But its cumulative effect was "the most impressive work of art that we have yet to show in prose fiction," a story "in its stark simplicity, its profound sincerity" comparable to *Anna Karenina* and *Lord Jim*. It was a tale American in "scene and human material, and yet so European in its method," a judgment that put Mencken definitively on the side of literary cosmopolitans in their rivalry with literary nationalists.

One reason for connecting Dreiser more to European than American literature was the novel's lack of morality. *Jennie Gerhardt* had "no more moral than a string quartet or the first book of Euclid." Its philosophy of life was a "dark pessimism," the sort also found in the novels of Thomas Hardy, Émile Zola, and Russian writers. This was not the "jejune" pessimism of the Romantics, "the green sickness of youth, but that pessimism which comes with the discovery that the riddle of life, despite all the fine solutions offered by the learned doctors, is essentially insoluble." Dreiser's style only reinforced this outlook. He demonstrated no "painful groping for the exquisite, inevitable word." Instead, he was content with the "common, even the commonplace coin of speech." Even despite its "gross crudities" and "incessant returns to C major," the novel depicted American life "with extreme accuracy" and criticized it with "extraordinary insight."

For anyone who knew Butterick Publications, which was not many, the review of *Jennie Gerhardt* might have also looked like a way for the reviewer to repay Dreiser's favor of putting him on the *Smart Set*'s radar. Indeed, because of their personal and professional relationship, some might have legitimately questioned Mencken's judgment and integrity. The questions might have persisted had readers also known that Mencken was looking for an author to promote in order to boost his own status as literary critic. Technically speaking, Dreiser was no longer on the staff of the *Delineator*. Because of the undue attention he directed at the eighteen-year-old daughter of one of his fellow editors at Butterick Publications, in 1910 Dreiser lost his job. But he and Mencken continued to socialize, sometimes for dinner with Dreiser and his wife, Sara, at other times in the city's beer halls.

Mencken found Dreiser fascinating, someone he called "a polygamist on a really wholesale scale." He admitted in his private correspondence that he saw Dreiser's women as much as he did the novelist. He also wondered how the novelist managed to escape paternity suits. The only explanation was Dreiser's sterility. Their friendship revealed Mencken's own Puritanism, though he would have hated such a depiction. For all his iconoclastic ways, Mencken had "a prejudice against adultery" as a "breach of faith." What separated him from the Puritans, aside from the difference between prejudice and doctrine, was that Mencken refused to inflict his prejudices on others. For that reason, he continued to frolic with Dreiser, all the while marveling at his exploits and making mental reservations about the novelist's bad form. As Fred Hobson put it, Mencken was the "well-born child of the *gelehrten*" (scientist or professor), while Dreiser was merely a "peasant," one of those German Americans that Mencken's father and grandfather had regarded as beneath their good breeding and refined sense. Even so, the more he spent time with Sara Dreiser, the more he empathized with Theodore's dilemma:

> "How," I asked myself . . . , "would *you* like to be married to a red-haired Christian Scientist from the Great Plains? How would *you* like to go home to her every night . . . ?" Who, indeed, was I, to pronounce judgment upon a man who was my elder and my better . . . ? If the needs of his extremely difficult and onerous trade required him to

consume and spit out a schoolma'm from the cow country, then it was certainly to be lamented—but that was as far as I could go in logic, or in such ethical theory as I subscribed to.

Mencken's review of *Jennie Gerhardt*, then, was as much the product of his complicated relationship with Dreiser as it was a critical assessment. Mencken knew, for instance, that after leaving the *Delineator*, Dreiser was hard pressed for cash and needed royalties from his second novel to fill the gap. Soon after the review, Dreiser made Mencken the executor of his literary estate. Aside from the circumstances of their friendship and professional relationship, Dreiser and Mencken constituted a team of literary terrorists who were hell-bent on destroying the monuments of American letters. Teachout observes that Menken "longed for an American writer to praise, a man unafraid to face the ugliness of modern life . . . a connoisseur of shabbiness and fear." Dreiser fit the profile:

> Everything about *Sister Carrie*—its comparative frankness about sexual matters, its refusal to observe the moral niceties of punishing Carrie Meeber for her sins, its fearsomely honest portrait of Hurstwood, a middle-aged man in decline—was as far removed as possible from the genteel tradition. . . . *Sister Carrie* was a deeply moral book, but it offered the soft-mouthed reader no reassuring vision of virtue triumphant, only a harsh portrayal of lost souls caught in the web of life.

In other words, what American literature lacked, "an awareness of the common life," "the saloonkeepers and prostitutes and crooked politicians and murderers"—all the people that Mencken had met when he was pounding the pavement as a reporter—Dreiser supplied. The irony was that Mencken only knew this world professionally; he was not from the wrong side of the tracks but inhabited a Victorian middle-class world that gladly lived by the moral code of mainstream American fiction. Dreiser himself picked up on the irony when he wrote to Mencken: "unlike yourself, I am biased. I was born poor."

Mencken could try to explain away these differences, but they were likely apparent to him as long as he followed his ambition. He tried to downplay their differences by reminding Dreiser of the gap between their standing when they had first met. Mencken recalled that Dreiser was wearing a Hart, Schaffner and Marx suit and used a gold-lead pencil. Dreiser's polish as editor of the *Delineator* meant that Mencken never noticed the novelist's "proletarian" background. To Mencken Dreiser was always "a kind of literary J. Pierpont Morgan." That perception probably helped Mencken to feel less responsible for using Dreiser to advance his own career as a book man. For the Baltimorean knew that instead of merely damning American literature he needed books and authors to champion, not only to set a new course for American writing but also to prove himself as an evaluator of talent. Mencken himself admitted that what he needed "was an author who was completely American in his themes and his point of view," who was not too obvious but simple enough to be read by the masses, and who "knew how to concoct and tell an engrossing story." Dreiser fit the bill. In fact, as Teachout points out, three years to the month after Mencken had started writing for the *Smart Set*, Mencken had "finally found a new American novelist for whom he was willing to bang the gong."

The literary world was listening. The *New York Post* noticed Mencken's praise for Dreiser, and Harpers, the publisher of *Jennie Gerhardt*, featured Mencken's review in advertisements for the novel, the first time Mencken's endorsement was put to commercial purpose. Even more remarkable is that Mencken's praise seemed to work. Dreiser's novel sold well. Soon thereafter, Dreiser repaid the favor by entertaining Mencken for a meal with his wife, an engagement that did not prevent the novelist from leaving the apartment for an hour or more to accommodate one of his paramours. While the novelist was away, Sara Dreiser complained to Mencken about her unfaithful husband. Even though he disapproved of such infidelity, he still decided to "stand with the devil's party." As he explained, Theodore, not Sara, was his friend, and "she had done nothing to lift me, or even to interest me." That take on the Dreiser couple, in connection with Mencken's exuberant evaluation of Dreiser's writing, suggests that the book reviewer for the *Smart Set* "heard the still small voice of careerism whispering in his inner ear."

Whatever Mencken's motivation in promoting Dreiser, he was following his own script of literary criticism in America. In an essay published a few years later about the state of criticism, Mencken identified four primary schools of thought. One group of critics held that literature was supposed to "encourage the virtuous and oppose the sinful," and the reviewer's job was to "police the fine arts and so hold men in tune with the moral order of the world." An important figure in this group was W. C. Brownell, a critic for the *Nation*, whose imitation of Matthew Arnold earned him the Menckenian nickname "the Amherst Aristotle."

Mencken explained that Brownell's standards were "as iron-clad as the Westminster Confession." The other groups were less conspicuous and powerful. One said that art had nothing to do with morality but everything to do with beauty. Another regarded literature as chiefly a path toward psychological awareness, both in the author and in the reader. The last adopted a scientific approach and established standards "that resemble algebraic formulae." The school that bothered Mencken most was the established one, those critics who regarded literary criticism as little more than "a branch of homiletics." These writers, most of them academics, judged a work of art "not by its clarity and sincerity, not by the force and charm of its ideas, not by the technical virtuosity of the artist, not by his originality and artistic courage, but simply and solely by his orthodoxy." "We are," Mencken lamented, "a nation of evangelists; every third American devotes himself to improving and lifting up his fellow-citizens, usually by force":

> "Here is a novel," says the artist. "Why didn't you write a tract?" roars the professor—and down the chute go novel and novelist. "This girl is pretty," says the painter. "But she has left off her undershirt," protests the head-master—and off goes the poor dauber's head. . . . [A]t its worst, it is comstockery, an idiotic and abominable thing. Genuine criticism is as impossible to such inordinately narrow and cocksure men as music is to a man who is tone-deaf.

To counter this state of affairs, Mencken proposed not a school but literary criticism as "catalytic," a word he borrowed from chemistry. A catalyzer was a "substance that helps two other substances to react." This was how Mencken understood his work as critic. His duty was to "provoke the reaction between the work of art and the spectator":

> The spectator, untutored, stands unmoved; he sees the work of art, but it fails to make any intelligible impression on him; if he were spontaneously sensitive to it, there would be no need for criticism. But now comes the critic with his catalysis. He makes the work of art live for the spectator; he makes the spectator live for the work of art.

Mencken believed that the fruit of such criticism was "understanding, appreciation, intelligent enjoyment." Did it hurt if in the process the critic made a name for himself as big as the novelist's?

From Writer to Editor—but Still in Baltimore

By 1911, at the relatively young age of thirty-one, Mencken had carved out a reputation in both worlds of journalism and literary criticism. To do so, he needed to work in two cities. Work for the *Smart Set* took him several nights each month to New York City, where he counseled publishers and cajoled writers by day, and enjoyed life as a bachelor by night. In Baltimore, as an editor at the *Sunpapers* and writer of his Free Lance column, Mencken was the dutiful family member who continued to live with his mother and siblings at the family home on Hollins Street, and an active member of the Saturday Night Club, a gathering of professional and amateur musicians who assembled weekly to eat, drink, and above all play symphonic music. (Mencken held down duties as *secondo* of the four-hand piano—two pianists playing parts to fill in for lacking instruments.) Friends often speculated that the reason Mencken remained single had less to do with his own romantic exploits than with the comfortable circumstances he found in a home where his mother took good care of her children. And since August Mencken had taken care of his wife, Anna, in his will, Mencken's responsibilities at Hollins Street were more managerial—overseeing property and sometimes directing trips—than financial. None of this was a burden, however, because Mencken, for all his bluster, was a "mama's boy." He later wrote that he owed to Anna "and to her alone, the fact that I had a comfortable home throughout my youth and early manhood."

No doubt, Mencken's domestic comforts also owed to a salary that would increase in 1913 together with a bachelor's overhead minus rent or mortgage payments. When the *Smart Set* changed owner's hands in 1911—from Colonel Mann to John Adams Thayer, a man who made his fortune on *Everybody's Magazine*—it also changed editors. Thayer had wanted Mencken to edit the *Smart Set*, but leaving Baltimore was not an option. Mencken did recommend that Thayer hire Willard Huntington Wright, a literary editor first for *Town Topics* and then the *Los Angeles Times*. Wright was an admirer of Mencken and had reviewed the Nietzsche book very favorably. Dreiser believed that Wright was too much enamored of Mencken. He complained to Mencken that Wright was a "third impression" of the Baltimore writer, "so overcome by your spirit that he even uses your language—almost verbatim." Even so, Mencken believed Wright's literary instincts were sound and that he was familiar enough with the world of advertising and publishing to reverse the

Smart Set's fortunes—the magazine was losing money. As editor, Wright followed the lead of European magazines by turning to Ezra Pound to spot overseas writers; through Pound the magazine published the likes of Joseph Conrad, D. H. Lawrence, and August Strindberg. Wright also paid writers more, a change that Mencken enjoyed when his monthly fee went from $50 to $100. Combined with his salary from the *Sunpapers*, in 1913 Mencken was making roughly $4,700—the equivalent of $80,000 in 2015. In his own words, this salary was "no mean revenue for a bachelor in those days," especially one still living with Mom.

Mencken and Wright enjoyed their professional relationship and even toured Europe together, and along with George Jean Nathan, wrote up their sampling of European urban nightlife in *Europe after 8:15*. Since Mencken enjoyed beer about as much as any writer in America, he took the Munich detail. Fred Hobson comments that Mencken was now writing with a "new confidence and vigor." Some of that confidence may have come from the bottle. After describing with eloquent precision the beer steins at the Hoftheatre Café—hexagonal with a pewter lid, an onyx handle, and metal thumbpiece—the vessels to deliver a "nut brown flood and fill the arteries with its benign alkaloids and antitoxins," Mencken uttered a confession:

[M]aybe I grow too eloquent! Such memories loose and craze the tongue. A man pulls himself up suddenly, to find that he has been vulgar. If so here, so be it! I refuse to plead to the indictment; sentence me and be hanged to you! I am by nature a vulgar fellow. I prefer "Tom Jones" to "The Rosary," Rabelais to the Elsie books, the Old Testament to the New, the expurgated parts of "Gulliver's Travels" to those that are left. I delight in beef stews, limericks, burlesque shows, New York City and the music of Haydn, that beery and delightful old rascal! I swear in the presence of ladies and archdeacons. When the mercury is above ninety-five I dine in my shirt sleeves and write poetry naked. I associate habitually with dramatists, bartenders, medical men and musicians.... Not, of course, that I have no pruderies, no fastidious metes and bounds. Far from it. Babies, for example, are too vulgar for me; I cannot bring myself to touch them. And actors. And evangelists. And the obstetrical anecdotes of ancient dames. But in general, as I have said, I joy in vulgarity, whether it take the form of divorce proceedings or of "Tristan und Isolde," of an Odd Fellows' funeral or of Munich beer.

Unfortunately for Mencken's traveling companion, Wright, the *Smart Set*'s editors were having a disproportionate amount of fun given the magazine's revenues. Wright had failed to right the publication's finances and was even running a $20,000 deficit only a year into his tenure as editor. Back in the United States, Wright received his pink slip from Thayer, who in turn tried to persuade Mencken to take over the *Smart Set*. He failed, but he did find someone else to buy the magazine, Eugene F. Crowe, one of the magazine's debtors. He hired Eltinge F. Warner as publisher (he had been publisher of *Field and Stream*), who was responsible for finding an editor to replace Wright. Warner approached George Jean Nathan, who countered with a plan to make Mencken and Nathan coeditors. Mencken did not refuse outright but insisted on keeping his Free Lance column and residing in Baltimore. Nathan conceded and agreed to run the *Smart Set*'s office and let Mencken act as the first reader of manuscripts from Baltimore. The latter did agree to travel to New York City twice a month for editorial meetings. Mencken later wrote that New York seemed "a most uncomfortable city," and that he liked Baltimore "much better." Financial inducements included the editors receiving a one-third interest in the Smart Set Company and a $100-per-month salary in addition to their fees for continuing to write the monthly columns on literature (Mencken) and theater (Nathan).

The arrangement, at least as Mencken described it, was equitable, no-nonsense, and surprisingly functional:

> Our authority as editors is exactly equal; nevertheless, we are never in conflict. I read all manuscripts that are sent to us, and send Nathan those that I think are fit to print. If he agrees, they go into type at once; if he dissents, they are rejected forthwith. This veto is absolute, and works both ways. It saves us a great many useless and possibly acrimonious discussions.

Their editorial policy was also surprisingly cooperative:

> [O]ur purpose, of course, has not been altruistic. We are surely not uplifters, either as critics or as editors. We have run our magazine as we have written our books—primarily to please ourselves, and secondarily to entertain those Americans who happen, in general, to be of our minds. We differ radically in many ways. For example, Nathan

is greatly amused by the theater, even when it is bad, whereas I regard it as a bore, even when it is good. Contrariwise, I am much interested in politics, whereas Nathan scarcely knows who is Vice-President of the United States. But on certain fundamentals we are thoroughly agreed, and it is on the plane of these fundamentals that we conduct the *Smart Set*, and try to interest a small minority of Americans. Both of us are against the sentimental, the obvious, the trite, the maudlin. Both of us are opposed to all such ideas as come from the mob, and are polluted by stupidity: Puritanism, Prohibition, Comstockery, evangelical Christianity, tin-pot patriotism, the whole sham of democracy. Both of us are against socialism and in favor of capitalism, believe that capitalism in the United States is ignorant, disreputable, and degraded, and that its heroes are bounders.

Mencken and Nathan agreed that the name of the magazine was a defect. People assumed "it is a society paper . . . devoted to tales of high life." But the nature of the legal and financial arrangements made a change undesirable, something that would create as many problems as it might solve.

As clear as Mencken was about editorial matters, he was arguably even more forthright about the business of magazines. He understood the difference between subscriptions and newsstand sales, and that because the *Smart Set* depended on over-the-counter sales, printing costs were much higher than if the magazine had a stable and reliable set of subscribers. Mencken also had a keen sense of what the reading public would bear and that the audience for his cage rattling had limits. He faulted the previous editor, Thayer, for running "'daring' stuff, often of a highly sexual and sophomoric character." Under the new editors, the magazine changed course, but Mencken feared that Thayer had "scared off" many old readers who continued to believe that the magazine was "full of *risque* stories." Mencken had no illusions about popularity. But he did believe that "no other American magazine [was] trying to do precisely what we are trying to do." Mencken's feud with idealism extended to his own estimate of his efforts—no boosterism permitted.

At the same time, the magazine made less of a lasting impression on American letters than it provided Mencken with a stepping-stone to greater notoriety. Malcolm Cowley would later write that the *Smart Set* failed to attract Europe's best writers. "As long as [Mencken and Nathan] were given their own pages to fill as they pleased," Cowley smirked, "they were willing to edit the rest of the magazine for people who liked fiction with a little tang to it and relish a bit of subtlety now and then—in other words, for drugstore cowboys." In fact, Mencken was able to lure James Joyce to publish two short stories in the magazine, the Irish writer's first appearance in print in the United States. Mencken and Joyce also discussed serializing *A Portrait of the Artist as a Young Man*, but Nathan and Mencken had decided against publishing anything in serial form and held to that policy. Joyce had come the *Smart Set*'s way through the encouragement of Ezra Pound, with whom Mencken corresponded in search of European authors and whose poetry began to appear in the magazine as early as 1915 (though not as much as Mencken wanted because Nathan used his veto powers to reject verse that left him cold). Other notable authors included James Branch Cabell, Willa Cather, Aldous Huxley, Somerset Maugham, Eugene O'Neill, F. Scott Fitzgerald, Joseph Wood Krutch, Lewis Mumford, and James Gibbons Huneker. But for every author who was either recognizable or would go on to be recognized, Nathan and Mencken also had to fill the magazine's pages with young, unknown authors, many of whom were of mediocre talent. The reason was simple. The *Smart Set* was a financial mess when they started, and they lacked the funds to pay the authors whose work they valued.

Even so, the defects of the magazine were not simply circumstantial. Since the editorial policy was to publish what pleased both Mencken and Nathan, criticisms of the *Smart Set* were ultimately reactions to their own taste. Here, as Terry Teachout observes, the scorecard is not in Mencken's favor:

> While he insisted that "an author should be judged by what he tries honestly to do, not by what anyone else, whether critic or not, thinks he *ought* to do," [Mencken's] own taste was constrictingly narrow. American literature before Mark Twain was a closed book to him, European modernism a joke. (In one of his columns he made a point of bragging about never having read *The Brothers Karamazov*.) Most of the time he wrote amusingly about bad books of no importance, and on the occasions when he had respectable ones to review, he was, like most working critics, wrong as often to do so. . . . He thought poetry "beautiful balderdash," preferring naturalistic novels that unflinchingly portrayed "the harsh facts of life," a phrase into which he packed the whole of his homemade Darwinism.

In his own words, Mencken used book reviews and literary criticism as a way to issue "truculent dissent from the *mores* of my country."

Expressing that dissent and giving it a platform was one of Mencken's chief contributions, and this was only the first chapter of his career. In his book on artistic modernism in the United States, *The End of American Innocence*, Henry May cites the appropriation of Nietzsche by the nation's intellectuals as arguably the factor most responsible for upending Victorianism in American letters. "Scattered groups of intellectuals," May wrote, rejected the values that were beginning to make America one of the most powerful players in world affairs—"humanitarian progress, comfort, and conventional morality." Of course, Mencken had already signaled the direction of this assault on the genteel tradition with his book on Nietzsche. May credits Mencken with foreshadowing the entire modernist revolution in American letters by using Nietzsche to question the idea that a natural morality was "engraven indelibly upon the hearts of man." Within the *Smart Set*'s pages, Nathan and Mencken published authors who, according to May, "battled" the censors, "baited" the bourgeoisie, and "boomed" the writers. This meant that more than anyone else of his generation, Mencken repudiated the chief dogmas of America's attempt at civilization—a commitment to moral standards, the importance of refined culture, and a belief in progress. But Mencken did more than poke at the zoo's inhabitants, according to May. Contrary to Mencken's self-chosen role of "the aloof, amused observer, the superior man who took for granted and genially enjoyed the follies of democracy," his best writing was "about Bryan and the American language and the whole culture of the American small town." This meant that Mencken cared about America in ways that his "alienated contemporaries" did not. Whether that care owed to his own comfortable middle-class life in West Baltimore or to the debt he owed to the news business, it added a layer of insight to his critique of American moralism that his admirers and fans have often missed.

CHAPTER FOUR

Philistinism—Another Name for Puritanism

Mencken was unable to succeed as a writer of fiction, but he found an outlet for his creative talents in the construction of epigrams. In fact, in 1916 he produced two books, one a collection of essays and sketches, *A Book of Burlesques*, the other a collection of epigrams about women, religion, and public life, *A Little Book in C Major*. Both were commercial failures. But the latter contained some of the material that continues to keep Mencken before the reading public—his eminently quotable one-liners. *A Little Book in C Major* collected some of Mencken's memorable thought experiments:

> Archbishop: a Christian ecclesiastic of a rank superior to that attained by Christ; see also bishop and archdeacon.

> Women may be divided into two classes: those who know how to rouge and those who know how to blush.

> Fugue: one damned fiddle after another.

> Women usually enjoy annoying their husbands, but not when they annoy them by growing fat.

> Theology is an effort to explain the unknowable by putting it into terms of the not worth knowing.

One of the best and most quoted epigrams of Mencken is his quip about Puritanism:

Puritanism is the haunting fear that someone, somewhere, may be happy.

That line did not come to light in *A Little Book in C Major*. Mencken did write about Puritanism in the collection, but the epigram was hardly up to his later effort:

> At the bottom of Puritanism one finds envy of the fellow who is having a better time in the world, and hence hatred of him. At the bottom of democracy one finds the same thing. This is why all Puritans are democrats and all democrats are Puritans.

The shorter and much more memorable line about Puritanism came from *A Book of Prefaces*, a book published a year after the *Little Book* that included an important essay, "Puritanism as a Literary Force."

The logic of Mencken's earlier epigram was undoubtedly simplistic, almost as crude as the pop psychology that allowed Mencken to reduce the political imperatives of democracy to jealousy. If mothers have often consoled children by reassuring them that their attackers are merely envious of their abilities, Mencken's diagnosis of Puritanism and democracy hardly seems insightful. But beyond the cheap shot was a more important point, one that equated the ills of American letters and political life with a similar hostility to social rank or superiority. That Mencken's animus against Puritanism and democracy came together during the years of World War I was hardly accidental. While attempting to consolidate his standing as a literary critic, an effort that meant questioning New England's control of the nation's literature (both in composition and instruction), Mencken also found himself suffocating from a political idealism that was taking the United States into war. The method to Mencken's crude association of Puritanism with democracy was to throw a Molotov cocktail into the parlor of American letters and see if the patrons of the house could rearrange the furniture after cleaning up. Underneath Mencken's conventional and comfortable life and the demons of his ambition was a bitter frustration with American standards. Democracy encouraged notions of equality, which in turn nurtured cultural inferiority. Mencken's diagnosis—tracing democracy to Puritanism—may have lacked analytic rigor, but it was one of those points that repaid repeated consideration.

Becoming German American

The conventional alter ego to Mencken's bad-boy swagger was partly evident in his review of Theodore Dreiser's next novel, *The "Genius"* (1915). Mencken's review appeared at the end of 1915, but for most of the previous calendar year the two writers had fallen out. The *Smart Set* editor disapproved of Dreiser's abandonment of his wife and subsequent move to Greenwich Village to live with a twenty-two-year-old actress. Mencken had always had trouble with self-styled bohemian literary affectations such as "fashionable radicalism" and "unconventional lives." Dreiser kept this affair from Mencken. He must have sensed that his Baltimore friend preferred a thoroughly conventional "bourgeois life." When Mencken finally learned about Dreiser's decision and visited the New York apartment, he called the change in Dreiser a "grotesque transmogrification—a German peasant turned Bohemian." Dreiser knew that he did not measure up to the standard of respectability in Mencken's neighborhood in Baltimore, as if he had "gone over to the red ink family." Mencken shot back, "Do you take me for a Methodist deacon—or a male virgin?" He wanted to avoid the charge of Puritanism but also believed that Dreiser's life was too closely resembling his art. *The "Genius"* in fact contained sexually provocative material that would gain the disapproval of censors.

Yet, Mencken's objections to the novel—a savage, almost 180-degree turn from his assessment of *Jennie Gerhardt*—avoided entirely the book's moral failings and hammered away instead on Dreiser's literary failure. The opening to Mencken's review said it all. He noted that on page 702, when the so-called genius, Eugene Tennyson Witla, was about to receive help for his mistreatment of women from a Christian Scientist, a point well into the book—some ninety-seven chapters and three hundred thousand words into it—Dreiser decided to feature details of both Christian Science and the Christian Scientist's house. Mencken wrote:

> The stagehands stand ready to yank down the curtains; messieurs of the orchestra, their minds fixed eagerly upon malt liquor, are up to their hips in the finale; the weary nurses are swabbing up the operating room; the learned chirurgeons are wiping their knives upon their pantaloons; the rev. clergy are swinging into the benediction; the inexorable embalmer waits in the ante-chamber with his inev-

itable syringe, his Mona Lisa smile. . . . And then, at this painfully hurried and impatient point, with the *coda* already under weigh and even the most somnolent reaching nervously for his goloshes, Dreiser halts the whole show to explain the origin, nature, and inner meaning of Christian Science.

Readers also learned that the apartment house in question was of "conventional design," had a "spacious airway" that was outlined by "cream-colored brick," with a front door protected by a wrought-iron gate, that the lobby was "usual," that the elevator man was "indifferent and impertinent," and that the lobby also was home to a telephone switchboard. "Such is novel-writing as Dreiser understands it," Mencken lamented, "a laborious and relentless meticulousness, an endless piling up of small details, an almost furious tracking down of ions, electrons, and molecules." He added:

> One has heard of a tree so tall that it took two men to see to the top of it. Here is a novel so huge that a whole shift of critics is needed to read it. Did I myself do it all alone? By no means. I read only the first and last paragraphs of each chapter. The rest I farmed out to my wife and children, to my cousin Ferd, and to my pastor and my beer man.

By the time Dreiser had completed *The "Genius"* and he and Mencken had aired their differences, the review was punctuation on an acrimonious relationship. In addition to Mencken's disapproval of the novelist's domestic arrangements, Dreiser had turned on the *Smart Set*. Almost two issues before Mencken's damaging review, Dreiser had complained that the magazine under Mencken and Nathan had entered a "non-disturbing period of persiflage and badinage." The *Smart Set* was "as innocent as the Ladies Home Journal." Mencken conceded that the magazine was a bit of a compromise but also insisted that it was not meant to start a revolution. Different attitudes toward marriage and sexual relations were likely responsible for the animosity since Mencken had tried to steer the *Smart Set* away from the racy content favored by Willard Huntington Wright (the previous editor). In addition to rendering an aesthetic judgment, Mencken's determination to refrain from sexually charged material may have reflected his own experience in the world of Baltimore's street life and a sense that what a New York editor considered risqué was actually tame. More than likely, however, it reflected the financial constraints under which the magazine operated and the editors' desire to avoid offending censors who could, because of one off-color story, shut down the *Smart Set*.

The threat of censors was real, as Dreiser soon learned. In 1916 the New York Society for the Suppression of Vice pressured the novelist's publisher, John Lane, to withdraw *The "Genius"* on grounds of lewdness and obscenity.[1] Despite their fractured relationship, Mencken rallied to Dreiser's defense. The editor secured signatures from 458 writers from the Authors League of America to protest the Society's action (which included Booth Tarkington, Willa Cather, James Branch Cabell, Edgar Lee Masters, and Sherwood Anderson—William Dean Howells, whom Mencken referred to as that "notorious coward," did not sign). Mencken spearheaded the effort and shelled out of his own pocket—according to his own estimate—$300 to defend the novelist. When the case finally went to court, partly owing to Dreiser's own suit against Lane for breach of contract, judges refused to decide whether the novel was obscene. It languished in bowdlerized form until 1923 when it was republished. By then Dreiser was a name associated less with literary greatness than with freedom of speech. In the meantime, Mencken's efforts to see the novel published said more about his commitment to civil liberties than about the novelist's genius.

One factor in Mencken's rallying to the controversial novelist was the overwhelming anti-German sentiment that prevailed in the United States even before the nation went to war against Germany and the Axis Powers. Mencken claimed that a man "accused of being a German has no chance whatever in a New York court at this time." Indeed, Mencken's defense of Dreiser, even at the expense of his literary reputation,

1. Among the seventy-five pages tagged as obscene was the following: "She leaned back against his shoulder stroking his hair, but finally ceased even that, for her own feeling was too intense to make movement possible. She thought of him as a young god, strong, virile, beautiful—a brilliant future before him. All these years she had waited for someone truly to love her and now this splendid youth had apparently cast himself at her feet. He stroked her hands, her neck, cheeks, then slowly gathered her close and buried his head against her bosom.

"Angela was strong in convention, in the precepts of her parents, in the sense of her family and its attitude, but this situation was more than she could resist. She accepted first the pressures of his arm, then the slow subtlety with which he caressed her. Resistance seemed almost impossible now for he held her close—tight within the range of his magnetism. When finally she felt the pressure of his hand upon her quivering limbs, she threw herself back in a transport of agony and delight."

capped a switch in cultural allegiance that would shape the rest of the Baltimorean's career as well as his standing in American letters. Mencken's own upbringing had nurtured a sense of superiority over German Americans, the immigrants from whom his grandfather had wanted to disassociate. At the same time, Mencken readily acknowledged his "mongrel" status—a "melting pot American" with Scottish, Irish, and French blood—even as he looked to his German ancestors for signs of family distinction. As late as 1911, Mencken wrote editorials that were critical of Germany and that praised the English: "few powers will venture into the Sea of Strife so long as our country and England shall say to them, 'Peace, Be still.'" But by 1913 he was writing about the "new" Germany and complimenting it for its "enormous practicality," "sharp common sense," "straightforwardness and ruthlessness." With his trip to Europe still in mind, Mencken remarked, "Munich has never seen a vice crusader. . . . In all Munich there is not a single uplifter, social server or other such moral bichloride tablet." Unlike the English or their American cousins who endured life, Germans enjoyed it.

The war begun in 1914 confirmed Mencken's outlook. In England, a friend wrote that people were blaming the armed conflict on Nietzsche—"the intellectual author of the war." Mencken also conceded later in life that the war helped him understand himself. He located the source of his outlook as "fundamentally anti–Anglo Saxon" and said that if he had "any spiritual home at all it must be in the land" of his German ancestors. For Mencken, England represented a form of self-righteous smugness that he associated with democracy and egalitarianism while Germany still upheld the ideal of the superior man and distinguished civilization unadorned by the sentimental trappings of equality. He followed with a series of editorials in the Free Lance column in which he praised war in Nietzschean terms for its contribution to a healthier body and a cleaner mind, for a way to reenact the law of natural selection. He soon moved to editorials in which he defended and prosecuted the case for Germany in the war: "Convinced, after long and prayerful consideration, that the Germans are wholly right, and that they deserve to win, and that they *will* win, I go, as the saying is, the whole hog." The war had become in Mencken's mind not a conflict between two rival European powers, but a Nietzschean-styled culture war between sentimentality and hypocrisy, between the "post-exodus Jews'" morality and the "master morality of the Periclean Greeks."

Mencken found an outlet for his Germanophilia in the pages of the *Atlantic Monthly*, which by 1914 was owned and edited by Ellery Sedgwick, a well-connected Boston Brahmin who had taken notice of Mencken a decade earlier. Although an Anglophile himself, Sedgwick solicited Mencken to write about the war in Nietzschean categories. The result was an essay "as extravagantly immoral" as Sedgwick had hoped. Indeed, "The Mailed Fist and Its Prophet," which appeared in November 1914, fused Mencken's admiration for Nietzsche with his growing disdain for the Anglo-Saxons, a combination that produced a glowing assessment of the new Germany as the embodiment of the German philosopher's ideas. In Mencken's hands, Nietzsche's *Thus Spoke Zarathustra*, published in 1892, was the mission statement for the next phase of German history:

> It was as if a new Luther had begun to speak with the tongue of a new Goethe; as if a new David had been sent into Germany to kindle her against the false gods of the past . . . a new gospel to take the place of the old gospel of brotherhood which the Socialists were turning so plausibly to their uses, an evangel of the counter-reformation.

In the sciences, the Germans were far surpassing their national rivals. German scientists "were swiftly getting a virtual monopoly of all those forms of industry which depended upon scientific exactness,—for example, the manufacture of drugs, dye-stuffs, and optical goods." Germany was catching up to Europe's colonial powers by establishing its own outposts in Africa and Oceania. Meanwhile, in the arts Germany had reached a golden age of music and literature, between Brahms and Richard Strauss, and Sudermann and Hauptmann. Even in politics, the new Germany found a way to appropriate democracy without the moralism:

> It was founded upon no romantic theory that all men were natural equals; it was free from the taint of mobocracy; it was empty of soothing and windy phrases. On the contrary, it was a delimited, aristocratic democracy in the Athenian sense—a democracy of intelligence, of strength, of superior fitness—a democracy at the top.

"On all sides there was this vast enrichment of the national consciousness," Mencken wrote, concluding his cultural survey, "this brilliant

86

shining forth of the national spirit, this feeling of new and superabundant efficiency, this increase of pride, achievement, and assurance."

The question that American readers who had not yet thrown their copy of the magazine into the trash bin were likely asking was what any of this German achievement had to do with Nietzsche. Mencken's answer was that the philosopher provided the intellectual constitution for the new Germany's growing confidence. "Germany began to grow cocky, skeptical, self-sufficient, brusque, impatient of opposition," he wrote. "It held up its head among the nations." But Germany lacked the intellectual justification for its new superiority. "What it needed, of course, was a philosophy to back it up, as the vast unrest of the American colonies needed the Declaration of Independence, with its sharp, staccato asseverations, its brave statement of axioms." Nietzsche was the missing ingredient. "[He] was the sufficient excuse and justification for their racial aspiration, the Magna Carta of their new intellectual freedom, the gospel of their new creed, of progress." Nietzsche's philosophy was dramatic, eloquent, persuasive, vigorous, romantic—"the principles that the Germans had been applying, dubiously, experimentally, to their new problems." But did Nietzsche require a complete break with Christian morality? From Mencken's reading, the enlightenment championed by Nietzsche was an acquired taste for superior men. The lower castes could still have their old beliefs. "Did they cling sentimentally to Christianity, unable to rid themselves of their yearning for a rock and a refuge? Then let them have it!" To take it away forcibly was "an offense against their sense of well-being," even "against human progress as well."

As for the war, Mencken could not have linked Germany's aggression to Nietzsche's ideas any better, ironically, than William Jennings Bryan did, Mencken's nemesis of the 1920s. "Germany becomes Nietzsche; Nietzsche becomes Germany." If you read *Zarathustra*, Mencken warned, you find notions such as "I tell you that a good war hallows every cause!" But where Nietzsche scared Bryan, he thrilled Mencken. "Barbarous? Ruthless? Unchristian? No doubt. But so is life itself. So is all progress worthy the name. Here at least is honesty to match the barbarity, and, what is more, courage, the willingness to face great hazards, the acceptance of defeat as well as victory." Mencken even saw an upside to a German victory—more and better music: "What did Rome ever produce to match the Fifth Symphony?"

So far Mencken's understanding of Germany was based largely on his reading of Nietzsche, his love of German music, and his dislike of Anglo-Saxon moralism. When in December 1916 the *Sunpapers* sent him to cover the war, the editors clarified that Mencken went to ascertain the "true inwardness of the German situation." "His intimate knowledge of the country and its people," the paper also explained, enabled Mencken "to do this probably better than any other newspaper man from this side of the water." Little did his colleagues understand that Mencken's affections for Germany were recent and concocted to give him a rooting interest against Anglo-Saxon morality and culture. As a thirty-six-year-old, Mencken admitted that his reason for the trip was "to get some excitement . . . into a life that had begun to grow unendurably stagnant."

When Mencken arrived in Berlin in early January 1917, he was the only American correspondent there. Because Bismarck's mother had been a Mencken, the American journalist earned himself "extra politeness." He received permission to go to the eastern front in Lithuania. He spent only five days there because of the danger. He was only a few hundred yards from the Russian forces and experienced a moment "when it seemed to me to be all up with Henry." If a brush with bullets and shrapnel was insufficient to shake up his stagnant life, temperatures that descended to forty below zero and inflicted temporary frostbite must have made his office back on Hollins Street look appealing. Mencken managed to stay alive by sleeping in peasants' homes, near the stove, but always expected "to be cremated before morning." The German officers with whom he ate and drank were admirable, while the Russians across the trenches were "stupid."

After five days at the front, Mencken returned to Berlin, where he learned that Germany had announced a new policy of unrestricted submarine warfare, a move that would likely draw the United States into the conflict. He took in as much of Berlin as he could, but the Germans' detainment of him and other foreign journalists restricted his movement as well as his reports. It took four weeks for Mencken to gain clearance to return to the United States. In the meantime, he dined with German friends (some of Jewish descent) and was surprised to see so little anti-American feeling. Mencken worried about the animosities that the United States' entry into war would provoke. He could not think of the Germans he knew "as enemies." When he finally left Germany on February 11, 1917, Mencken referred to a "new Europe," one that was "much duller and sadder."

In the United States, the scene was by no means dull or sad—more like alarmed and hateful, or so was Mencken's experience. War hysteria had unleashed American hostility to all things German, when sauerkraut became "liberty cabbage"; Bach, Beethoven, and Brahms were no-shows at American symphony performances; and Saxon-sounding names drew suspicion. As an American of German descent (on one side), Mencken was suspect; as a reporter who had written positively about Germany and attacked England, he was more so. Some of Mencken's German American friends went to jail, a prospect he feared. He found that his mail from overseas had been opened before reaching him. He also discovered that the Justice Department had opened a file on him. To be safe, Mencken collected sensitive documents, placed them in a lockbox, and buried it in his backyard. He even refused to travel to New York City except when absolutely necessary because he did not want to leave his mother and sister at home without a male presence. At least some of the federal investigators, like Billups Harris, regarded Mencken as no threat. In one report, Harris wrote that Mencken's pro-German outlook was a "sort of affectation." He added that most of the journalist's friends had broken "close relationships with him on account of his pronounced pro-German feeling." Still, Harris added, "hardly any of them think that Mencken himself would engage in any activity against this country." Too controversial for the pro-British owner and editors of the *Sunpapers*, Mencken was barred by the paper's top brass from its pages during the war. The only newspaper that would take him was the *New York Evening Mail*, on the condition that he not write about the war. Mencken could not help but notice that the officer in charge of this assault on citizens' freedoms was the Presbyterian moralist who occupied the White House, President Woodrow Wilson:

> The Germans among us, in those first soul-wracking days needed a friend who stood above the tumult. They faced a mob aroused to intolerable fury, their every effort to defend themselves was denounced as treason and worse. Ah, that a genuinely first-rate man had been in the White House, with a first-rate man's sense of justice and a first-rate man's courage.

To understand the roots of these discomforts, Mencken turned to Puritanism.

Puritanism Exposed

Prior to the war, Puritanism was barely on Mencken's radar, or at least he had not opened a file in the *P* drawer where he placed moralizing Protestant annoyances. But sensitivities to differences between Germans and English during the war were a large factor in his discovery of English Protestantism as the source of America's impoverished politics and culture. As it turned out, Mencken's hiatus from the *Sunpapers* and writing about the war freed up his prose for an avalanche of columns and books that included some of his most significant arguments. One of those was entitled "Puritanism as a Literary Force," published in 1917 by Alfred A. Knopf, then a new kid on the block of New York publishing houses, and a Jewish American with whom Mencken established a close professional relationship even while privately remarking about Knopf's racial tics. *A Book of Prefaces*, which included essays on Joseph Conrad, James Huneker, and Theodore Dreiser, remained in print until 1933 and sold over fifteen thousand copies. Neither Mencken nor Knopf could object to their literary transaction.

Although he took a decidedly antagonistic perspective on the New World's original English Calvinists, Mencken was in good company in recognizing for good or ill Puritanism as a large presence in American letters. Henry F. May, for instance, argues that the US custodians of high culture, sometimes called the "genteel tradition," sometimes Victorianism, "linked the defense of [traditional] culture to Puritanism." This was not because Puritans valued culture for its own sake, but because these English Protestants "took culture seriously." For W. C. Lawton, who wrote at the turn of the century a work entitled *Introduction to American Literature*, Puritanism was responsible for a spirit that "breathed" in the works of William Ellery Channing and Ralph Waldo Emerson. The "sane" expressions of Puritanism, the kind that informed John Milton, "condemned nothing merely because it sweetened life." Instead, in its better forms, Puritanism opened "the gates to the whole world of imagination." Barrett Wendell, who taught literature at Harvard, likewise attributed to Puritanism the spirit that was responsible for the renaissance of American literature in nineteenth-century New England. In his *Literary History of the United States* (1900), the likes of Emerson, Hawthorne, and Melville had kicked away the training wheels of Puritanism's dogmatism and intolerance. But as a "lifelong effort to recognize and follow ideals which can never be apprehended by unaided human senses," the best American writers were still Puritans "at heart."

Mencken's long-form explanation of Puritanism was not as funny as his memorable epigrams, but it was no less blunt.[2] English Calvinists, the logic ran, were so preoccupied with God and pleasing such a demanding deity that they never developed an aesthetic or literary sense. Here Mencken followed the argument of Leon Kellner, whose history of American literature, originally published in 1913 in German and translated in 1915, gave the newly minted German American the ammunition he needed. Van Wyck Brooks had already written a book critical of Puritans, *The Wine of the Puritans* (1908), but Mencken likely neglected it, even though he was critical of Puritans for being provincial and utilitarian, as all pioneers inevitably are. Brooks was likely tarnished because he drew heavily on the instruction received as a Harvard undergraduate from Barrett Wendell, one of the academics Mencken suspected of moralistic uplift masquerading as literary scholarship. Kellner was a different matter, someone who was German and not infected with New England ancestor worship. According to Kellner, who was writing well before the post–World War II rediscovery of Puritan poets such as Anne Bradstreet and Edward Taylor:

> The God of the Puritans was in this respect a jealous God who brooked no sort of creative rivalry. The inspired moments of the loftiest souls were filled with the thought of God and His designs; spiritual life was wholly dominated by solicitude regarding salvation, the hereafter,

2. By the time Mencken cowrote with George Jean Nathan *The American Credo: A Contribution toward the Interpretation of the American Mind* (New York: Knopf, 1921)—a book that Mencken wrote chiefly himself—the Puritan had switched to Presbyterian. But his estimate of Calvinism was the same:

> The man of morals has a certain character, and the man of honour has a quite different character. No one not an idiot fails to differentiate between the two, or to order his intercourse with them upon an assumption of their disparity. What we know in the United States as a Presbyterian is pre-eminently the moral type. Perhaps more than any other man among us he regulates his life, and the lives of all who fall under his influence, upon a purely moral plan. In the main, he gets the principles underlying that plan from the Old Testament. . . . Sin is to the Presbyterian the salient phenomenon of this wobbling and nefarious world, and the pursuit and chastisement of sinners the one avocation that is permanently worth while. . . . Every single human act, he holds, must be either right or wrong—and the overwhelming majority of them are wrong. (*The American Credo*, 51, 52, 53)

grace; how could such petty concerns as personal experience of a lyric nature, the transports or the pangs of love, find utterance? What did a lyric occurrence like the first call of the cuckoo, elsewhere so welcome, or the first sight of the snowdrop, signify compared with the last Sunday's sermon and the new interpretation of the old riddle of evil in the world? And apart from the fact that everything of a personal nature must have appeared so trivial, all the sources of secular lyric poetry were offensive and impious to Puritan theology.

When Kellner concluded that America had "no belletristic literature" prior to 1800, Mencken was inclined to believe him and to attribute the defect to Calvinism. That Kellner was Jewish or a philologist who would not necessarily have been a recognized authority on American literature did not trouble Mencken. He likely had discovered the Austrian professor at Chernivtsi University, a new institution founded in 1875 by Franz Joseph I (today in Ukraine), during Mencken's initial efforts on the American language. No matter the source, Kellner's point made sense of the disparate pieces of America's literary tradition.

If his description of Calvinism's influence sounded extreme, Mencken understood that Puritanism needed the sort of critical exposé that muckraking journalists had been applying to the nation's corporations and cities. That the Dreiser incident was still much on Mencken's mind was in little doubt, even though the chapter on the American novelist in *A Book of Prefaces* was not as schoolgirlishly glowing as his first review in *Smart Set*. (Mencken still admired *Jennie Gerhardt* and *The Titan* but said of *The "Genius"* that "nothing worse is to be found in the newspapers.") Only three paragraphs into the roughly twenty-thousand-word essay, Mencken used reviews of Dreiser's novels to demonstrate the moralistic literary impulse of American criticism (that he laid at the doorstep of Calvinism). "Fully nine-tenths of the reviews of Dreiser's 'The Titan,'" Mencken wrote, "were devoted chiefly to indignant denunciations of the morals of Frank Cowperwood, its central character." Even though he was "superbly imagined and magnificently depicted," and despite his creation rising to the level of "an artistic achievement of a very high and difficult order," reviewers could only fault the novelist for a defective character. Mencken had also included a chart in his essay on Dreiser that showed which public libraries in the country's largest cities had acquired the novelist's titles. The municipalities guilty of a special reluctance to make Dreiser available were Boston, Hartford,

Providence, Washington, and Baltimore (which had only one or two of Dreiser's then seven titles); only New Orleans had refused to carry any of Dreiser's novels.

Puritanism's pinched aesthetic even afflicted Mencken's childhood favorite, Mark Twain. He was, Mencken conceded, a great artist who displayed "that prodigality of imagination, that aloof engrossment in the human comedy, that penetrating cynicism, which one associates with the great artists of the Renaissance." But Twain's nationality hung on him like a "millstone," and he could never escape the philistinism that plagued American authors. *The Innocents Abroad* was a funny book, but Twain completely tripped over the profundities of Christendom:

> May not a civilized man, disbelieving in it, still find himself pro-
> foundly moved by its dazzling history, the lingering remnants of its
> old magnificence, the charm of its gorgeous and melancholy love-
> liness? In the presence of all beauty of man's creation—in brief, of
> what we roughly call art, whatever its form—the voice of Mark Twain
> was the voice of the Philistine.

Had Twain been born in France, he would have "conquered the world." As it was, he was afflicted by "Puritan smugness and cocksureness, the Puritan distrust of new ideas, the Puritan incapacity for seeing beauty as a thing in itself, and the full peer of the true and the good."

The reason was that Americans generally assessed literature and creative expressions through a moral grid. That moralistic tendency may have hampered Puritans themselves, but by the Victorian era it had left the United States with a "new" Puritanism led by "the moral expert, the professional sinhound, the virtuoso of virtue." Indeed, the modern version of Puritanism was a check not simply upon good literature but also upon a decent society. The broader sweep of Puritanism in Mencken's day also explains why he so easily segued from discussions of books to a defense of booze. In the new era of American Puritanism,

> the special business of forcing sinners to be good was taken away
> from the preachers and put into the hands of laymen trained in its
> technique and mystery, and there it remains. The new Puritanism
> has created an army of gladiators who are not only distinct from the
> hierarchy, but who, in many instances, actually command and intim-
> idate the hierarchy. This is conspicuously evident in the case of the

Anti-Saloon League, an enormously effective fighting organization, with a large staff of highly accomplished experts in its service.

Mencken recognized that the new Puritanism was a secularization of the old. Instead of being enforced by clerics and professors, Puritanism now enjoyed a raft of social science and policy experts, persons who had lost the "flavor of sacerdotalism," whose chief business was the "chase and punishment of sinners."

For readers who may have wondered if Mencken was simply interested in preserving his own inordinate love of beer, the legal consequences of the new Puritanism for editors was not entirely different from the pressure that brewers and bar owners felt. Comstock's laws against pornographic literature were simply the beginning of a more general assault on vice. Mencken conceded that initially the laws passed in the 1870s were simply aimed at explicitly pornographic materials. But in time crusaders applied them to the ancients and then to modern literature. Once Zola, Balzac, and Hardy had qualified as pornographic, editors like Mencken were left always worrying whether what they decided to print would land them in court.

I am, in moments borrowed from more palatable business, the editor of an American magazine, and I thus know at first hand what the burden is. That magazine is anything but a popular one, in the current sense. It sells at a relatively high price; it contains no pictures or other baits for the childish; it is frankly addressed to a sophisticated minority. I may thus assume reasonably, I believe, that its readers are not sex-curious and itching adolescents, just as my colleague of the *Atlantic Monthly* may assume reasonably that his readers are not Italian immigrants. Nevertheless, as a practical editor, I find that the Comstocks, near and far, are oftener in my mind's eye than my actual patrons. The thing I always have to decide about a manuscript offered for publication, before ever I give any thought to its artistic merit and suitability, is the question whether its publication will be permitted—not even whether it is intrinsically good or evil, moral or immoral, but whether some roving Methodist preacher, self-commissioned to keep watch on letters, will read indecency into it. Not a week passes that I do not decline some sound and honest piece of work for no other reason. I have a long list of such things by American authors, well-devised, well-imagined, well-executed, respectable as human documents and as works of art—but never to be printed in mine or any other American magazine. . . . [T]hey simply cannot be printed in the United States, with the law what it is and the courts what they are.

However readers may have disagreed with Mencken's views on decency or civilization, his complaint against Comstockery was not simply a mocking gesture to wake up the animals. The beasts, as Mencken knew full well in Dreiser's case, were alive and still on the prowl. For serious writers and editors, whose morals might be questionable in the eyes of many Christians, the nation's laws posed a real threat. Once scholars in academic programs such as American civilization or American studies came along to refresh Puritanism's image, Mencken's blaming Calvinism for American literature's defects may have looked simplistic and even tendentious. But at the time, it seemed plausible. Americans may have thought they lived in an enlightened land far removed from the Roman Inquisition or the strictures of the Ottomans. Folks like Dreiser and Mencken disagreed.

Mencken's understanding of Puritanism and American literature would not significantly change. "Puritanism as a Literary Force" was his most sustained treatment of New England Calvinism, and it functioned as his *bête noire* for the rest of his life. In the 1920s he complained that the literary critics who sustained the "literary Brahmins" of New England always assumed ethical criteria for evaluation. "You will spend a long while going through the works of such typical professors as More, Phelps, Boynton, Burton, Perry, Brownell and Babbitt before ever you encounter a purely aesthetic judgment upon an aesthetic question." The power of Puritanism to corrupt Americans was also evident when Mencken opined about the republic's manners of sociability:

> [T]he thing that makes us enjoy the society of our fellows is not admiration of their inner virtues but delight in their outward manners. It is not enough that they are headed for heaven, and will sit upon the right hand of God through all eternity; it is also necessary that they be polite, generous, and, above all, trustworthy. . . . It is the tragedy of the Puritan that he can never inspire this confidence in his fellow men.

Mencken continued his assault upon the release of the letters of Barrett Wendell, professor of literature at Harvard. In response to the point that

Puritans were actually lovers of beauty and that the charming cottages on Nantucket proved this delight, Mencken noted that the houses in question were not built "until the Puritan theocracy was completely demoralized and impotent—until Boston had a theatre, and was already two-thirds of the way to hell." If any culture had emerged in New England, it had come at the hands of anti-Puritans, or at least from "Puritans who had gone out into the wide, wide world and savored its dreadful and voluptuous marvels—Puritans who had come back from the Eastern seas with gaudy silks in their sea-chests, and the perfume of strange gals upon their whiskers, and a new glitter to their eyes."

Of course, the professors who occupied chairs in the halls of learning that Puritans had founded were unwilling to concede a point about the stifling nature of the nation's literary standards to such an editorial lowbrow as a Baltimore journalist (even if they themselves had difficulty reconciling the original Puritans' theology with New England's later creative works). Stuart Sherman, whom Mencken had called the "archetype of the booming, indignant corrupter of criteria, the moralist turned critic," drew the short straw among the academic establishment to respond to the attack on Puritanism. A professor at the University of Illinois and a regular contributor to the *Nation*, Sherman's support for America's entrance into the European war and his belief in literature's power to sustain moral convictions made him a likely replacement for Brander Matthews at Columbia. It also colored his response to Mencken, since he devoted almost a third of his critique to identifying the Baltimorean with his German heritage and love of German music and philosophy despite being of "mixed blood." To the matter of literature and morality, though, Sherman was unambiguous:

> He is anti-Christian. He is for the *Herrenmoral* and against the "Sklavmoral that besets all of us of English speech." He holds with Blake that "the lust of the goat is also to the glory of God." Finally there are his national and racial feelings and convictions. He holds that the Americans are an "upstart people," and that "formalism is the hall-mark of the national culture." He holds that the Anglo-Saxon civilization excels all others as a prolific mother of quacks and mountebanks.

Of course, none of this was untrue of Mencken's essay. Nor was it a refutation. But Sherman seemed to think he could win over his readers simply by noting that Mencken was immoral and un-American (which for Sherman may have been a redundancy). Even so, perhaps Sherman did not feel compelled to argue against Mencken because the Baltimorean's essay was not exactly an argument. As Sherman himself noted, Mencken's "continuous tirade against everything respectable in American morals, against everything characteristic of American society, and against everything everybody distinguished in American scholarship and letters" hardly qualified as "*aesthetic* criticism." In fact, an "unsympathetic person" like Sherman might conclude that Mencken had not engaged in literary criticism "at all, but mere scurrility and blackguardism . . . [or] infatuated propagandism."

Sherman could not also refuse to comment on Mencken's power as a writer. Not only did Mencken use words that sent "the vulgar reader to the dictionary," but he also eruditely dismissed the entire literary and moral history of the United States. To underscore his incredulity, Sherman paired adverbs such as "gently," "nobly," "adequately," and "felicitously" with Mencken's attacks on Dryden, Puritanism, abolitionism, Emerson, and Howells, as if to demonstrate how far Mencken fell from the ranks of the great English writers. "The sheer verbal loveliness of writing like this can never pass away," Sherman smirked. "It is the writing of a sensitive intellectual aristocrat . . . the quality and tone of high breeding." Such sarcasm might have endeared Mencken to Sherman, since it was a departure from the general platitudes that characterized much of the literary criticism to which the *Smart Set* editor objected. But the combination of assumed ethnic and educational superiority along with warmongering against Germany and Germans meant that Mencken would never forgive Sherman (even though the Illinois professor would by the 1920s want to make peace).

The exchange between Mencken and Sherman was one of the most public skirmishes in a battle of the books that pitted Victorians (and the "genteel tradition") against literary modernists. As David J. Hoeveler describes it, this war of culture involved more than questions of the author's moral responsibilities as opposed to his aesthetic judgments. It also included the place of contemporary literature in the canon of great (read classical) texts. Puritanism, with its moral and philosophical seriousness, had been one theoretical device for literary academics to assert continuity between the ancient Greeks and Romans and American writers. Mencken represented a significant challenge to the literary establishment even as he paved the way as editor and critic for writers who would not conform to Protestant sensibilities. In the long run, Mencken may have been the victor by championing a new set of authors who portrayed human existence not ideally but realistically. But in the contest over Puritanism, Mencken's victory was incomplete. To undergraduates such as Perry Miller, Mencken's bombast was welcome intellectual provocation. In 1959 the Harvard professor reminisced:

> I had commenced my work within an emotional universe dominated by H. L. Mencken. My contemporaries and I came of age in a time when the word "Puritan" served as a comprehensive sneer against every tendency in American civilization which we held reprehensible—sexual diffidence, censorship, prohibition, theological fundamentalism, political hypocrisy, and all the social antics which Sinclair Lewis, among others, was stridently ridiculing. Because I too had been an adolescent campaigner in this anti-Puritan rebellion, I dared not profess, even in a sentence, that I considered the intellect of Puritans worth serious examination.

But by 1959, not only was Mencken dead but Miller, his colleagues, and students had almost completely routed the smart-alecky rendering of Puritanism that Mencken made famous.

Beat Reporter as Literary Critic

When Mencken looked back on the publication of *A Book of Prefaces*, he recounted in a matter-of-fact way the sales figures, the book's longevity, and how much he made—$1,864 (the equivalent of $34,100 in 2014). He did concede that the book's "indirect benefits" were much greater than the numbers' significance. It gave him "a kind of authority" that he lacked merely on the basis of his work at the *Smart Set*. Other authors continued to discuss Mencken's book, so much so that he speculated that "[i]t will probably be a long while before anyone will be able to write a history of American literature without mentioning it, or, at all events, stealing from it." Best of all, the book "shook the professors as they had never been shaken before"—especially Sherman. In other words, Mencken had arrived as a literary critic. James Gibbons Huneker, a literary journalist Mencken admired more than any other, wrote to him that "You are the big critical centre now" and deserve "a wider audience."

For that reason Huneker advised that Mencken assume literary editorship of New York's *Sun-Herald*. Considering that he had begun this trek only a dozen or so years earlier while reviewing theater and musical performances in the provincial city of Baltimore for its second-string newspaper and equipped with a vo-tech high school diploma, Mencken's landing in the country of American letters was hardly matter of fact.

As a connoisseur of books, Mencken lacked, as Sherman argued, an aesthetic theory, but he had a firm sense of what made a novel good (and why American novelists performed so poorly). He had been working out this understanding since his early days as a reviewer for the *Smart Set*. Mencken's literary history of the United States within "Puritanism as a Literary Force" is revealing. In the early national period, the stories of the Washington Irvings, the James Fenimore Coopers, and the Nathaniel Hawthornes were "completely disassociated from life as men were then living it." "Irving told fairy tales about the forgotten Knickerbockers; Hawthorne turned backward to the Puritans of Plymouth Rock; Longfellow to the Acadians and the prehistoric Indians," Mencken continued, while "Emerson took flight from earth altogether." The Civil War changed the machinery of literary moralism but did not fundamentally divert the nation's letters. Walt Whitman led a revolt of sorts, but his "countrymen could see him only as immoralist." No one fully grasped Whitman's stature as an artist or knew that "such a category of men existed." "[T]he sentimental rubbish of 'The Blue and the Gray' and the ecstatic supernaturalism of 'The Battle Hymn of the Republic' were far more to the public taste." The emergence of William Dean Howells, Henry James, Bret Harte, and Mark Twain during the 1880s promised a better day for American literature, but with Twain's *The Gilded Age* the American novel "slipped back into romanticism tempered by Philistinism."

> The American scene that they depicted with such meticulous care was chiefly peopled with marionettes. They shrunk, characteristically, from those larger, harsher clashes of will and purpose which one finds in all truly first-rate literature. In particular, they shrunk from any interpretation of life which grounded itself upon an acknowledgment of its inexorable and inexplicable tragedy.

The result was that books were still judged "not by their form and organization as works of art, their accuracy and vividness as representations of life, their validity and perspicacity," but by their "conformity to national prejudices." What critics want is a "clean," "inspiring," and "glad" book.

In the 1920s, when Mencken started to crank out books with a flourish, he continued to talk about the need for good novels to conform to "real" life. As he put it in an essay about women novelists, the primary aim of the novel is "the representation of human beings at their follies and villainies, and no other art form clings to that aim so faithfully." Why a Christian sensibility like Puritanism that stressed human depravity would shy away from such an aim is a question that did not seem to dawn on Mencken. That conundrum notwithstanding, Mencken's penchant for realism was part of the assault of literary modernists against the formality and gentility of American letters.

This was a decidedly different modernism from the one that was blossoming in the mainstream Protestant churches and occupied one wing of the fundamentalist-modernist controversy. Protestants on both sides of that conflict were committed to the morality that Mencken identified with Puritanism, whether the sunny outlook of Victorian novels or the political paternalism of Prohibition. Even the modernists who wrote for and edited the *Christian Century* were not amused by Mencken and "the Young Intellectuals." In two separate notices on *Civilization in the United States: An Inquiry by Thirty Americans*, edited by Harold E. Stearns, in which Mencken wrote the chapter on politics (Conrad Aiken on poetry, George Jean Nathan on theater, and Van Wyck Brooks on literature), the *Century*'s editors sneered at the young intellectuals' "smug conceit" and "garish smartness." What stood out for comment was not their "flippancy," "comic logic," or "incredible vulgarity." Instead, what the *Century*'s progressives could not abide was a religious education based on Tom Paine, Robert Ingersoll, and "the Mencken version of Nietzsche—what a background for a modern university man!" If the nation's universities and colleges followed suit, they would leave young people "morally bankrupt" and "spiritually illiterate." In fact, "[i]t is a queer outcome of our education," the *Century* warned, if it produced people who regarded "morality with 'loathing,' or else with 'perfunctory hypocrisy,'" and the "eternal verities" as little more than "sentimental fictions to be tossed aside."

In a sequel that mentioned the complaints of "our young intellectuals" that Prohibition was turning the United States into the land of the Turks, the *Century*'s editors singled out Mencken, "who raids the trenches of the bourgeoisie exploding grenades and stink bombs, to an accompaniment of uproarious laughter, just as if this were not a dry land at all." They took offense at his calling Americans "a 'race of goose-steppers' led by 'jitney-messiahs'" and so were "bogged in 'absurdities so immense that only the democratic anaesthesia to absurdity' can save us." "After this manner our artists and young intellectual leaders," the editors sneered, "help us in the eternal battle for decency." The *Century* concluded that the new writers sought "ugliness" where the old authors desired "loveliness." The new writers were "strangely fascinated by the garbage cans and back alleys of modern life." "What we regret is not their realism, nor yet their radicalism, but their unspeakable vulgarity."

Mencken was clearly on the side of the young in the *Century*'s scheme, even if he had hit middle age, but to him the world of literature was more complicated than a simple division between the vulgar youth and the decent elderly. He recognized at least four schools of literary criticism after the Great War: the moralists who "encourage the virtuous and oppose the sinful," the amoralists who hold that "the arts have nothing to do with morality whatsoever," the psychologists who argue that a literary work is valueless if it does not "help men to know themselves," and finally those seek the author's original intent. Mencken identified the latter school of criticism with J. E. Spingarn, a Jewish American who taught at Columbia University and ran afoul of the institution's administration when he sided with a colleague fired for breach of promise. Mencken thought Spingarn's approach had merit except that it required critics to be "civilized and tolerant," qualities he believed to be in short supply among the professoriate. The worst kind of literary criticism was that which dominated the United States—a "branch of homiletics" that judged a work "not by its clarity and sincerity, not by the force and charm of its ideas, not by the technical virtuosity of the artist, not by his originality and artistic courage, but simply and solely by his orthodoxy." "In its baldest form," Mencken continued, "it shows itself in the doctrine that it is scandalous for an artist—say a dramatist or a novelist—to depict vice as attractive." The folly of this approach was patent. "The fact that vice, more often than not, undoubtedly *is* attractive—else why should it ever gobble any of us?—is disposed of with a lofty gesture. . . . The artist is not a reporter, but a Great Teacher. It is not his business to depict the world as it is, but as it ought to be."

In the end, Mencken came closest to Spingarn in his understanding of literary criticism, though the *Smart Set* editor admired James Huneker's work about as much as that of any American critic. Simply to oppose moralism was to establish another kind of morality. For this reason, the "really competent critic must be an empiricist." He needed to work "within the bounds of his personal limitation" and "produce his effects with whatever tools will work." In Mencken's case, this rule meant that he saw his own criticism as merely "catalytic"; he was a sort of literary middleman between the reader and the artist who added value to the literary work. This may have been an editorial task that authors like Dreiser were unwilling to cede. It was as if the artist needed a mediator comparable to Moses making Yahweh's ways known to the Israelites. But for Mencken, it compensated for his own inadequacy as a storyteller or poet. As literary critic, as he later explained, his judgments were unimportant because over time they became archaic. "But if, in stating them, he has incidentally produced a work of art on his own account, then he is read long after they are rejected, and it may be plausibly argued that he has contributed something to the glory of letters."

Mencken's critics like Stuart Sherman or the editors at the *Century* saw no glory in his literary contributions. To the old guard, Mencken was more emetic than catalytic. But in his own unlikely way Mencken was making a mark on American letters. The surest sign was the 1919 publication of *The American Language*, a book that was among the first to distinguish the English spoken by Americans from that spoken by the English, and that would occupy Mencken's attention throughout his life (it went through four editions, the last published in 1943). The work put the author in the odd role of scholar even though it did not endear him to pedants. As early as 1910, he had become aware of differences between England and the United States when reviewers in London and Edinburgh complained of the Americanisms in his book on Nietzsche. And as Mencken explained in the preface, his years of work as an editor forced him to read British newspapers, magazines, novels, and literary criticism, and during the process he began to collect instances of linguistic differences. *The American Language* was less an occasion for Mencken to employ his catalytic function than it was an opportunity for him to assume his older role as reporter. He described himself as "neither teacher, nor prophet, nor reformer, but merely inquirer."

Although Mencken had less to say in the first edition of *The American Language* about religion, the topic surfaced in surprising ways. For instance, he devoted a section to "Honorifics" and catalogued the different ways that the British and Americans referred to clergy:

> In general, ecclesiastical titles are dealt with somewhat loosely in the United States. In England an archbishop of the Established Church is *the Most Rev.* and *His Grace*, and a bishop is *The Right Rev.* and *His Lordship*, but there are no archbishops in the American Protestant Episcopal Church and bishops are seldom called *His Lordship*. . . . Among Catholics, by the prevailing interpretation of a decree of the Sacred Congregation of Rites, an archbishop who is not a cardinal is now *the Most Rev.* and *His Excellency* (*Excellentia Reverendissima*), and so is a bishop. Formerly an archbishop was *the Most Rev.* and *His Grace*, and a bishop was *the Right Rev.* and *His Lordship*. A cardinal, of course, remains *His Eminence*.

That Mencken refused to mock any of these titles was a testimony to his attempt at objectivity. But he undoubtedly had fun with his pose as neutral observer when he turned to the section on expletives and recounted the uncanny creativity that Americans displayed when invoking "hell":

> It is not only employed constantly in its naked form; it is also a part of almost countless combinations, many of them unknown to the English. . . . The use of *hell* in such phrases as "He ran like *hell*" is apparently an English invention, but when *like hell* is put first, as in "*Like hell* you will," the form is American. So is "The *hell* you say." So is the use of *hell* as a verb, as in "*to hell* around." So is the adjective *hellishing*, as "He was in a *hellishing* hurry." So is the general use of *hell* as an intensive, without regard to its logical meaning, as in "it was colder than *hell*," "The pitcher was wilder than *hell*," "What in *hell* did you say?" and "*Hell*, yes." So is its use as a common indicator of inferiority or disagreeableness, as in "A *hell* of a drink," "A *hell* of a note," and "A *hell* of a Baptist."

Changes in American law and the decline of Victorian standards gave Mencken greater room to document American uses in later editions than when he started *The American Language*. Mencken himself bore a special responsibility for challenging and eventually toppling the older generation of literary moralists. But his brief against Puritanism was merely the initial round of a skirmish that would occupy most of the next decade.

"The impact of such lovely country upon a city boy barely eight years old was really stupendous. Nothing in this life has ever given me a more thrilling series of surprises and felicities."

H. L. Mencken and siblings Charles Edward, Anna Gertrude, and August at summer house in Mount Washington, 1892 (*Enoch Pratt Free Library, Maryland's State Library Resource Center. All Rights reserved. Used with permission. Unauthorized reproduction or use prohibited.*)

"At a time when the respectable bourgeois youngsters of my generation were college freshmen, oppressed by simian sophomores and affronted with balderdash daily and hourly by chalky pedagogues, I was at large in a wicked seaport of half a million people, with a front seat at every public show..."

H. L. Mencken in Baltimore Herald temporary office after great Baltimore fire of 1904 *(Enoch Pratt Free Library, Maryland's State Library Resource Center. All Rights reserved. Used with permission. Unauthorized reproduction or use prohibited.)*

"I read all the manuscripts that are sent to us, and send Nathan those that I think are fit to print. If he agrees, they go into type at once; if he dissents, they are rejected forthwith. The veto is absolute, and works both ways."

H. L. Mencken and George Jean Nathan on Long Beach in Long Island, New York, September 12, 1915 *(Enoch Pratt Free Library, Maryland's State Library Resource Center. All Rights reserved. Used with permission. Unauthorized reproduction or use prohibited.)*

"These friends delight me. I turn to them when work is done with unfailing eagerness. We have the same general tastes, and see the world much alike. Most of them are interested in music, as I am. It has given me more pleasure in this life than any external thing."

H. L. Mencken and Saturday Night Club members at Philip Green's place on the South River in Maryland *(Enoch Pratt Free Library, Maryland's State Library Resource Center. All Rights reserved. Used with permission. Unauthorized reproduction or use prohibited.)*

"When I think of anything properly describable as a beautiful idea, it is always in the form of music. . . . Nothing moves me so profoundly as the symphonies of Beethoven and Brahms."

H. L. Mencken at piano in Hollins Street home, circa 1928 *(Enoch Pratt Free Library, Maryland's State Library Resource Center. All Rights reserved. Used with permission. Unauthorized reproduction or use prohibited.)*

"In all their dealings with the question of free speech the newspapers of the country, and especially the larger and more powerful ones, have been infinitely pusillanimous, groveling, dishonest and indecent."

H. L. Mencken photographs of himself at Sixth Avenue penny arcade in New York City, 1927 *(Enoch Pratt Free Library, Maryland's State Library Resource Center. All Rights reserved. Used with permission. Unauthorized reproduction or use prohibited.)*

CHAPTER FIVE

Educated Toryism

Mencken had always worked hard. His work ethic set him apart from other reporters (not to mention his gift with words) at the *Sunpapers*, and that same drive accounts for the variety of assignments he took on—book reviews, editing, writing books—that also catapulted him onto the national stage. Even so, by the time Mencken turned forty in 1920, he was, in his own words, "frightfully overworked." He was still writing columns for Baltimore's *Evening Sun* and coediting the *Smart Set*, either of which, as Fred Hobson observed, would have been a full-time job for most people. Mencken was also responsible, as part of his duties with the Smart Set Company, for overseeing several of the firm's pulp magazines. His recently established relationship with Alfred Knopf further added to his work, which included acting as a consultant to the New York publishing house. Mencken had also begun to write for the *Nation* as a contributing editor—an arrangement that must have stung Stuart Sherman. On top of this Matterhorn of activity, Mencken continued to write books, articles for other magazines, and chapters for other books such as Harold Stearns's *Civilization in the United States*. In fact, the 1920s witnessed the production of six volumes of *Prejudices* (recently republished by the Library of America), a series of books that collected some of Mencken's reviews, essays, and columns, in some cases improved them, and overall made accessible in book form the sort of invective and observation that up to that point had largely been confined to magazines and newspapers. (*A Book of Prefaces* was more or less the model for *Prejudices*.) Mencken estimated that he was working between twelve and fourteen hours a day. Compounding this load were physical ailments and a degree of hypochondria that made work difficult. Mencken's "Illnesses" file for the 1920s included influenza, bronchitis, colds, sore throats, hay fever, stomach discomfort, and "severe lumbago."

The one part of his load from which Mencken sought relief was the *Smart Set*. By 1923 the magazine had run its course, and Nathan, Mencken, and the publisher, Eltinge F. Warner, were trying to unload it but were unable to do so. Mencken and Nathan wrote a satirical piece in late summer 1923 about President Harding that Warner believed to be in bad taste—Harding had died on August 2. When the publisher spiked the essay, Mencken and Nathan left the *Smart Set*, and did so claiming that they had accomplished what they originally wanted to, which was to "break down some of the difficulties which beset the American imaginative writer." But the end of the *Smart Set* did not mean the end of magazine editing. Knopf was waiting in the wings with another Mencken-Nathan venture—the *American Mercury*, which came out with its first issue in January of 1924. Mencken's idea was to expand beyond the arts and include all of American life, a notion on which Nathan was not keen. Mencken still wanted to provoke, even to "drive a wedge" between, liberals and conservatives. But he still imagined that he was producing a magazine for the nation's "civilized minority." The thought of a fresh publication, he wrote, "makes me young again." Only a year into the venture editorial differences divided Mencken and Nathan, with the latter wanting to confine the magazine to literary life. Mencken's political interests were not the only issue. He was dissatisfied with Nathan's management of the magazine. By 1925 Knopf and Mencken had demoted Nathan to writing about theater and overseeing the *American Mercury*'s Clinical Notes. None of the magazine's readers seemed to notice the editorial breakup. When the second issue went to the newsstand, the *American Mercury* had over fifteen thousand subscribers.

Mencken's interest in affairs beyond publishing and literature was hardly unusual for a writer who started in journalism and wrote weekly columns on a variety of subjects, including local and national politics. (After a hiatus of sixteen years, in 1920 Mencken covered the Democrat and Republican national conventions, and continued to do so until the end of his career.) Furthermore, his understanding and experience of American letters were bound up with his own dealings with authors, publishers, and laws regulating decency and patriotism. Indeed, Mencken could not help but view Puritanism as a force that not only stunted the American imagination but also restricted basic civil liberties. As he wrote in *A Book of Prefaces*, underneath the various legislative aspects of Comstockery was "the dubious principle—the very determining principle, indeed, of Puritanism—that it is competent for the community to limit and condition the private acts of its members." This involved the "inevitable" and equally shaky corollary that "there are some members of the community who have a special talent for such legislation, and that their arbitrary fiats are, and of a right ought to be, binding upon all." With a new magazine and several book projects in the works, Mencken would have lots of space to explore the imbecilities of Americans' cherished beliefs about government of the people, by the people, and for the people—especially the religious ones.

Democracy's Malcontent

Mencken may have complained stridently about the effects of Comstockery on his efforts to improve the nation's letters, but Woodrow Wilson's idealist policies, especially in foreign affairs, affected the writer's life much more directly than an urban association with a mission to eliminate vice. Under Wilson's administration not only did the United States intervene in the Great War on the side of the Allies, but income tax rates soared from 7 to 77 percent, the manufacture and sale of intoxicating liquor became illegal, and Espionage and Sedition Acts proscribed any "disloyal, profane, scurrilous or abusive" utterances about pubic officials. What was a provocateur like Mencken to do? His losses were considerable. Owners of the *Sunpapers* refused to let him write out of fear that he would print seditious matter. He also lost his car—proceeds from its sale went to stocking up on wine, beer, and alcohol before Prohibition went into effect. Mencken also endured the loss of some of his privacy since the agents of the postmaster general often read his mail before he did. Mencken even worried about being drafted for the war. As a bachelor, even of thirty-seven, he was conceivably eligible for military service. The alternative was to lay low during the war. His routine at the family home was to go over correspondence and *Smart Set* submissions during the mornings, work on house renovations in the afternoons, and write primarily at night before ten o'clock, when he stopped for reading, drinking, and conversation. Mencken's reduced income prompted complaints that he might have to "go back to cigar-making." In fact, even before the war he was making plenty from nonnewspaper work, especially with the *Smart Set* and its related publications. In 1918 he earned just under $7,000 before the federal government took its share to pay for the war and related expenses.

Mencken also held his tongue on the chief executive that he blamed for such hardships—Woodrow Wilson, the Presbyterian president who embodied Puritanism as Mencken understood it. During the twenty-eighth president's two terms—especially during the war—Mencken had little room to comment on Wilson's affairs. If he felt pressure from local vice squads when considering risqué short stories, how much more from a federal government that was imprisoning critics of the war? Not until after Wilson left office did Mencken start to dissect the former president's defects. One of his first comments came in a review of a William Bayard Hale book, *The Story of a Style*, a study of Wilson's rhetoric. Since Hale had written a biography of Wilson and had also coauthored with Wilson *The New Freedom*, he was by no means out to undo Wilson. In fact, Mencken complimented Hale for saying "very kind things about Woodrow—a man probably quite as mellow and likable within as the next man, despite his strange incapacity for keeping his friends." But such admirable personal qualities did not prevent Hale from noting the "extreme badness of the Woodrovian style," and gave Mencken an excuse to single out those fools who were responsible for giving the impression that Wilson's verbal dexterity was on a par with "the Biblical prophets." These hacks "were not men who actually knew anything about the writing of English, but simply editorial writers on party newspapers, i.e., men who related themselves to literary artists in much the same way that Dr. Billy Sunday relates himself to the late Paul of Tarsus." Then Mencken went for the jugular:

> [R]eading [Wilson's] speeches in cold blood offers a curious experience. It is difficult to believe that even idiots ever succumbed to such transparent contradictions, to such gaudy processions of mere counter-words, to so vast and obvious a nonsensicality. Hale produces sentence after sentence that has no apparent meaning at all—stuff quite as bad as the worst bosh of the Hon. Gamaliel Harding. . . . The result was the grand series of moral, political, sociological and theological maxims which now lodges imperishably in the cultural heritage of the American people, along with Lincoln's "government for the people, by the people," etc., Perry's "We have met the enemy, and they are ours," and Vanderbilt's "The public be damned." The

important thing is not that a popular orator should have uttered such grand and glittering phrases, but that they should have been gravely received, for many weary months, by a whole race of men, some of them intelligent.

Still, the defects in Wilson were not as glaring as those in Teddy Roosevelt, another Progressive politician whose policies smacked of sanctity. The prevailing American theory of government in the early decades of the twentieth century held that "political heresy should be put down by force." This orthodoxy was not Wilson's creation but Roosevelt's. The twenty-sixth president, the first Progressive to occupy the Oval Office, came into politics as a reformer, shocked by the "discovery that his town was run by men with such names as Michael O'Shaunnessy and Terrence Googan—that his social inferiors were his political superiors." That notion of superiority, Mencken believed, partook of the same outlook that had informed Friedrich Nietzsche. Mencken detected Nietzschean convictions in Roosevelt's early speeches, so much so that the American Progressive was a pale imitation of Kaiser Wilhelm:

> Both dreamed of gigantic navies. . . . Both preached incessantly the duty of the citizen to the state, with soft pedal upon the duty of the state to the citizen. Both praised the habitually gravid wife. Both delighted in the armed pursuit of the lower fauna. Both heavily patronized the fine arts. Both were intimates of God, and announced His desires with authority. Both believed that all men who stood opposed to them were prompted by the devil and would suffer for it in hell.

Such affinities with matters German could not spare Roosevelt or the Progressives from Mencken's dismissal. Perhaps the journalist's disdain stemmed from the veneer of democracy that gave Progressives purchase upon the electorate. For Roosevelt "believed in strong centralization—the concentration of power in few hands, the strict regimentation of the nether herd, the abandonment of democratic platitudes." But to come to power, Roosevelt had to mimic the democratic ideals of the populists and western Progressives, thus swallowing "at one gigantic gulp, and out of the same herculean jug, the most amazing mixture of social, political and economic perunas ever got down by one hero . . . a cocktail made up of all the elixirs hawked among the boobery in his time, from woman suffrage to the direct primary, and from initiative and referendum to the short ballot, and from prohibition to public ownership."

This drinking stunt put Roosevelt and Wilson atop "the most tatterdemalion party ever seen in American politics." Some of the initial Progressives, "the quasi-religious monkey-shines that marked the first Progressive convention," may have truly believed in democracy. But Roosevelt believed "in government . . . a hard concentration of power . . . a rigid control from above, a despotism of inspired prophets and policemen." Of course, Mencken dissented from democracy and favored a society that allowed for the cultivation of superior and civilized men. But he was not in favor of Progressivism because he preferred old-fashioned liberalism—"free speech, unhampered enterprise, the least possible governmental interference." Under the new powers of the federal government, however, the American theory of "a federation of free and autonomous states" had "broken down by its own weight." Mencken lamented that "we are moved toward centralization by forces that have long been powerful and are not quite irresistible." So too were the United States' days of freedom from foreign entanglements a fiction. The nation "can no longer hope to lead a separate life in the world, undisturbed by the pressure of foreign aspirations." In a line that once had meaning but today sounds almost trite, Mencken warned that "[h]owever unpleasant it may be to contemplate, the fact is plain that the American people, during the next century, will have to fight to maintain their place in the sun."

To top off these complaints, Mencken also faulted professional historians for failing to step up and provide perspective on such fundamental changes in American government. He groused that the nation's historians were "ten times more cruelly beset by the ruling politico-plutocratic-social oligarchy than ever the Prussian professors were by the Hohenzollerns." Here Mencken still had the recent war in mind, and the members of the academic establishment, including the American Historical Association's president, J. Franklin Jamison, and the University of Chicago's Samuel Harper, who vouched for the Sisson Documents, a set of forged Russian documents issued to show ties between the German government and the Russian revolutionaries. Mencken believed he was merely supplying ballast to academics who were justifying the nation's rulers in ways that echoed Eusebius's praise for Constantine. Still, the lack of truthfulness about United States politics went beyond the war and its exigencies. Americans, professors included, were generally gullible about national figures and their policies because of an almost religious conviction about the sanctity of their elected officials. Where, Mencken asked, "is the first-rate biography of Washington—sound, fair, penetrating, honest, done by a man capable of comprehending the English gentry of the eighteenth century"? The only decent political biographies produced by Americans that rivaled John Morley's study of William Gladstone or Winston Churchill's biography of his father were William Graham Sumner's book on Andrew Jackson and Daniel Coit Gilman's exploration of James Monroe. Otherwise, Mencken's shelf was empty:

> One thinks of Dr. Woodrow Wilson's biography of George Washington as one of the strangest of all the world's books. Washington: the first, and perhaps also the last American gentleman. Wilson: the self-bamboozled Presbyterian, the right-thinker, the great moral statesman, the perfect model of the Christian cad. It is as if the Rev. Dr. Billy Sunday should do a biography of Charles Darwin.

When Mencken turned from politicians to policy, he discovered that the same starry-eyed optimism in the face of sober realities was responsible for the other major political inconvenience of the era—Prohibition. The part to which he objected least was the "forward-looker," rather than the "right-thinker." While the latter was "privy to all God's wishes" and "never wrong," the former was "heir" to all God's promises and "never despairing." Mencken preferred forward-looking if only because it showed "courage and originality." It took "long practice and considerable natural gift" to believe in the outcomes promised by various utopians. Such "sad, mad, glad folks," at once "pathologically sensitive to the sorrows of the world" and "pathologically susceptible to the eloquence of quacks," were convinced that Prohibition would rid the world of evil. The federal abolition of alcohol was "obviously a colossal failure." It had "not only not cured the rum evil" but had made it "five times as bad as it ever was before."

> [T]o confess that bald fact would be to break the forward-looking heart . . . it cherished the sorry faith that somehow, in some vague and incomprehensible way, Prohibition will yet work. When the truth becomes so horribly evident that even forward-lookers are daunted, then some new quack will arise to fool them again, with some new

and worse scheme of super-Prohibition. It is their destiny to wobble thus endlessly between quack and quack.

To the right-thinkers who advocated Prohibition, Mencken was not so patient. In fact, he returned to the theme he first encountered in Nietzsche and by which he would explain democracy and Puritanism, namely, the inferior man's hatred of his superiors (or that Puritanical fear that someone somewhere may be having fun). In a piece he wrote in the early days of dry America, Mencken opined that the typical proponent of Prohibition was "a man full of religious excitement, with the usual sadistic overtones." "He delights in persecution for its own sake," Mencken explained, he "likes to see the other fellow jump and to hear him yell." The thrill of the chase, not the instruction of Holy Writ, was what Billy Sunday and the Methodists understood so well. If unjust, the pursuit of sinners is even more fun, "for to do injustice with impunity is a sign of power." In Mencken's Nietzschean calculus, "power is the thing that the inferior man always craves more violently."

The simplistic analysis, almost as Manichean as Billy Sunday's, continued to dominate Mencken's critique of democracy, but to his credit he added observations about Prohibition-era America that encouraged readers to look past his own hollowness. For instance, he remarked that one of the blessings of Prohibition was to reveal the appeal of urban life. Contrary to the notion that farm boys came to cities to make a higher wage—which to Mencken did not make sense since boys worked as hard in the city as they did on the farm with low wages to boot, and since most wealthy Americans were city born and bred—Prohibition showed that rural folk moved to cities in pursuit of "the gay life." "[T]hey yearned for a semester or two in the theaters, the saloons and the bordellos." This "gorgeous bait dragged them out of their barn-yards," only to have Puritanism in the form of Prohibition "eat the bait." Another unforeseen consequence of the federal legislation was that it functioned as a deterrent to marriage. Here Mencken painted a verbal picture that rivaled the real ones that Norman Rockwell later drew:

> It was alcohol, in the past, that was the primary cause of perhaps a majority of alliances among civilized folk. The man, priming himself with cocktails to achieve boldness, found himself suddenly bogged in sentimentality, and so yielded to the ancient tricks of the lady. Ab-

solutely sober men will be harder to snare. Coffee will never mellow them sufficiently.

At the same time, Prohibition would in the long run increase marriages among the upper class because "the life of a civilized bachelor will become intolerable." Going to a club without the prospect of having a drink was as unappealing as a "beautiful girl without hair or teeth."

Cheek by jowl with Mencken's complaints about democracy was his resentment of Puritanism and the hypocrisy that followed from it. In one essay on Prohibition published in 1920, he observed that the "Puritan Commonwealth, now as always, has no traffic with heretics." But he knew that the United States had plenty of lapsed Puritans and that many of them were officers in the commonwealth. Indeed, a regular feature of Mencken's reporting on the national political conventions was his observations about hotels and the availability of alcohol. In 1924, for instance, when the Democrats met in New York City and considered the merits of New York governor Al Smith, Mencken speculated that the decision to hold the convention at Madison Square Garden owed in part to the ability of local party officials (Tammany Hall) to ply delegates with "enough sound drinks at reasonable prices to keep pleasantly jingled." Mencken had also heard rumors that the Coolidge administration had "hurled hundreds of Prohibition agents into Manhattan" to keep the town "bone-dry." But Mencken's New York friends were optimistic. "There are, indeed, so many saloons in the town that all the Federal judges east of the Mississippi, working in eight-hour shifts like coal miners, could not close them completely." Even Prohibition agents were conceding that the price of scotch was declining thanks to cheap imports from the Bahamas. Meanwhile, Mencken had sources telling him that the Republican convention in Cleveland was undergoing "elaborate preparations" to "slack the thirst of visitors." Because Ohio was the home of the Anti-Saloon League, the agents of the "Only True Christianity" would likely drive bottles of bad scotch up to $15 and "more than one delegate [would] go home in the baggage car, a victim to methyl alcohol."

In contrast to New York and Cleveland, San Francisco, site of the 1920 Democratic convention, reflected "the difference between entertaining human beings and entertaining horned cattle." There administrators at city hall had ordered sixty barrels of "excellent" bourbon and charged it to the local smallpox hospital. When the "Methodist mullahs" discovered and exposed the transaction by proving that the hospital had not had a patient for four years, they campaigned hard against the Republican mayor James Rolph and his administration. But the electorate returned the mayor to office by "immense majorities." Despite local variations, Mencken attributed the hypocrisy of Prohibition to the American invention of "right-thinking." This was first the creation of theologians, but only in the United States had Americans extended to every area of human relations the idea that "there is a body of doctrine in every department of thought that every good citizen is duty bound to accept . . . a right way and a wrong way to think about the beverages one drinks with one's meals, and the way children ought to be taught in schools, and the manner in which foreign alliances should be negotiated." Such a demand for rectitude prevented "the man of vigorous mind and stout convictions" from securing public office. Instead, American politics had room for only two kinds of men, either "the blank cartridge who has no convictions at all and is willing to accept anything to make votes" or "the mountebank who is willing to conceal and disguise what he actually believes."

The problem with mixing Christianity and politics, aside from the cover it gave to democracy, was that the effort to create a nation of right-thinkers depended on thoughts that did not add up. In many cases, Mencken was not necessarily opposed to the reforms Christians advocated. But he could not abide the do-gooders' methods. For instance, about birth control and sex education, Mencken was almost as skeptical of the reformers' arguments as he was of Moses's account of human origins. Sex education materials exhibited a singular pedagogical error; namely, they took something mysterious and alluring and accounted for it "as a plumber might explain a leaky faucet." The only sure outcome of scientific elaborations of sexual desire was to make science "obscene." But because efforts to suppress birth control turned coercive, Mencken could not side with Christians. "If the debate were open and fair, I'd oppose the birth controllers with all the subtlest devices of rhetoric, including bogus statistics and billingsgate." But as long they were denied their rights—"so long as those rights are denied them by an evil combination of theologians and politicians—I am for them and shall remain so until the last galoot's ashore."

In a similar fashion Mencken defended capital punishment, a subject that by the 1920s was dividing liberal and conservative Christians. He thought the logic of ending capital punishment—that it was cold-blooded and did not deter crime—may have stemmed from Christian charity but made no sense. Imagine, he speculated, how cold-blooded a federal judge tasked with enforcing Prohibition had to be. He had to assume that "the great body of wet and enlightened Christian men—are all criminals," and that "a pack of spies and blackmailers, the corps of Anti-Saloon League snouters and Prohibition agents—are truth seekers and altruists." Still, a sound case for capital punishment owed less to Christian notions of justice than to the Aristotelian sense of catharsis (*katharsis*), a form of blowing off steam or discharging emotions, such as the schoolboy at odds with his teacher who sets a tack on the teacher's chair and laughs when she sits down only to jump back up. After a murder or heinous crime, the public craves "the satisfaction of seeing the criminal before them suffer as he made them suffer." Punishment was a way of restoring "peace of mind" or "squaring accounts." Mencken explained, "I do not argue that this yearning is noble; I simply argue that it is almost universal among human beings."

Perhaps Mencken's greatest objection to his fellow Christian citizens was their optimism about human nature, a concern that ironically put him closer to Augustinian notions of depravity than his churchgoing opponents. Mencken observed perceptively that causes like Prohibition and Comstock depended on the "doctrine that virtue and ignorance were identical—that the slightest knowledge of sin was fatal to virtue." Consequently, the way to prevent drunkenness was not through moderate consumption of alcohol, but through complete avoidance of it. So too the way to preserve the sexual innocence of schoolgirls was to keep them ignorant about sex. In turn, Comstock ran up against a school of uplifters who contended that schoolgirls sinned precisely because they were ignorant about the specifics of sexual relations. This led to the production of sex hygiene books that alerted innocents to allurements of sexual attraction and the consequences of consummation. Mencken conjectured that the knowledge of sex was actually partly responsible for the rise of frank sexual material in the modern novel. "The most virtuous lady novelists," he noted, "write things that would have made a bartender blush to death two decades ago." Either way, Christian reformers operated on the assumption that sin and virtue were largely intellectual categories, with education or wholesome thoughts being the remedy for avoiding temptation. Mencken sensed, in contrast, that virtue and vice had little to do with common sense but tapped into something deeper and darker in the human soul. Reason was an asset to humans trying to negotiate their way through a complicated universe but no match for the basic urges that drove human experience. For that reason, in Mencken's world justice was always tinged with revenge, sex could not be divorced from reproduction, and decency everywhere came with a helping of vice.

Mencken's sober outlook may also account for his positive coverage of a Roman Catholic presidential candidate, Al Smith, the one Christian politician he favored. Instead of raising the specter of a Roman Catholic ayatollah, Mencken had no more trouble with the prospect of an American president in fellowship with the bishop of Rome than he had with a self-righteous Presbyterian like Wilson in the White House. Mencken was accustomed to religious convictions cluttering the political process. But his Protestant fellow Americans were not so adaptable since they adhered to the right thinking that Mencken detected and could only view their own religious outlook as normal and non-Protestant views as abnormal. Anti-Catholicism in the United States, of course, had a long history. It owed a debt to real theological and liturgical differences that split the Western Church at the Reformation. Those Protestant objections gained greater currency during the eighteenth century when Enlightenment thinkers regarded Roman Catholicism as an enemy of free thought and liberal society. Some of the fiercest instances of anti-Catholicism flared during the 1840s when immigrants from Ireland and Germany (many Roman Catholic) flooded cities like Philadelphia and Boston. During the decades of the greatest influx of immigrants from Europe (1870 to 1920), which coincided largely with Mencken's life, anti-Catholicism among Protestants may not have been as violent as in the 1840s, but it was much better organized. Institutions like the Evangelical Alliance (1864) and the Federal Council of Churches (1908) still listed Roman Catholicism as one of the major threats to Christian civilization in the United States (along with other categorical errors such as socialism, atheism, and materialism).

Protestant anti-Catholicism came to a head for Mencken with the political career of Al Smith, the four-time governor of New York who was neither a typical Roman Catholic ruler (like, say, the Austrian emperors) nor predictably the product of urban political corruption. He did emerge from the political networks of Tammany Hall in New York City, a political machine that in the minds of Progressives stood for political patronage and graft. After graduating from Tammany Hall to the New York State Assembly in 1904, Smith embraced a number of reforms such as reducing child labor and expanding government support for public schooling. In 1918 he became governor of New York and, after losing reelection in 1920, returned to office in the 1922 election and remained through two more two-year terms. This track record made him an attractive nominee by the Democrats for president, a process that also prompted Smith to explain his obligations to the Roman Catholic Church as a public official in the United States.

In an article during the early rounds of the 1928 presidential campaign, Smith needed to give an account of his faith after Charles C. Marshall penned a letter, published in the *Atlantic Monthly*, that questioned whether a Roman Catholic could uphold the US Constitution while also in subjection to the pope, at one time a foreign prince with temporal power. Marshall quoted from various encyclicals to prove his point. A regular churchgoer who did not follow the magisterium closely, Smith wondered in private, "what the hell is an encyclical?" But in his published response, Smith was quick to say that he had never experienced any tension between his faith and his political loyalty and service. In a statement that prefigured John F. Kennedy's explanation of his church membership to Texas Baptists thirty-two years later, Smith said in so many words that Roman Catholicism was as American as generic Protestantism:

> I am unable to understand how anything that I was taught to believe as a Catholic could possibly be in conflict with what is good citizenship. The essence of my faith is built upon the Commandments of God. The law of the land is built upon the Commandments of God. There can be no conflict between them. Instead of quarreling among ourselves over dogmatic principles, it would be infinitely better if we joined together in inculcating obedience to these Commandments in the hearts and minds of the youth of the country as the surest and best road to happiness on this earth and to peace in the world to come. This is the common ideal of all religions. What we need is more religion for our young people, not less; and the way to get more religion is to stop the bickering among our sects which can only have for its effect the creation of doubt in the minds of our youth as to whether or not it is necessary to pay attention to religion at all.

Smith concluded by summarizing the American creed to which he professed (which resembled greatly the Americanism that Pope Leo XIII in

1898 had mildly condemned as a heresy). Smith said that he affirmed "the worship of God according to the faith and practice of the Roman Catholic Church," the "absolute freedom of conscience for all men," the "absolute separation of Church and State," the "public school as one of the cornerstones of American liberty," and the "common brotherhood of man under the common fatherhood of God."

Mencken worried that Smith's explanation of his faith a full year before the convention and general election may have been a blunder. His other weakness, from the vantage of Baltimore, was the Roman Catholic hierarchy in the United States. Mencken lamented that gone were the days of Archbishop John Ireland or James Cardinal Gibbons, two clerics who lobbied for a church better adapted to republicanism and received a mild slap on the wrists from Leo XIII in his 1898 encyclical that condemned "Americanism." Without a savvy episcopate in the United States, Smith would be at the mercy of lesser clerics and forever "bound up with the acts and attitudes of the church." As much as Mencken hoped Smith would win the White House, if only to rebuke "the Methodist-Baptist tyranny which now oppresses the Republic," the journalist was not hopeful that the American clergy could rally. Smith's performance in the pages of the *Atlantic*, which Mencken claimed to be widely recognized as the product not of the governor himself but of a priestly ghostwriter, "was well-aimed and immensely effective." It was, "in essence, a defiance of the Pope—or, at all events, it was so interpreted in the South." Smith served notice to Rome "that, in all matters of civil government, he was prepared to wrap the flag about him and defy the whole College of Cardinals."

By the spring of 1928, Mencken was writing about the potential of a civil war breaking out in the "Solid South" over Smith's candidacy. One issue was, of course, Prohibition, a topic that alienated Smith from southern Protestants. Mencken did not understand Prohibition to be directly an expression of religious conviction. In his Nietzschean division of humankind, Prohibition was the outgrowth of the yokels' jealousy of city folk. If a city man drinks to excess, the worst that happens is the police arrest him, his wife "beats" him, and he loses his job. But a farmer who drinks uncontrollably loses his livestock (the cows' udders burst and the hogs starve), his priest denounces him as an atheist, and "he is ruined." Prohibition protects the "yokel" from himself and "harasses his superior and enemy, the city man." Only after such rural jealousy of urban life did religious conviction emerge to justify

Prohibition. Once the "yokels and their spiritual advisers" saw that city folk were still capable of finding their favorite drinks, Prohibitionists fell back on "the doctrine that Prohibition is ordained of God." To the urban dweller such a belief was risible since "the chief agents of revelation are Methodist bishops," and the city man "has heard too much balderdash from them to have any confidence." Conversely, Mencken believed that Smith, if elected, could help to unravel Prohibition even if he had to work with a Congress dominated by drys. Presidential authority in appointing federal judges might balance police and federal regulators who enforced the law.

Smith's religion, however, was a greater obstacle to his electoral victory than his opposition to Prohibition. In fact, Mencken predicted that Smith's Roman Catholicism would only divide the country:

> His defeat will be a smashing affront to all Catholics, who will be notified thereby that the majority of their fellow-citizens do not regard them as sound Americans. And if he is nominated and elected it will be a no less smashing affront to those millions of Protestants who believe in all sincerity that Catholicism is inimical to free government, and that the election of a Catholic President will sound the death-knell of the Republic.

In fact, Mencken contended that religion always made political contests more partisan. He recalled a time when Prohibition could be discussed "good-humoredly." People could even talk civilly about Carrie Nation. "But the moment the Baptist and Methodist pastors began taking jobs with the Anti-Saloon League," Mencken observed, "the contest became a bloody riot." If he were merely reflecting on the increase in crime during the 1920s, Mencken had a point. In many of the largest cities murder rates doubled and the federal inmate population increased by nearly 550 percent. Mencken may have overshot the mark by chalking up the criminalization of alcohol to religious bias. But it was another indication of the way an agnostic tried to make sense of Protestant hegemony in the United States.

Mencken was in the habit of shooting from the hip, but in this case he had done his homework. During the 1928 campaign, beginning in July, he subscribed to a large pile of southern secular and denominational newspapers. At first, Mencken found that the pastors were engaged in disputes among themselves, with some editors even battling their own editorials. For instance, the man in charge of Georgia's *Christian Index* warned in one editorial of the danger of bringing politics into the pulpit, but he printed several articles covering church meetings to rally support for Prohibition and opposition to Smith. Mencken also noticed that for two weeks after Smith's nomination the southern editors were silent about the Democrat's religion. But then the drumbeat of articles against the papacy ensued with objections to Roman Catholic infidelity and the church's history of mixing church and state. Even so, Mencken could not resist taking delight in "certain Romish practices" finding a home in "the Bible Belt." The *Biblical Record* of Raleigh, North Carolina, for instance, devoted a front-page story to "an account of a *retreat* at Ridgecrest, N.C. in June! More than sixty Baptists took part in it." By Mencken's reckoning, retreats were common among not Protestants but Roman Catholics.

By September Mencken was still slogging through the Baptist and Methodist papers. He estimated that two-thirds of them still carried on stridently about the campaign. Half of the stories concluded that "anyone who is against Prohibition is against God." The other half simply damned the pope. In both cases, southern Protestants exhibited a dubious logic. On the one hand, Prohibitionists excused law enforcement on the ground that the use of alcohol was a moral question, and "they are bound by their oaths to horn into all moral questions," except, of course, when they did nothing "while the Klan was flogging and barn-burning all over the South." On the other hand, they defended their attacks on the pope by deducing that the Roman Catholic Church was "a political machine with pretensions to secular power," all the while forgetting that "secular power is what [Protestants] are trying to get themselves." The campaign wound up revealing less about the political order of the United States than about the hollowness of American ideals:

> Every American is taught in school that all Americans are free, and so he goes on believing it his whole life—overlooking the plain fact that no Negro is really free in the South, and no miner in Pennsylvania, and no radical in any of a dozen great States. He hears of equality before the law, and he accepts it as a reality, though it exists nowhere, and there are Federal laws which formally repudiate it. In the same way he is taught that religious toleration prevails among us, and uncritically swallows the lie. No such thing really exists. No such thing has ever existed.

Mencken was not happy about these inconsistencies, but he was glad that the campaign had exposed that "millions of Americans, far from being free and tolerant men, are slaves of an ignorant, impudent and unconscionable clergy," and that they were beholden to "theological ideas so preposterous that they would make an intelligent Zulu laugh." The only relief for thoughtful Christians reading Mencken was his hopeful contention that Protestant politics was "the complete antithesis of any recognizable form of Christianity."

Mencken professed that he was a "life-long Democrat," though his distaste for Bryan and Wilson makes it hard to believe that he always voted for the party of Jackson. But in the case of Smith, Mencken's choice was transparent. A month before the election he tried to explain the governor's appeal. One theory was that the American people "loved and admired a man with a red face." Another was that Smith "wins by his free and unashamed sweating." Mencken did not agree with either. Smith's voice and gestures were also insufficient to account for his popularity. He waved his hat "mechanically," and "there is nothing of the tenor clarity of Wilson's" or "cello like quality of Bryan's" in Smith's voice. His physique was undistinguished, with shoulders "that sloped like a woman's" and a "body too long for his legs." In the end, Smith had what "the movie folk call IT—and the movie folks discovered long ago that it could not be described with any precision." In fact, Smith had "IT" as "no American politician has had it since Roosevelt." The American public delighted in him (except when Smith resorted to "such dullness as resides in official statistics"). Smith "somehow thrills them and makes them happy." When the governor cast "his magic over them it penetrates to their gizzards." Less than a week before the November 1928 election, Mencken rhapsodized:

> It seems to me that it is not enough that a President of the United States should be full of learning and rectitude; it is also important that he have good humor in him, and be likeable as a man. His business is not merely discharging words of wisdom; he must also manage men. If he is too vain and haughty to do it, as Wilson was, then the result is bound to be turmoil and disaster. If he is too idiotic, as Harding was, then it is a riot and scandal. If he is too boorish, as Coolidge was, then it is sour and witless burlesque. . . .
>
> Frank, amiable, tolerant, modest and expansive, he has the faculty of taking men into the camp. They trust him at sight, and the

better they know him the more they trust him. No man in American politics has ever had firmer friends among his enemies. His career, indeed, has been made by their aid, and it is Republicans who are his most devoted partisans today. He would bring to the White House the equipment of a genuine leader. He would face Congress with assurance and break it to his will. And he would give us the liveliest, gaudiest, most stimulating show ever seen in Washington since the days of Roosevelt.

Of course, Mencken's endorsement did not help Smith. Even in defeat, though, Mencken continued to shower praise: "he went down to defeat with every flag flying and the band playing on deck. He was, is, and will remain a man. There are not many in public life in America. They are so few, indeed, that the American people have got out of the habit of looking for them, and of following them when found."

What Ails Democracy?

Mencken believed he knew why the American voters would not elect Smith, even though he sounded hopeful in his coverage of the 1928 campaign. As much as anti-Catholicism turned the Solid South Republican, the problem went deeper. Democracy itself was fundamentally flawed, and Mencken attempted to make that point in his 1926 book *Notes on Democracy*. It was the first of a trilogy (politics, religion, and morality) in which Mencken decided to strike a more philosophical and less journalistic pose. He attributed this new phase of writing to age (or possibly maturity):

> I have passed into the middle forties, and am no longer the artless youth I once was. That youth was chiefly interested in the gaudy spectacle of life, i.e., the superficial effects of ideas. The ageing man who now confronts you is chiefly interested in the immemorial instincts and emotions that lie under them. So this is a good time, perhaps, to draw a line. The show is not over, I hope, but there is a climax and a new beginning.

The question was not whether people would read and pay attention to *Notes on Democracy* or any other books by Mencken that ventured into matters of more serious reflection. The question was whether a man who had gained confidence as a writer by covering the seamy side of Baltimore and then created a following by lampooning his nation's ideals in some of the most vigorous prose since the days of Mark Twain and Ambrose Bierce could reinvent himself. The other question was whether Mencken was capable of systematic thinking about human nature, society, and power, or would fall back on getting a laugh.

Mencken had already gleaned insights about Western civilization from his book on Nietzsche and about the United States from his assessment of Puritanism. *Notes on Democracy* built on these themes, but the edifice was low and artless. In fact, the book revealed that Mencken's mature reflection at least at this stage was fairly thin. He began by observing that the origins of democracy were recent and ignoble. The first democratic man was interested in "something concrete and highly materialistic—more to eat, less work, higher wages, lower taxes." He had "no apparent belief in the acroamatic virtue of his own class, and certainly none in his capacity to rule." But once "the pikes were out," being a tribune of the people was far more dangerous than defending the old order. By 1828 in the United States and 1848 in Europe, every "Christian government" adhered to the central axioms of democracy, namely, that the masses have "an unalienable right" to govern themselves, and that "they are competent to do it." Mencken's aristocratic prejudice questioned the second axiom. In fact, he observed parts of human existence every day that dramatically disproved democracy's dogma.

Aside from noting the formal similarities between Christianity and democracy, Mencken also used Christianity to explain the appeal of popular sovereignty. Democracy relied upon the premise that human beings were created in the image of God. This contention placed democracy on the same footing as the Genesis accounts of human origins and with the same leverage that the "sacred faculty" used to argue that without a divine aspect to human nature men and women would be no better than brutes. Democracy, then, was a form of theology, and the antidemocrat was "not merely mistaken; he [was] also wicked." Modern defenders of democracy were "full of Christian juices," fundamentalists "by instinct." The specific human instincts that fueled democracy were fear and envy. Human beings entered life with a collective sense of fear—"Make a loud noise behind an infant just born, and it will shake like a Sunday-school superintendent taken in adultery." Properly executed, an education would rid many humans of such native or "phylogenic" fears. The trouble was that all men were not equal. Intelligence, for Mencken, was largely responsible for sorting the superior out from the inferior. This inequality made democracy inherently susceptible to demagoguery. Such Christian politicians as Wilson and Bryan obtained office by alarming the mob against their superiors. Instead of Christian statesmen, they became merely "witch-hunters," politicians who promoted "melodramatic pursuits of horrendous monsters, most of them imaginary." This concoction of fear and envy led Mencken inevitably back to his main point that democracy thrived on the inferior man's jealousy of his superiors, which was remarkably similar to his view of Puritanism—the haunting fear that someone, somewhere may be happy. "In precisely the same way democratic man hates the fellow who is having a better time of it in this world," he wrote. "Such, indeed, is the origin of democracy," and "such is the origin of its twin, Puritanism."

Any reader familiar with Calvinism might have wondered if Mencken's and Calvinism's views of human nature were similar. Humans entered the world fearful, envious, and inherently selfish. Only education and the trappings of civilization could domesticate any person. But where the Calvinist saw such defects in all persons, Mencken attributed them overwhelmingly to rural folk; for him the city dwellers were superior. The peasant stock, in Mencken's classification, were filled with envy—a kind of hatred—of their superiors. The farmer "hates the plutocrats of the cities, not only because they best him in the struggle for money, but also because they spend their gains in debaucheries that are beyond him." The Mann Act was predictably the result of six million farmers being "forced to live in unmitigated monogamy with wives whose dominant yearning is to save the heathen hordes in India from hell fire." The man in the city was not necessarily better by nature but participated in a wider set of social conventions that "mitigated and mellowed" his desires. The city "proletarian" may live a life that is "swinish." But in good times, "there is actual money in his hand, and immense and complicated organizations offer him gaudy entertainment in return for it."

As thin and unsatisfactory as Mencken's book was, his reputation forced reviewers and pundits to pay *Notes on Democracy* attention. The author himself admitted privately that he had written a poor book, "probably the worst" (the personal reasons for such an admission come in the next chapter). In his assessment for the *Saturday Review*, Walter Lippmann faulted Mencken for registering against "the divine right of demos" the same attack that political philosophers had employed against kings, nobles, and priests rather than recognizing some of the advantages of democracy. Lippmann also wondered aloud whether Mencken was "more an artist than a metaphysician," and so not up to serious intellectual work. There was nothing wrong with not being a philosopher. Mencken's contribution, according to Lippmann, was still positive—"a personal force in American life which has an extraordinarily cleansing and vitalizing effect." But the book was not political philosophy. Edmund Wilson in the *New Republic* was more critical than Lippmann. Mencken's caricature of democratic man was little more than the one-dimensional figures of Swift. Worse, Wilson detected the same old Mencken "melodrama, with the gentleman, the man of honor, pitted against the peasant and the boob." One of the few readers to enjoy *Notes on Democracy*, unsurprisingly, was the former German kaiser, who, as Fred Hobson observes, sent Mencken a letter of congratulations and two autographed photographs.

To Mencken's credit and unstinting work ethic, he had consulted some of the noted commentators on American democracy such as Alexis de Tocqueville and Henry Adams. Both authors would have provided support for Mencken's dim view of democracy. Even if Tocqueville also attributed some of the genius of American politics to the Puritans, he too asserted, as Mencken did, that democracy and liberty were inherently antithetical. Whether Tocqueville would have put it as graphically as Mencken did—"the only sort of liberty that is real under democracy is the liberty of the have-nots to destroy the liberty of the haves"—the French visitor would not have been surprised by the illiberal circumstances that Mencken endured under majority rule. Even so, both Tocqueville and Adams, much more experienced with elitism than Mencken, the aristocrat manque, diagnosed the dangers of democratic political forms in ways comparable to those of their younger critic—the self-interest that haunts both voters and officials, the unlikelihood of superior persons emerging from the electoral process, the power of material interests, and disrespect for authority and achievement.

Part of the trouble was that Mencken's style was not suited for the high-minded plaints of aristocrats like Adams and Tocqueville, nor was his critique appealing to his egalitarian-minded contemporaries. Two of the more important writers to comment on democracy in Mencken's day were Vernon Louis Parrington and Charles Beard. The former's history of the nation's letters, *Main Currents in American Thought*, which in 1928 won the Pulitzer Prize for History, mirrored Mencken in drawing a contrast between rural and urban America. For Parrington, though, the heartland was the soil from which the democratic or Jeffersonian ideals of America had grown, ideals that were responsible for the nation's greatness. For Beard, the fundamental tension in American politics also followed rural-urban opposition, with Jeffersonian egalitarianism pitted against Hamiltonian privilege. Although Beard's earlier work emphasized the class interests of both farmers and elites, by the time of *The Rise of American Civilization* (1927) he had rallied to the side of the American people and their belief in progress. Mencken's book on democracy may have enjoyed a measure of credibility if readers were aware of Adams's and Tocqueville's critiques.

The discordant note that Mencken's observations about democracy struck sounded even more jarring to Christian readers. Editors of Protestant and Roman Catholic magazines may have considered Mencken too unedifying to take notice of his book, but Christian authors themselves never dared to ponder democracy's darker side. Harry Emerson Fosdick, arguably the nation's most popular liberal preacher, opined in *Christianity and Progress* (1928) that democracy "elevates us into self-esteem." Its genius, he explained, "is to believe in men, their worth, their possibilities, their capacities for self-direction." The old politics "depressed men into self-contempt," but democracy "exalted men into self-exaltation." William Adams Brown, a professor of theology at Union Theological Seminary in New York City, was no less committed to democracy. His 1922 book *The Church in America: A Study of Its Present Condition* assumed that in the great conflict between autocracy and democracy, the church fully sided with the latter. Brown also concluded that democratic society could well expect the churches to supply *"a unifying spiritual influence, springing from a common faith, and issuing in common action."* Whether that common action included laws that infringed on Mencken's work as editor or his drinking habits after hours was not a question that Brown considered. So widespread was Christianity's uncritical support for democracy that G. K. Chesterton could conclude his travelogue on the United States with the dogmatic conviction that democratic society had no hope unless founded upon belief in "the divine origin of man." He added that so far "as democracy becomes or remains Catholic and Christian, that democracy will remain democratic." That kind of support for democracy gave Mencken little chance of persuading Christians. The best he could do was engage the editors and readers of secular outlook.

Baltimore Patriot

Mencken often received questions about why he did not join the ranks of the American intellectuals and writers who were unable to endure their nation's political and cultural follies and so relocated to civilized Europe. He admitted that he had sympathy for their position, and some of his criticisms went further than theirs:

> It is . . . one of my firmest and most sacred beliefs, reached after an inquiry extending over a score of years and supported by incessant prayer and meditation, that the government of the United States, in both its legislative arm and its executive arm, is ignorant, incompetent, corrupt, and disgusting—and from this judgment I except no more than twenty living lawmakers and no more than twenty executioners of their laws.

Mencken was no less dismissive of the nation's judges—"stupid, dishonest, and against all reason and equity"—or America's foreign policy—"hypocritical, disingenuous, knavish, and dishonorable." To round out his complaints, he regarded the American people to be "the most timorous, sniveling, poltroonish, ignominious mob of serfs and goose-steppers ever gathered under one flag in Christendom since the end of the Middle Ages."

Despite this, Mencken remained "on the dock, wrapped in the flag" when the expatriates set sail.

> [H]ere I stand, unshaken and undespairing, a loyal and devoted Americano, even a chauvinist, paying taxes without complaint, obeying all laws that are physiologically obeyable, accepting all the searching duties and responsibilities of citizenship, unprotestingly, investing the sparse usufructs of my miserable toil in the obligations of the nation. . . . [H]ere am I, contentedly and even smugly basking beneath the Stars and Stripes, a better citizen, I daresay, and certainly a less murmurous and exigent one, than thousands who put the Hon. Warren Gamaliel Harding beside Friedrich Barbarossa and Charlemagne, and hold the Supreme Court to be directly inspired by the Holy Spirit, and belong ardently to every Rotary Club, Ku Klux Klan, and Anti-Saloon League, and choke with emotion when the band plays "The Star-Spangled Banner."

Why? Because he was happy and America afforded him opportunities unimaginable elsewhere to be so disposed. Mencken had three requirements for happiness: a comfortable material existence, a sense of superiority "to the masses of my fellow-men," and being entertained. For this reason it was impossible not to be happy in the United States, since it was easy to make a living (especially after the war "brought the loot of all Europe to the national strong-box"). What made Mencken even happier was living in Baltimore, where he "lived, voted, and had his being." Though Mencken commuted to his magazine offices in New York City, he contended that the Big Apple was "fit only for the gross business of getting money" while Baltimore was a "place made for enjoying it." And what made Baltimore so enjoyable was the domestic life it nurtured. Mencken admitted that he had lived in one home for forty-five years, and to lose it would have been like losing a leg. Such stability of home life gave to human relations "a solid permanence." "A man's circle of friends becomes a sort of extension of his family."

Although dependent on his domestic circumstances in Baltimore, Mencken had no trouble feeling superior in America or enjoying the amusement that came with it:

> Here the general average of intelligence, of knowledge, of competence, of integrity, of self-respect, of honor is so low that any man who knows his trade, does not fear ghosts, has read fifty good books, and practices the common decencies stands out as brilliantly as a wart on a bald head, and is thrown willy-nilly into a meager and exclusive aristocracy.

This sense of superiority ironically added to Mencken's enjoyment of the United States, which was "incomparably the greatest show on earth." In fact, Americans had such an entertaining knack for turning what was dull in other "Christian countries" into "such vast heights of buffoonery that contemplating them strains the midriff almost to breaking." Mencken's chief example was worship:

> Here we not only have bishops who are enormously more obscene than even the most gifted of the English bishops; we have also a huge force of lesser specialists in ecclesiastical mountebankery—tin-horn Loyolas, Savonarolas and Xaviers of a hundred fantastic rites, each performing untiringly and each full of a grotesque and illimitable

whimsicality. Every American town, however small, has one of its own: a holy clerk with so fine a talent for introducing the arts of jazz into the salvation of the damned that his performance takes on all the gaudiness of a four-ring circus. . . . Their proceedings make me a happier American.

As much as Mencken clothed his invective in the fabric of invective, his was a naysayer's that defied categories. It was one part village atheist and one part town drunk. He loathed the legislation that the devout passed, especially since the laws affected him directly. But he was an amiable critic who, rather than letting his believing inferiors get the better of him, decided to play along. Mencken was fully patriotic and arguably among the most anti-American of Americans.

One possible explanation is that American Christianity was chiefly responsible for this bipolarity.

CHAPTER SIX

The Mencken Show

H. L. Mencken may have taken consolation from sitting in the front row of the show produced by the United States. But during the 1920s he left his center-aisle seat and walked into the limelight. His performances took their toll and were responsible for his poor showing in *Notes on Democracy*. Even so, fame compensated for his failings as a political philosopher. In 1925, for instance, Walter Lippmann hailed Mencken as "the most powerful influence on a whole generation of educated Americans." To one editor, he was "America's Dr. Johnson"; to another, "the nearest thing to Voltaire that America has ever produced"; and to still another, "the Genghis Khan of the Campus." Indeed, with a circulation of sixty thousand, Mencken's *American Mercury* was the item for undergraduates to be seen carrying around campus as a badge of independent thought, if not naughtiness. But his celebrity crossed over the world of language and letters into uncharted waters of popular culture. A story in New York's *Daily News* concluded on the basis of interviews with female readers that Mencken was the third most fascinating man in the world, tied with Rudolph Valentino, Charlie Chaplin, and Douglas Fairbanks. Fred Hobson puts it well when he says that Mencken had reversed expectations in American literary life. "Perhaps for the first time in American life a critic, rather than a novelist or a poet, was the most famous and most influential American writer." This fame did not mean, of course, that Americans across the board considered Mencken a gift to national life. The Justice Department's file on him included testimony that Mencken was a "Bolshevik." A Methodist minister called him a "menace" because "his ghastly fingers of death" were wrapped around the throats of America's youth. Even Lippmann had to admit that Mencken was an "outraged sentimentalist."

The phenomenon of H. L. Mencken also meant the start of a line of books about the author. In 1925 Mencken was the subject of two assessments. The first book, a slim volume just under one hundred pages by the Irishman Ernest Boyd, evaluated Mencken as a critic and a philosopher. The second, by a former colleague at the *American Mercury*, Isaac Goldberg, was a biography, or as Hobson put it, a "three-hundred-page encomium" that even Mencken could not resist helping in order to enhance his reputation. One reviewer of the Goldberg book announced that the "canonization of H. L. Mencken has begun."

In addition to compromising the first volume of his projected trilogy on life's most important questions, celebrity also diminished Mencken as a reporter. Even if he enjoyed the adulation and needed to turn down numerous invitations that came with fame, Mencken could no longer attend an event without drawing attention to himself. That was especially true in two of the more famous episodes of the 1920s' culture wars that pitted the modernists of the literary and artistic worlds, along with their liberationist cheerleaders, against the Victorians who had overseen the nation's cultural life since the 1870s. The first of those events took place in the South, a region that Mencken had long ridiculed, the second in Boston, the capital of his archenemy, Puritanism. In both cases, he once again confronted a cultural Christianity that on paper supported a free republic even while imposing serious restrictions on the work that made Mencken's life in Baltimore pleasant.

Showdown in Dayton

The trial of John T. Scopes during the summer of 1925 has occupied a place in America's legends right alongside the Salem witch trials, the legal proceedings against Henry Ward Beecher for adultery, and the Senate hearings conducted by Joseph McCarthy. The reasons for Scopes's fame have much to do with the easy way the trial fits into the narrative of reason prevailing over faith in the war of science and theology. Just as important is the publicity surrounding the trial. It was the first nationally broadcast courtroom proceeding that showed the remarkable power of the new medium of radio. Mencken was among the tsunami of reporters to flood the small town of Dayton, Tennessee, and cover the state's case against the local high school biology teacher for using a text-book that clearly violated legal prohibitions against teaching evolution. In the play *Inherit the Wind* (1955), which Jerome Lawrence and Robert Edwin Lee later wrote to memorialize this important victory for freedom of thought, Mencken's activities in Dayton were the inspiration for the character of the reporter E. K. Hornbeck, played in the movie of the same name (1960) by Gene Kelly. As it turned out, the courtroom drama had little suspense on the merits of the case. Scopes was guilty, and the jury had no trouble reaching that decision even if the judge waived the $100 fine. The real suspense was the trial's import for the larger contest be-tween secular elites like Clarence Darrow, the lead defense attorney, and Mencken, and popular Protestantism represented by William Jennings Bryan, the chief prosecutor. But as Edward Larson has so well shown in the Pulitzer Prize–winning book *Summer for the Gods: The Scopes Trial and America's Continuing Debate over Science and Religion* (1997), the overt contest between faith and reason was merely a cover for a constel-lation of other issues that included the sovereignty of state legislatures, Dayton's commercial cheerleaders who wanted a boost in publicity and business, majority rights in a democratic government, and the implicit if not straightforward embrace of the idea of a superior breed of humans put forth by Darwinism's defenders, including Mencken.

Nor was the trial a simple matter of law enforcement. Tennessee's legislature in 1925 had passed the Butler Act; Tennessee was the fifth state, after Kentucky (1922), South Carolina (1922), Oklahoma (1925), and Florida (1925), to enact legislation that banned evolution from pub-lic school curricula. The specific law that took John T. Scopes to court read:

> That it shall be unlawful for any teacher in any of the Universities, Normals and all other public schools of the State which are supported in whole or in part by the public school funds of the State, to teach any theory that denies the Story of the Divine Creation of man as taught in the Bible, and to teach instead that man has descended from a lower order of animals.

Conceivably prosecutors could have initiated proceedings against any biology teacher in these states since the textbooks available contained Darwinist instruction. But Tennessee was different because the Amer-ican Civil Liberties Union (ACLU), already advocating academic freedom in colleges and universities, advertised in the *Chattanooga Times* its willingness to assist any Tennessee schoolteacher willing to challenge the law. George W. Rappleyea, a chemical engineer in Dayton and an opponent of the Butler Act, noticed the ACLU's advertisement and rallied local Daytonians to accept the challenge. He worked with two city attorneys, Herbert E. Hicks and Sue Hicks, and the school board superintendent, Fred Robinson, who owned the drugstore where the team deliberated, to identify a schoolteacher. John T. Scopes was a welcome defendant since, as a single, winsome, and young man, he had little stake either in the merits of the law or in the consequences for Dayton. He was by no means passive in the proceedings. Scopes did teach evolution and disapproved of the new law. But he was not a radical or a spokesman for evolution. Scopes was the marionette manipulated by puppeteers much more powerful and experienced than he was. It did not hurt that the trial promised to put a small town, whose business leaders wanted to attract visitors, on the map.

While Daytonians assembled a local cast, Mencken was meeting with a different set of figures to discuss the situation in Tennessee. The place for the meeting was the home of James Branch Cabell, a southern writer whom Mencken greatly respected and had visited on other occasions. To Mencken, Cabell represented the aristocracy of the Old South and possessed the literary sensibility in novels such as *Jurgen* (1919) to prove it. In 1921 the Virginian had hosted a dinner party in Mencken's honor. Four years later Mencken was paying a visit to Cabell; this visit coincided with a meeting of the American Psychiatric Association where Darrow was scheduled to speak. By then the carnival aspect of the trial had emerged since the prosecutors in Tennessee, again to draw attention to the spectacle, had lined up William Jennings Bryan to lead the prosecution. The Great Commoner was all Darrow and Mencken needed to involve themselves in Tennessee's affairs. Mencken himself was not a fan of Darrow, since the attorney had distinguished himself as a "violent Hun-hater" during the war and valued the common man almost as much as Mencken defended the superior gentleman. Mencken would later remark that he had never had a "high opinion" of Darrow, since he was not a lawyer but an "orator" whose "frequent pronunciamentoes on legal and social questions were usually banal." In fact, Mencken could not understand why Darrow wasted time by touring the country to debate fundamentalists and defenders of Prohibition. Mencken found alarming Darrow's support for Bryan as president. But in this case, Mencken was happy for the cooperation and used the auspices of Baltimore's *Evening Sun* to post bail for Scopes. A few weeks later, Mencken met with one of Darrow's professional associates to plan a strategy for the defense. By this point, Scopes was a pawn in a larger scheme to trap Bryan, a man who repulsed both Mencken and Darrow. Even the ACLU's hopes of protecting intellectual freedom became a sacrificial lamb on the altar of a plan to expose Bryan. And with the heavyweights on the bill, Mencken captured the event's aura with the label, "the Monkey Trial." Whether that was a reference to humanity's origins or Bryan's smarts kept some guessing, and many laughing.

Given Mencken's hostility to Bryan, a native of Illinois and politician from Nebraska, readers of the former's Dayton reporting might have reasonably thought that the three-time Democratic nominee for the presidency was a southerner. In an earlier essay that established Mencken's reputation as an iconoclast, he had savaged the South as "the Sahara of the Bozart," a phrase that became an easy way for those in the know to identify the nation's most backward region. Its opening imagery about the South's wasteland was vintage Mencken:

> Down there a poet is now almost as rare as an oboe-player, a dry-point etcher or a metaphysician. . . . Nearly the whole of Europe could be lost in that stupendous region of fat farms, shoddy cities and paralyzed cerebrums: one could throw in France, Germany and Italy, and still have room for the British Isles. And yet, for all its size and all its wealth and all the "progress" it babbles of, it is almost as sterile, artistically, intellectually, culturally, as the Sahara Desert. If the whole of the late Confederacy were to be engulfed by a tidal wave to-morrow, the effect upon the civilized minority of men in the world would be but little greater than that of a flood on the Yang-tse-kiang.

The theme of the civilized minority overwhelmed by the unwashed and uncouth majority was a familiar one, but Mencken's essay had an apt bearing on the debates in the Scopes proceedings. Rather than attributing the South's inferiority to religion, Mencken chalked it up to genetics. The Old South, a region that had cultivated a natural aristocracy, was thoroughly admirable. This was the region that had captured James Branch Cabell's imagination and Mencken's fancy. But the Civil War had destroyed that cultural regime and allowed "the worst blood of western Europe" to prevail. Mencken put it succinctly: "the vast bloodletting of the Civil War half exterminated and wholly paralyzed the old aristocracy, and so left the land to the harsh mercies of the poor white trash, now its masters." The prevalence of Celtic genes also accounted for the South's faith, which was "almost precisely identical with the religious thought of Wales"—the same "naive belief in an anthropomorphic Creator but little removed, in manner and desire, from an evangelical bishop," the same "submission to an ignorant and impudent sacerdotal tyranny," the same "sharp contrast between doctrinal orthodoxy and private ethics," a piety compatible with "the theory that lynching is a benign institution." Still, the South's bloodletting was as much the product of aristocratic migration as of reproduction and intermarriage—Saxons marrying their inferiors or the southern gentry's preference for "mulatto mistresses." The arts, such as they still existed in "the lower reaches of the gospel hymn, the phonograph and the Chautauqua harangue," were all but dead, an ancient tradition of civility "broken down, alas, by the hot rages of Puritanism."

Explanations based on a people's biological traits were, of course, partly what drove eugenics and its cousins, which included Margaret Sanger's ideas about birth control, white supremacist notions of race, prohibitions against interracial marriage, anti-Semitism in most forms, and Protestant support for efforts like Planned Parenthood to encourage fewer births among Roman Catholics. That Mencken dabbled in such metaphors or thought was no surprise since most of America's educated elite embraced these ideas at some level. For instance, just two years after the Scopes trial the United States Supreme Court would uphold laws that required the sterilization of the intellectually unfit (*Buck v. Bell*, 1927). Oliver Wendell Holmes, by no means a shoddy or reactionary thinker, wrote in the decision, "society can prevent those who are manifestly unfit from continuing their kind." He added, "[t]hree generations of imbeciles are enough." The surprise about the Scopes imbroglio was that Bryan, for all his moralistic squint, saw the link between Darwinism and such genetics-based tyranny. For the very textbook that Tennessee had approved for John T. Scopes to use in class offered an explicitly eugenicist application of evolution:

> If such people were lower animals, we would probably kill them off to prevent them from spreading. Humanity will not allow this, but we do have the remedy of . . . preventing intermarriage and the possibility of perpetuating such a low and degenerate race.

Bryan's problem was that the Menckens and Darrows of the world regarded him as an intellectual inferior.

Aside from the social implications of Darwinism, the trial also touched upon the perennially sticky American debate about the sovereignty of states. Did the legislators of Tennessee, no matter how benighted they may have been, have the authority to legislate classroom instruction in the very schools they oversaw and funded? Mencken believed they did, or so he argued in the pages of the *Nation* just a few weeks before the trial: "No principle is at stake in Dayton save the principle that school teachers, like plumbers, should stick to the job that is set for them." Mencken added that the issue of free speech was "quite irrelevant." But Mencken's gambit in Dayton was not the law technically, but the "boobs" who passed and prosecuted the law, "to make Tennessee forever infamous." Bryan's presence was particularly attractive. Mencken took credit for the idea of putting Bryan on the witness stand and thereby making "a monkey of him before the world." The Great Commoner took a different and arguably naive view: "They came here to try revealed religion. I am here to defend it."

Mencken did not consider Bryan's task of defense—in actuality, prosecution—all that difficult, since Dayton was firmly situated in the Bible Belt and the locals who populated the jury were equally firm in their loyalty to Holy Writ. But in one of his first stories on the trial for the *Sun*, Mencken did admit a measure of surprise about Dayton's civic leaders. Instead of a "squalid Southern village, with darkies snoozing on the horse-blocks, pigs rooting under the houses and the inhabitants full of hookworm and malaria," Dayton was actually a "country town full of charm and even beauty." Mencken was also surprised to learn that Dayton lacked "that poisonous spirit which usually shows itself when Christian men gather to defend the great doctrine of their faith." The evolutionists and their opponents were "on the best of terms" and even hard to tell apart. Rhea County, Mencken discovered, was proudly tolerant. "The klan has never got a foothold here," he explained. The men who ran Dayton were "well-heeled Free-masons," believed in "keeping the peace," and even treated the "stray Catholics" politely, "though everyone naturally regrets they are required to report to the Pope once a week." In fact, Mencken began to suspect that the stratagems of Daytonians were every bit as sophisticated as his plans with Darrow in Cabell's parlor: "the gentlemen who are most active in promoting [the trial] are precisely the most lacking in hot conviction." Why else were the local preachers so silent?

Those orchestrating the trial behind the scenes could not, however, control the selection of the jury. The court's proceedings began with prayer from a local pastor and instruction from the judge about the importance of protecting the schools. Everyone interviewed was "hot for Genesis." The best that Darrow could do was to "sneak in a few men bold enough to declare publicly that they would have to hear the evidence against Scopes before condemning him." In sum, Dayton's citizens were "simply unable to imagine a man who rejects the literal authority of the Bible." This meant that the jury would hardly be impartial or the proceedings fair. At the same time, Mencken was not all that hopeful for the posttrial trial after Scopes was convicted and "ordered to the hulks." At that point, the jury would be "that great fair, unimpassioned body of enlightened men which has already decided that a horse hair put into a bottle will turn into a snake and that the Kaiser started the late war." For Mencken, Dayton was little more than another act in the great carnival of American buncombe.

In fact, Mencken found true entertainment outside the courthouse and far from Dayton's town center. In the days before the trial he decided to attend a camp meeting conducted in a rustic location he could have called "Hills of Zion." The service he found was mesmerizing, completely unlike any religious observance he had yet witnessed. "Even the Baptists no longer brew a medicine that is strong enough for the mountaineers," he claimed. "The sacrament of baptism by total immersion is over too quickly for them. . . . What they crave is a continuous experience of the divine power, an endless series of evidence that the true believer is a marked man, ever under the eye of God." Not even an annual revival would suffice. The "Holy Rollers" Mencken had found were ready with an answer to this spiritual craving. His depiction of a young female who had come forward to a form of the anxious bench suggested that a journalist with lots of knowledge of the world's ways still had one layer of innocence left:

> At a signal all the faithful crowded up the bench and began to pray—not in unison but each for himself. At another they all fell on their knees, their arms over the penitent. The leader kneeled, facing us, his head alternately thrown back dramatically or buried in his hands. Words spouted from his lips like bullets from a machine gun—appeals to God to pull the penitent back out of hell, defiances of the powers and principalities of the air, a vast impassioned jargon of

apocalyptic texts. Suddenly he rose to his feet, threw back his head and began to speak in tongues—blub-blub-blub, gurgle-gurgle-gurgle. . . . The climax was a shrill, inarticulate squawk, like that of a man throttled. He fell headlong across the pyramid of supplicants.

Did Mencken find this funny? His best analogy was that of "peeping through a knothole at the writhings of people in pain." By the time he recovered his wits, though, he could reassure readers that he was merely describing "what the great heritage of mankind comes to in regions where the Bible is the beginning and end of wisdom, and the mountebank Bryan, parading the streets in his seersucker coat, is pointed out to sucklings as the greatest man since Abraham."

Mencken's reporting featured the fate of free speech more than the value of scientific inquiry. Although Darwinism confirmed his crude notions of superior men and civilized races, Mencken was generally skeptical of claims to certainty, whether wrapped in the gauze of faith or presented on the disinfected tray of science. For instance, the effort to make sex scientific, as proponents of sex hygiene attempted, was only to take something mysterious and pleasurable and treat it "either as something inert and banal, like having one's hair cut, or as something painful and dangerous, like having one's appendix out." He regarded sociology as "a monkey-shine which happens to pay." Psychology was similarly "guesswork, empiricism, hocus-pocus, poppycock." In fact, people generally frowned on efforts at psychological research because "they do not offer us any nourishment, there is nothing in them to engage our teeth, they fail to make life more comprehensible." Economics for Mencken was the "dismal science" if only because economists were too invested in their own subject, namely, "the science of the ways and means whereby [scholars] have come to such estate, and maintain themselves in such estate, that they are able to hire and boss professors." Furthermore, even if Mencken himself dabbled with notions that floated in the same currents as eugenics, he thought that as a science of superior breeds, it was decidedly inferior. Nietzsche was, for instance, a great man but died insane and did little with his ideas other than to "preach a gospel that to most human beings remains unbearable." In fact, the scientific evidence for the biological superiority of the better sort of human beings was "very slight."

When Mencken did write positively about science, he often contrasted it with poetry or theology, which were products of human emotions rather than reason. In the case of human origins, the conflict was simply between the known and the mysterious. "No one knows Who created the visible universe," Mencken asserted, and "[n]o one knows why man has his present form." But when it came to the material evidence, scientists knew facts that theologians did not. When "hordes of theologians come marching down from the Southern mountains, declaring raucously that God created the universe during a certain single week of the year 4004 B.C., . . . science cannot suffer them gladly, nor even patiently." "Theological raiders" started the conflict that was playing out in Dayton by invading "the field of science."

To be sure, Mencken thought evolution was a scientific fact, but the point he repeatedly made in his accounts of the trial was the legal one of free speech in a polity protected by the Bill of Rights. The effects of free speech were everywhere evident when a preacher "of any sect that admits the literal authenticity of Genesis" gathered a crowd and disputed the claims of science. "But the instant a speaker utters a word against divine revelation he begins to disturb the peace and is liable to immediate arrest and confinement in the calaboose beside the railroad tracks." Mencken blamed the legislators in Tennessee for allowing this state of affairs. They knew what "nonsense" preachers were ramming and hammering "into yokel skulls." What is more, he found nearby Chattanooga to be a lovely city with a large "civilized minority." Even Rhea County, home to Dayton, was "very tolerant" by Bible Belt standards. "The Dayton Babbitts" managed to honor Darrow with a banquet, "despite the danger from lightning, meteors and earthquakes." But Tennessee's enlightened citizens had ignored "what was going on in the cross roads of Little Bethels." They mistook "buffooneries" for humor. As a result, in places like Dayton, "the ordinary statutes are reinforced by Holy Writ, and whenever there is a conflict Holy Writ takes precedence."

The trial itself was fair, but only by the standards of biblical teaching. Mencken was surprised that public opinion in Dayton saw no impropriety in the trial being opened with a prayer by a "clergyman known by everyone to be against Scopes." Nor did the public seem to notice the inequity of Bryan assuming the "character of public evangelist" whenever he spoke outside the courtroom while also functioning as one of the attorneys of record. These anomalies indicated that the people, from whom the jury was selected, were against Scopes not merely as one who broke the law but also as a heretic. Despite the great advantage that the prosecution had, Bryan and his team contested every point of

procedure and took advantage of their acquaintance with local protocol. When the defense put Maynard M. Metcalfe from Johns Hopkins on
the stand, who gave "one of the clearest, most succinct and withal most
eloquent presentations of the case for the evolutionists," Bryan sat with
his gaze fixed on the witness, sometimes his face "darkening," at other
times his eyes "flashing." Before Bryan started to question Metcalfe, he
came out from behind the prosecution's table and planted himself ten
feet directly in front of the witness. By the time Bryan was finished, the
jury had heard nothing of Metcalfe's testimony, which "went whooping
into the radio and . . . banging into the face of Bryan."

When the verdict came against Scopes—with little suspense—
Mencken's thoughts went chiefly to the civilized minority in Tennessee. How could the trappings of civility and decency flourish in a state
where fundamentalists had the enlightened citizens outnumbered? Although he found the townspeople of Dayton to be agreeable, Mencken
did not care much for them since "Darrow's ribaldries" had not shaken
them out of beliefs that they are "not mammals," that "they know more
than all the men of science," and that "the earth is flat and that witches
still infest it." The rest of the state's residents were not so easily dismissed. Mencken worried about the "agreeable folk" of Chattanooga
who "led civilized lives, despite Prohibition," and "were interested in
civilized ideas, despite the fog of Fundamentalism." Pastors, priests,
rabbis, attorneys, and newspapermen with whom Mencken empathized
still endured "pathetically under the imbecilities of their evangelical
colleagues." In response to the proceedings in Dayton, these civilized
people asked for "suspended judgment, sympathy, Christian charity."
Mencken thought they deserved it. But he also believed that Tennessee's intelligent minority was responsible for its own troubles. They
were guilty of being "too cautious and politic— . . . too reluctant to of-
fend the Fundamentalist majority." They were also insufficiently critical
of their "somewhat childish local patriotism." They feared they would
bring the derision of the rest of the country on them if they attacked
the buffooneries of fundamentalism. The gambit had failed. "Now they
have the derision, and to excess—and the attack is ten times as difficult
as it ever was before."

Mencken's capacity to distinguish between Tennessee's good and
not-so-great citizens evaporated by the time he wrote on William Jennings Bryan's death, an occurrence that almost coincided with the
Scopes trial and colored perceptions of the three-ring circus in Dayton

with the sobriety of a funeral. Five days after John T. Raulston handed down Scopes's verdict of guilty and set the fine at $100, Bryan, who had remained in Tennessee to give speeches, returned from church and a Sunday dinner to his hotel room, where he died in his sleep (the likely causes were diabetes and fatigue). Mencken had already treated national readers of his reports on Dayton to less than flattering depictions of Bryan's abilities and motivations. At the outset of the trial Mencken took stock of Bryan's health. "He is a bit mangey and flea-bitten, but no means ready for his harp," Mencken observed. "He may last five years, ten years or even longer." That prospect bothered Mencken because Bryan was capable of doing in the South what no city man with access to the national media could do:

> [Bryan] is full of such bitter, implacable hatreds that they radiate from him like heat from a stove. He hates the learning that he cannot grasp. He hates those who sneer at him. He hates, in general, all who stand apart from his own pathetic commonness.

A little later in the trial, Mencken observed that Bryan turned to "yokels" for "consolation in his old age, with the scars of defeat and disaster all over him." But to the simple townsfolk, "he is a prophet of the imperial line—a lineal successor to Moses and Abraham." Mencken could not resist one further assessment of Bryan toward the end of the trial. In it he credited Bryan with once having "one leg in the White House" and the nation trembling "under his roars." But in Dayton Bryan "is a tinpot pope in the coca-cola belt and a brother to the forlorn pastors who belabor half-wits in galvanized iron tabernacles behind the railroad yards."

> The Bryan of today is not to be mistaken for the political rabble-rouser of two decades ago. That earlier Bryan may have been grossly in error, but he at least kept his errors within the bounds of reason: it was still possible to follow him without yielding up all intelligence. The Bryan of today, old, disappointed and embittered, is a far different bird. He realizes at last the glories of this world are not for him, and he takes refuge, peasant-like, in religious hallucinations. They depart from sense altogether. They are not merely silly; they are downright idiotic.

Little did Mencken realize that no matter how much Bryan may have appeared to be at the end of his tether, his assessments of the prosecutor's career were a warm-up for arguably the most controversial column that Mencken would ever write. Perhaps unaware of the log in his own eye, Mencken reduced Bryan's life to one of hatred. The journalist had thought such bigotry was the product of evangelical Christianity, which "as everyone knows, is founded upon hate, as the Christianity of Christ was founded upon love." But even evangelicals were capable of "loose[ning] their belts and belch[ing] amicably." Bryan's defect was not his faith but his "lust for revenge." "The men of the cities," Mencken explained, "had destroyed him and made a mock of him; now he would lead the yokels against them. . . . The hatred in the old man's burning eyes was not for the enemies of God; it was for the enemies of Bryan." Mencken was aware of a "national custom to sentimentalize the dead" but had no trouble avoiding it. Bryan's hatred for enlightened men called for "hatred to match it." Still, Mencken did not want to judge Bryan simply on the basis of his last few weeks of life:

> Bryan, at his best, was simply a magnificent job-seeker. The issues that he bawled about usually meant nothing to him. He was ready to abandon them whenever he could make votes by doing so, and to take up new ones at a moment's notice. For years he evaded Prohibition as dangerous; then he embraced it as profitable. At the Democratic National Convention last year he was on both sides, and distrusted by both. In his last great battle there was only a baleful and ridiculous malignancy. If he was pathetic, he was also disgusting. . . . [At Dayton he] seemed only a poor clod like those around him, deluded by a childish theology, full of an almost pathological hatred of all learning, all human dignity, all beauty, all fine and noble things. He was a peasant come home to a dung-pile. Imagine a gentleman, and you have imagined everything that he was not.

Marion Elizabeth Rodgers records that Mencken's vitriol was too much even for his editors back at the *Sunpapers*. In response to angry calls and advertisers who wanted their ads pulled, Mencken rushed into the office to change his copy—"fool" became "figure" and "mountebank" turned into "leader." In fact, the paper's managing editor stopped the presses during the printing of later editions. Mencken was not pleased but went along. He later wrote, "[f]or two weeks I denounced [Bryan] as a mountebank daily; now he must be praised. But not by me, by damn." The unexpurgated version, which would appear in collections of Mencken's essays, according to Terry Teachout was "among the great masterpieces of invective in the English language." But it also revealed a gaping inconsistency. As a defender of decency or as an amused spectator of American buffoonery, Mencken advised standards of decency and civility. He could not maintain them when confronted by Bryan. The hatred and envy that Mencken detected in Bryan were just as evident in the journalist's columns. To suggest that Mencken also envied Bryan is to dabble in pop psychology. But that interpretation is plausible if Mencken's own celebrity compromised his detachment. He was a writer who was a national figure and read all over the world but could not command the loyalty or following of someone he considered to be a second-rate politician and religious zealot. Mencken was indeed a celebrity. But Gene Kelly's E. K. Hornbeck was nevertheless a supporting role behind Frederic March's Matthew Harrison Brady (William Jennings Bryan).

War against the Comstocks

For all of Mencken's bravado, he was prone to introspection and depression. After turning forty, he claimed to have experienced a "full sense of human sorrow." His awareness of human mortality came with a recognition that he had lived longer than his father, that he had even eclipsed "the average span of the Menckenii for three hundred years." His ancestors were "a feverish race, launching out into life prematurely and wearing out before most [men] are full-grown." Writing was not always a consolation even if, as Fred Hobson remarked, it was the one place where Mencken could impose an order on a "random and meaningless universe." Mencken complained that the writing life reeked of "loneliness" and "melancholy." Sometimes he longed for a different occupation. "I wish I had studied drumming and taken to the road" because "it is a dreadful thing to sit in a room alone." Every interruption cut the writer "like a knife" and so magnified "enormously" every physical sensation. Events like the Scopes trial lifted his sometimes dark mood.

Another episode that drew him out of his brooding and further enhanced Mencken's notoriety was a confrontation with descendants of Puritanism in Boston. What has been called the "Hatrack" censorship case transpired during the spring of 1926; thus, within the span of nine months, Mencken was given a dose of Protestantism from both ends of its righteous spectrum. In contrast to Dayton where Mencken played a supporting role behind Darrow and Bryan, the "Hatrack" case pitted him directly against J. Franklin Chase, a Methodist minister who became secretary of the New England Watch and Ward Society. "Hatrack" was the title of an article that was fictional but had the feel of journalism, published in the April 1926 edition of the *American Mercury*, written by Herbert Asbury, a direct descendant of Francis Asbury, the so-called father of American Methodism. The piece featured the life of a prostitute in the small town of Farmington, Missouri. The legal fallout of publication of the article involved the arrest on March 30, 1926, of Felix Caragianes, a Greek American owner of a newsstand in Harvard Square, Cambridge, who sold copies of the April issue of Mencken's magazine. By that point the magazine had been on sale for the better part of a week and had almost sold out. But Chase wanted to teach Mencken a lesson, and the *American Mercury*'s editor was glad for the chance to defy the censor's instruction. After consulting his publisher, Alfred Knopf, he decided to fight Chase by arranging for a public sale of a copy of the banned magazine to Chase on the Boston Commons. Mencken's hope was to be arrested and then to challenge Chase's powers in court, aided by Arthur Garfield Hays, an attorney who was part of the legal team that defended John T. Scopes. On Monday, April 5, at 2:00 p.m., after an overnight train trip from Baltimore, Mencken arrived at the Commons to meet Chase, with over one thousand people on hand to watch the violation. Chase was late for the sale, but when he reached Mencken he purchased the magazine for a half-dollar. The editor mugged for the crowd by biting the coin to test its integrity. Chase in turn ordered Mencken's arrest. At police headquarters Mencken was arraigned and his trial set for the following day. Mencken expected to be found guilty. His hope was to win on appeal and expose Chase and his committee of censors the way Darrow had embarrassed Bryan and Tennessee in Dayton.

Mencken and Chase had a history. Since the *American Mercury* began publication, Mencken had been on the New England Watch and Ward Society's radar. (The society was by no means a fringe organization. It was founded in 1876, and its membership had included some of Boston's elite families, and for the year 1925–1926 had benefited from the services of former Harvard University president, Charles W. Eliot, as vice president.) Mencken himself had intended to use the magazine to shame organized outlets of censorship with which he had had firsthand acquaintance after the legal opposition to Theodore Dreiser's

The "Genius." Mencken explained that his aim was not to oppose the censors "in a pontifical manner" but to use satire for attack. In 1925 he had published two articles, "Keeping the Puritans Pure" (September) and "Boston Twilight" (December), that targeted and infuriated Chase. The April 1926 issue included an article, "The Methodists," that also offended the society's secretary, but Asbury's "Hatrack" became the story that Chase singled out. The article was not explicit, but Asbury's juxtaposition of holiness and vice was sufficiently provocative for the censors to think they had an offender. Asbury wrote:

> Six days a week Hatrack was a competent and more or less virtuous drudge employed by one of our best families, but Sunday was her day off, and she then, in turn, offered her soul to the Lord and went to the devil. For the latter purpose she utilized the Masonic and Catholic cemeteries, which were side by side, although their occupants presumably went to different heavens. Hatrack's regular Sunday night parade, her descent from righteousness to sin, was one of the most fascinating events of the week, and promptly after supper those of us who did not have engagements to take young ladies to church (which was practically equivalent to publishing the banns), went downtown to the loafing place in front of the Post Office and waited impatiently.

Chase, the censor, was the perfect foil to Mencken, the editor. The former was willing to defend "the new Puritanism" over against the latter's blaming Puritanism for the timidity and provincialism of American letters. Soon after the incident, Chase delivered remarks on this "new" Puritanism to Harvard's undergraduates of the Liberal Club. Were these some of the same students who proudly carried copies of the *American Mercury* under their arms? If so, they had a different understanding from the magazine about the meaning of *liberal*. But Chase cut through the subtleties of semantics. He boasted that he had read, in an official capacity to be sure, the novels of New York publishers and there found that novelists "have 57 varieties of creeping things and abominable beasts in their heart." The problem, however, was not the novelists' own depravity, but the effects that such books had on readers. For Chase not only read books but heard first-person accounts of moral tragedy. "A whole class of unwedded mothers may be the result of a lascivious book." From the creator of an immoral tale to the person who acted immorally, Chase saw a clear line that made the writer as responsible for vice as the sinner.

"An author who shocks the sense of public decency," he declared, "differs little from a lewd and lascivious person, a common night walker, both male and female." The task of monitoring bad books and preventing their circulation depended on local societies since the federal government, he complained, was of no help. But the problem with local oversight was that the "Tammany judges" in New York City gave the New York publishers too long a leash. Chase had no doubts about the value of his cause, even if it was in effect a Protestant version of the Roman Catholic hierarchy's practice of banning books. "In Boston we are fortunate in having a high minded set of booksellers and their association has appointed a Booksellers Committee," he explained, "which notifies the trade throughout the state and quietly the book is withdrawn."

After the police arrested Mencken on April 5, the municipal court set his trial for the next day at 10:00 a.m. Chase's case against the *Mercury* was predictable. The "Hatrack" story "viciously intimates that the preaching against immorality by the clergy acts as a boomerang, and that by warning their congregations against existing evils the ministers of God" unintentionally invite "visits to these places of sin." Perhaps just as bad were the "word pictures" of Asbury's story, which involved "filthy and degrading descriptions." Mencken arrived on time for the proceedings, but the courtroom deliberations took the better part of an hour to start. The defendant had to sit in the courtroom unaccompanied while his legal team consulted with court officials. Chase had arranged for Judge Michael J. Creed, a Roman Catholic Irish American who was friendly to the Watch and Ward Society, to hear Mencken's case. But because the people arranging dockets were sympathetic to Mencken, they chose instead Judge James P. Parmenter on the "specious" grounds that Creed's docket was too full.

When Parmenter finally arrived in court, the drama of the prosecution's thrust and the defense team's parry was hardly audible to the spectators who filled the room. Because the case involved matters considered obscene, procedures dictated that the attorneys conduct their arguments in hushed tones only within earshot of the judge at his bench. Eventually, the group huddled in a corner of the courtroom, where both sides made their arguments. The prosecution went first and called as its first witness John W. Rorke, an assistant to Chase, who argued that Asbury's story would corrupt the youth of America because it questioned the effects of revivals on small towns. Then came the police officer who had arrested Mencken and who testified that he had witnessed the sale of the *Mercury*; his evidence was the copy that Chase had purchased and the half-dollar spent. Chase also testified by explaining how he had heard about the story and his earlier efforts to have the bookseller in Harvard Square arrested. Chase also informed the judge that the theatrically arranged sale of the magazine at Brimstone Corner on Boston Commons was all Mencken's idea.

The defense called Mencken. He first described the magazine and its contents. The *Mercury*'s contributors included a bishop and a US Senator, so it was not exactly a seedy publication. Mencken explained as well that each issue cost fifty cents and so circulated among "persons of some education, and included many well-known men and women." He also told the judge that he had come to Boston because after the arrest of Caragianes—which Mencken thought unjust—he needed to defend his own property and good name. But the real issue was whether "Hatrack" was obscene. Mencken contended that the story was not indecent "within any rational meaning of the law" and that the magazine did not print "salacious matter." If he had attacked Comstockery in the *Mercury*, the critiques went directly after "its raids upon serious and meritorious publications."

The next to testify for the defense was a Boston attorney, H. Wadsworth Sullivan, who had studied law at Yale and informed the court that during his legal training a professor and classmates had used an article on divorce from the *Mercury*. The last witness for the defense was Asbury, the author himself. A reporter for New York's *Herald Tribune*, Asbury received a call from Mencken the day before the trial. The resident of Brooklyn caught an overnight train to Boston in time to inform the judge that the story was true. Asbury had grown up in Farmington and had known the original prostitute as well as the particulars of her profession.

The concluding arguments pitted an appeal to the Bill of Rights by Hays against a lesson about the law by Rorke. Mencken's attorney believed the case bore on the fundamental nature of civil liberties in the United States. The prosecution contended that no matter the high tone of Mencken's magazine, the laws against obscenity were indeed the law, and that civil liberty was not an excuse for license. The closing speeches had none of the drama that characterized arguments at Dayton. Judge Parmenter heard them "wearing an expression of profound judicial calm." Mencken later admitted that he was uneasy as he tried to read the judge's disposition. Parmenter closed the proceedings by explaining that he would read the magazine and return with a decision the following morning. From the courtroom Mencken and his associates went to lunch, where he learned from a local attorney that the municipal courts in Boston almost never flouted the Watch and Ward Society. He presumed that the judge would turn Mencken over to the criminal court and recommended a lawyer. Despite a growing sense that he would be found guilty, Mencken caught up on mail forwarded to his room at the Copley-Plaza Hotel.

The next day the defendant and his attorneys arrived at the courthouse in time for the 9:30 a.m. gathering. The judge entered the courtroom with only a copy of the *American Mercury*. With practically no flare for the dramatic, Judge Parmenter delivered his verdict extempore, which concluded: "I find that no offense has been committed, and therefore dismiss the complaint. You are free to go at once. Your bail is vacated. Next case." Because Mencken had expected a pronouncement of guilty, he needed time to "recover" his wits. When he did, he persuaded his attorney to ask the judge if he had prepared a text upon which he based his decision. The hope was to print the legal reasoning and so take further starch out of Comstockery. The judge refused and dismissed the request almost as quickly as he had denied the Watch and Ward Society's argument about indecency. Although the judge would not facilitate Mencken's desire to expose the flimsy grounds for prudery, Mencken left the court wondering about retaliation in the form of a libel suit. Mencken had one of his lawyers inquire about the Watch and Ward Society's assets—a $160,000 endowment and a posh home in West Roxbury. From the courthouse, Mencken went to Cambridge, where he was the honored guest of the Harvard Union. Felix Frankfurter was the emcee who announced, much to the packed room's glee, that the court had acquitted the *Mercury*'s editor. After the luncheon, which included a speech by Mencken, he left for New York City on the 5:00 p.m. train with an associate and a pint of bootleg whiskey.

Unlike the Scopes trial, which grabbed for the nation's attention by mass media during the better part of a week, the "Hatrack" case played out in dribs and drabs, with the municipal court's decision being the first round in a series of low-level legal contests that had Chase and Mencken waging a battle of wits up and down the Northeast corridor. During the initial courtroom proceedings in Boston, Mencken had noticed that Chase was absent. The reason was likely that the secretary of Boston's Watch and Ward Society knew that Judge Parmenter would give the *Mercury* a favorable verdict and so sacrificed magazine sales in Boston for postal distribution in New York. Postal regulations stipulated that a publication that enjoyed second-class circulation privileges needed to be inspected for indecency by the postmaster prior to mailing, or as Mencken put it, "to give the official smellers a chance" to sniff. Because the magazine was printed in Camden, New Jersey, and published in New York, its publisher sent four copies of each issue to the postmaster in both cities. Chase sensed that convicting someone for selling a magazine that contained "Hatrack" might not pass muster with Boston's municipal judges, so he vacated the city early and traveled to New York to have the *Mercury* banned from the mails. Chase's petition went all the way to US Postmaster General Harry S. New, who agreed that the magazine was not fit for postal distribution. Mencken only learned of this ruling from reading the newspapers on April 7 while catching up on magazine business.

It was an ingenious move on Chase's part and forced Mencken to fret over the May issue of the *Mercury*. It contained a piece by Bernard A. DeVoto entitled "Sex and the Co-Ed" that claimed college students were far more virtuous than many reports indicated. Because of the subject matter, Mencken feared it would inflame the "wowsers"; the resulting instigation would not necessarily be any worse than "Hatrack" except that if censors banned the May issue from the mails, the *Mercury* would lose its second-class status because it no longer could claim to be a "continuous publication." Mencken was fully aware that this was one of the tactics that the US government had used against radical magazines during the Great War. He could not afford (literally) to take this challenge lightly, and so decided to "scrap" the May issue, which was already at the press, printed and assembled, and only waiting for binding. He replaced the DeVoto piece with a story by Doris Stevens about playing the cello. The cost of reprinting was $8,000, a figure as high as any of the legal costs throughout the entire episode. But Mencken was still worried about the verdict of the postmasters in Camden and New York. He waited five days for a reply, only to learn that the postmasters were under no obligation to respond to inquiries. Either the publication went out or it did not.

The May issue would indeed go through the mails, but not before Mencken sought an injunction against Chase and the Watch and Ward Society in Boston. Along with his attorney, Mencken entered Boston's municipal court on April 11 to seek an injunction against the city's censors. Chase's attorney attempted to persuade the judge that "Hatrack" was in fact indecent. The defense's stronger argument was that Mencken was simply using the court to publicize his magazine. Mencken's lawyer, Hays, countered that no more copies of the April issue would be published even though demand was high, thanks to the legal proceedings. For Mencken it was primarily a question of censors without legal standing intimidating publishers and booksellers. When the Watch and Ward Society's lawyer stated, "if they will submit to us the May number in plenty of time, we will notify them whether it is objectionable or not," Mencken's attorney shot back: "They want to be censors of our business, and they have no right to do it. We will put in what we want, and we ask you to have us arrested if there is anything in it that is improper, and nothing more." In other words, Mencken and his publisher, Knopf, were seeking through this injunction to eliminate the censorship middleman. The police and the courts were within their rights to implement laws that governed indecency. They did not need help from "wowsers." The judge sided with Mencken:

> The defendants . . . secure their influence, not by voluntary acquiescence in their opinions by the trade in question, but by the coercion and intimidation of that trade through fear of prosecution if the defendants' views are disregarded.
>
> In my judgment this is clearly illegal. The defendants have the right of every citizen to come to the courts with complaints of crime. But they have no right to impose their opinions on the book and magazine trade by threats of prosecution if their views are not accepted.

Having used the courts to intimidate the Watch and Ward Society—and Mencken sometimes hinted that he was interested in securing damages against the society's endowment—the *Mercury*'s editor and publisher sought an injunction against the postmaster in New York for arbitrarily preventing the magazine's access to the mails. Those defending the postal administrators compared the situation to one of preventing the mailing of a bomb. In such a case, the postmaster had no reason to notify the sender that he was prohibiting the bomb's access to the mail. Mencken thought the analogy overdone and repeated his characterization of the *Mercury* as a "reputable, serious, solvent, and respected magazine." Complicating the debate was the introduction of new evidence of the *Mercury*'s indecency. An advertisement in the magazine—which also ran in publications such as *Harper's*—came from a New York bookseller who had been guilty of sending through the mails an obscene book. The advertisement did not include indecent titles for sale. It merely came from a bookseller who had previously sold books that the postal service had banned. This evidence was not sufficient to prevent the judge from issuing an injunction against the postal service. On appeal, a legal counterthrust that took another year to come before the court, the Second Circuit's Court of Appeals reversed the injunction. The reason was basically that the April 1926 issue was a onetime affair and that the damages caused to the magazine were limited to that occasion. Further restraints on the post office were unnecessary.

That ruling should have ended the legal bickering, which set the *Mercury* back by almost $20,000 in legal fees and production costs, but Mencken kept accurate score of how the press covered the affair. In his account, written a decade after the last courtroom ruling but not published until 1988, Mencken tabulated the results of the nation's newspapers. (The clipping service to which he subscribed and that filled dozens of scrapbooks gave Mencken access to press coverage.) The *Boston Herald*, the *New York Herald Tribune*, and the *New York Sun* were the most hostile to Mencken. Even Baltimore's *Sunpapers* were mixed—the *Evening Sun* took the *Mercury*'s side, but the morning edition, edited by J. Haslup, a liberal of the English variety and a Methodist, argued that "Hatrack" should not have been published even though the April 1926 issue of the magazine also should not have been barred from the mails. Indeed, Mencken's survey of clergy quoted in news stories ran decidedly against the *Mercury*. Boston's A. Z. Conrad declared that the "high ideals of life" were lost on Mencken. Likewise, a Roman Catholic priest in Denver called "Hatrack" "unredeemed dirt, an open sewer, without even the iridescent scum that sometimes half invites and half excuses a glance."

Even so, of all the clergy that Mencken quoted, more defended the magazine or sided with its legal point than condemned the story or the editor. In fact, Mencken was shocked to see stories in Chicago's *Congregationalist* and Richmond's *Christian Leader* either defend the rights of free speech or even laud the magazine. The latter, a Methodist publication, actually expressed "admiration for Mr. Mencken for sticking to his guns and fighting the battle of liberty." Overall, Mencken was disappointed that the press did not side overwhelmingly with him. If the nation's newspapers had scorned Tennessee's legislators in the Scopes trial, Mencken thought they should do the same with Boston's voluntary vice squad and the nation's postmasters. In both incidents, he believed, freedom of speech was at stake. He was on the right side in each, and so should the nation's editors and journalists.

The Little Guy and the Prosecutor

The parallels between Dayton and Boston were not in Mencken's mind only but took on providential proportions in several other respects. The editor of the *Mercury* may have thought the "Hatrack" trial was about him, but the real John T. Scopes of this affair was Felix Caragianes, the Harvard Square bookseller who was arrested for selling (as it turned out) thirty-five copies of the magazine. In the same municipal court where Mencken's trial took place in early April, Caragianes received a guilty verdict from a different judge, George Flynn. Like Scopes's fine in Dayton, the court required Caragianes to pay $100 and then released him on his own recognizance. That was not the end of the matter, for Mencken did not want to see Caragianes take the brunt of the law. Both sides orchestrated an appeal that was scheduled for June 1926. Mencken's attorneys believed they had a district attorney who would let the matter drop if Caragianes pled *nolo contendere*. But the judge proved to be hostile to the *Mercury*, even to the point of threatening the bookseller with jail if he continued to insist on his innocence. As a result, the verdict and fine stood. Mencken and his business partners paid the fine.

An additional parallel between Dayton and Boston was the fate of the chief member of the prosecution. Just as Bryan had died only a few days after the Scopes trial, J. Frank Chase was no match physically for the drama surrounding the "Hatrack" trial and its aftermath. The court's injunction against the Watch and Ward Society had damaged the institution's reputation, and the secretary, Chase, was worried about a suit for damages by the magazine. In October of 1926 the society's attorney entered into discussions with Mencken and company about a peace plan that would rescind the censors' earlier judgment against "Hatrack" and agree to give the publisher, Knopf, plenty of time to make adjustments after the society had inspected books and magazines. The hope was to vacate the injunction and undermine motivations for a suit. During these negotiations, Chase became ill and reports indicated that he needed rest. Then on October 25 came news that he had developed "pulmonary complications." These were the first signs of a bout with pneumonia. By November 3 Chase was dead, only months after the legal maneuvering had ended. Mencken admitted that he was superstitious and had always believed that "men who set out to do me evil not infrequently die suddenly." He did not compare Bryan to Chase directly, but he considered both men to be frauds. Bryan was the hoax of democratic man, the inferior who envied his superiors. Chase, in contrast, was the fraud of Christianity—"a Pecksniff" who "was fond of the dirty literature he professed to hold in such holy horror."

The untimely death of Chase, however, did afford the Watch and Ward Society a way to save face. Although embarrassed by the bad publicity of "Hatrack," its ongoing leadership could attribute the affair to the misguided enthusiasm of Chase. For the next few years, the society continued to monitor obscene publications with help from Roman Catholic clergy who used censorship laws to protect the faithful from questionable books, and from the Church of Christian Science, which attempted to ban the publication of a biography of Mary Baker Eddy. Again, Theodore Dreiser suffered for another book, *American Tragedy*, and Upton Sinclair experienced the effects of book banning with his novel *Oil!* But the proverbial straw that broke the camel's back was the arrest of a respectable Cambridge bookseller, James A. DeLacey, the owner of the Dunster House Bookshop, for selling D. H. Lawrence's *Lady Chatterley's Lover*. The negative publicity that surrounded the conviction of DeLacey prompted prominent members of the Watch and Ward Society to abandon ship; in 1929 Julian T. Coolidge, who taught at Harvard; Henry B. Washburn, the dean of Episcopal Theological School; and Bishop William Lawrence (Episcopal Church) resigned. Within a year the Massachusetts legislature approved an amendment to obscenity law that loosened the state's previously tight restrictions and that signaled to the Watch and Ward Society the need to change tactics. Although the politics of World War II would give room for additional campaigns to monitor indecency and obscenity, by 1948 the society had shifted from obscenity to gambling. By 1957 its name had become the New England Citizen's Crime Commission, and Mencken was dead, his remains in an urn. He had no chance to remark on the transformation. In his own estimation, he was the Scopes of the "Hatrack" affair, and his colleagues in the press failed to side with him as he had with Scopes. Between Dayton and Boston, Mencken had all the more reason to think he was a "party of one," an isolated, even if famous, voice in American culture.

CHAPTER SEVEN

The Stronger Sex

On December 13, 1925, roughly midway between the Scopes trial and the "Hatrack" imbroglio, which was arguably the peak of his fame, Mencken's mother Anna died. On his return from Tennessee, the family physician had warned Mencken that his mother was suffering from an advanced form of arteriosclerosis. The only treatment was to keep Anna as comfortable as possible. Mencken cut back on trips to New York for editorial meetings. He also regularly interrupted his writing at the Hollins Street family home to sit with and talk to his mother in the second-floor sitting room. Mencken later admitted that his mind "was filled with horrible imaginings" and resentment "that medicine could do so little for her." Her condition worsened during the fall—she needed medication to sleep and lost feeling in her limbs. In December she came down with acute tonsillitis and needed to have surgery to drain the infection. A week later the sixty-seven-year-old woman no longer had the strength to live. Her last words to her son were that she was feeling better. Always a tad superstitious, Mencken noted that Anna had died on the same day of the month as his father. She was buried next to her husband at Baltimore's Loudon Park Cemetery. The occasion gave Mencken an excuse to replace the "hideous" tombstone—because it bore the emblem of the Masons—that marked their graves with a new one that included the Mencken family coat of arms.

Anna's death devastated Mencken, who expressed his grief privately to friends even as he settled the estate and attended to his duties as the head of home. He lamented that the house felt "as empty as a cave" and that he felt "like a boy of 6." A few weeks after the burial, Mencken wrote to Theodore Dreiser:

I begin to realize how inextricably my life was interwoven with my mother's. A hundred times a day I find myself planning to tell her something, or ask her for this or that. It is a curious thing: the human incapacity to imagine finality. The house seems strange, as if the people in it were deaf and dumb. But all life, I begin to believe, resolves itself into a doing without.

That loss only intensified as Mencken grew older. Later, in his memoirs, he confessed that Anna's death was a "pure disaster" because she had always been loyal. "Her death filled me with a sense of futility and desolation." If the legal proceedings surrounding the "Hatrack" affair were partly responsible for Mencken's less than stellar performance in *Notes on Democracy*, Anna's death also contributed.

Yet, Mencken's work ethic carried him through the grief and allowed him not only to fulfill work responsibilities but also to carry out functions that he now faced as the head of the family. To the public he appeared the confirmed bachelor who came and went as he pleased, sometimes showed up in news stories with a female movie star, and lived a life dedicated to words and ideas. In fact, despite not being married, Mencken had lived the way many middle-class American husbands did. At home he still lived with his brother August and his sister, Gertrude. He also assisted his other brother, Charlie, and his family. August had a habit of bad driving and, in the midst of Mencken's worries about the *Mercury*, had a bad automobile accident. The same year, August came down with appendicitis so severe that it endangered his life. Meanwhile, Mencken was helping to arrange medical care for his brother Charlie's wife, Mary, who visited Baltimore from her home in Pittsburgh for surgery and related treatments for cancer. During the midst of Mary's visit to Baltimore's physicians in 1927, Mencken complained that his writing had "gone to pot" and that he scarcely had "time to shave."

In addition to shepherding his siblings and their families, Mencken had to manage the financial damages that attended the collapse of his father's old firm, Aug. Mencken & Bro. Days before his mother died, he received a note from his uncle with information that the company was "virtually bankrupt." Mencken never thought his uncle was a good businessman; in addition to his poor performance in the cigar business, his uncle had also made a foolish investment in a mining company. Mencken feared telling his mother about the company since she had always been proud of her husband's success. Her death spared Anna from the news, but Mencken needed to shoulder both the grief of losing his mother and managing the sale of the company's assets in a way that avoided "public scandal" for the proud Mencken clan.

This was arguably the period of Mencken's greatest fame and his deepest personal loss. Without his mother he was in serious need of the stability that female companionship might bring. The question was not whether he could come to terms with America's "new woman," but whether any American woman could fill Anna's void.

Ladies' Man

The period between the courtroom dramas of Dayton and Boston was not all work for Mencken. It included a trip to Hollywood in the fall of 1926, where he associated with movie stars, posed for photographers, and proved that a writer from the province of Baltimore could indeed become a national sensation. The trip across the lower half of the nation was partly professional—according to form, he wrote about his travels—partly for pleasure. A significant part of his enjoyment involved his relationship with Aileen Pringle, a Hollywood actress now barely known beyond the world of movie buffs but at the time one of the silent motion picture industry's leading ladies. (Her film credits for the 1920s alone include thirty different titles.) Mencken had met her in the summer of 1926 at a dinner party in West Chester, Pennsylvania. For Pringle, although married and estranged from her husband, who lived in Jamaica, meeting Mencken was almost love at first sight. She later wrote that the day she met him was "the most important day of my life." Mencken himself returned the favor when he wrote to her after their first acquaintance that the days were "dreary and dull without you."

While in California, Mencken spent most of his time with Pringle. Some of Mencken's recollections indicated that he spent the night in Pringle's home after a party, though not in her bedroom. Mencken may have detested Puritanism, but if he flouted Victorian sexual conventions, he was not going to do so openly. Another version says that he never spent a night in her home. Even if Mencken could not keep his stories straight, his relationship to Pringle extended to meeting the actress's mother while in San Francisco. After he returned to Baltimore, feelings intensified to the point that marriage emerged as one way to overcome the distance between them. Pringle was the first to broach the subject and discussed the possibility of moving to Baltimore, where she understood Mencken needed to work. Her romantic correspondent returned the favor by writing frequently and even signing off with "Love forever." After a visit from Pringle in the spring of 1927, Mencken wrote to her that she was "grand, lovely, gorgeous, incomparable, peerless, perfect." Pringle discussed ways to procure a divorce and confessed to Mencken, "I am prepared to marry you and suffer the consequences." In the end, both the intensity of Pringle's love—she was prone to utterances such as "Life without you would be unbearable"—and the reality of marriage spooked Mencken. Fred Hobson writes that Mencken balked at being "more pursued than pursuer."

One of the earliest of Mencken's flames, Marion Bloom, was a pursuit that may have helped take his mind off Pringle. Bloom was Mencken's first documented romance—with the stress on *documented*, since Marion saved the hundreds of letters he wrote to her. Mencken's understanding was that his ex-loves would destroy their correspondence, but Marion refused, a likely indication of her lifelong attachment to a writer she met in 1914 when Mencken was still working primarily on the newspaper. She was an unusual woman for Mencken, since she was neither as independent as the other ladies he romanced nor as accomplished. But she met Mencken before he had achieved greatness and celebrity, a time when an attractive female form might have been sufficient for a dalliance. In fact, the circumstances under which they met involved Marion inquiring at the newspaper with her sister, Estelle, about her sister's missing husband. Like her sibling, Marion suffered the consequences of their father's suicide; Marion was seven at the time. That death left the family in desperate financial straits. Both Marion and her sister left home in their late teens to work in the city of Washington and to look for suitable husbands. As Fred Hobson observed, Marion was right out of a Dreiser novel, "the proto-typical small-town girl, emerging from hardship, poverty, and religious piety, who went to the city to pursue her own idea of the American dream." She was definitely not Aileen Pringle. And in 1914, neither was he *that* H. L. Mencken.

After their meeting, Mencken corresponded with Marion and visited her in Washington. His interest was both romantic and professional, since she aspired to be a writer and Mencken offered advice and encouragement. For the next two years they saw each other frequently, in Washington, Baltimore, and New York. Mencken wrote Marion even more often and regularly sent gifts and mementos. She was his lone romantic interest as a bachelor in his midthirties. Meanwhile, because they came from opposite sides of the tracks, they frequently fought. One source of conflict was Mencken's unwillingness to accept Marion as she was. He wanted a woman of independence, sophistication, and accomplishment, and thought that with the right coaching Marion might become that. She often took offense at the instruction, even though she refused to give up the attention of such an accomplished and sophisticated writer and editor. The disparity between their stations in life made for a rocky relationship, even if Mencken's persistence with it suggested a degree of insecurity that undermined his aspirations to be the Nietzschean superior man.

Between 1914 and 1916 Mencken and Marion conducted an at-times intense romance that for intervals saw him writing her every day and visiting her as much as possible. When Marion moved to New York to live with her sister, Mencken could enjoy greater anonymity than in nearby Washington. Even so, when he stayed overnight in Marion's apartment at 274 West Nineteenth Street, he insisted that Estelle remain to supply the necessary seal of propriety. (Estelle would eventually become Theodore Dreiser's lover, and the novelist took delight in mocking Mencken's conventionality by calling him a "moralist," an epithet that may have even amused J. Franklin Chase, the head of Boston's Watch and Ward Society.) Marion grew to understand, however, that their relationship was as much the product of what Mencken saw in her as it was based on any attractiveness she possessed on her own. He continued to encourage her as a serious writer, to the point where Marion believed their romance depended on her literary performance. As long as Mencken could imagine Marion as a "woman of sophistication and writer of merit"—Fred Hobson's phrase—he remained romantically involved.

The war and Mencken's trip to Europe put the affair on hold, but after his return to the United States he continued to spend time with Marion, though her expressions of dependence and unworthiness often alienated him. But when Marion signed up to work as a nurse in the war and left for Europe, her show of independence lured Mencken. He wrote to her frequently and mourned his own loneliness in the wake of her absence. He admitted to longing for "a glimpse of a certain gal," and was amazed that he "should be so soft at my advanced age." Mencken's feelings of being deprived grew so intense that he even wrote about marriage and suggested that Marion move in with him, his mother, and brother at the Mencken home at 1574 Hollins Street. Had Marion returned to the United States in 1918, the couple might well have wed. But by 1919 Mencken's affections had cooled. He only rarely signed his letters "with love," even while he continued to correspond with Estelle and inquired about Marion. At one point he admitted to Estelle, Marion is "a remarkable girl, with an amazing talent for riling me."

After 1918 Mencken no longer broached the subject of marriage, and the reason owed greatly to Marion's conversion to Christian Science upon returning to the United States. Like many who witnessed the horrors of the Great War, Marion looked for a reason behind the suffering and desolation she had witnessed in France; she found it in the divinity of Mary Baker Eddy. Mencken dismissed most religious affirmations as denials of fundamental realities but could take some faiths more seriously than others. Christian Science fell in the camp of the ludicrous. As early as 1908 he called it the "most grotesque child of credulous faith and incredible denial." It would continue to function as one line in a litany of religious buffooneries or idealistic chicaneries. For instance, in his essay "Among the Avatars," included in the first collection of *Prejudices* (1919), Mencken cited Christian Science as evidence of Americans' impoverished efforts to maintain a culture:

> It may be, as they say, that we Americanos lie in the gutter of civilization, but all the while our eyes steal cautious glances at the stars. In the midst of the prevailing materialism—the thin incense of mysticism. As a relief from money drives, politics and the struggle for existence—Rosicrucianism, the Knights of Pythias. . . . In flight from Peruna, Mandrake pills and Fletcherism—Christian Science, the Emmanuel Movement, the New Thought.[1]

In another essay, "The Forward-Looker" (1919), Mencken included Christian Science in the menu of causes that progressives espoused:

> Give the forward-looker the direct primary, and he demands the short ballot. Give him the initiative and referendum, and he bawls for the re-

---

1. The Knights of Pythias are a nonsectarian fraternal order established in 1864; Paruna was a patent medicine marketed as a cure-all; mandrake pills were a nineteenth-century liver pill; and Fletcherism was the belief, advocated by Horace Fletcher, that lengthy mastication would improve physical health.

call of judges. Give him Christian Science, and he proceeds to the swamis and yogis. Give him the Mann Act, and he wants laws providing for the castration of fornicators. Give him Prohibition, and he launches a new crusade against cigarettes, coffee, jazz, and custard pies.

To Estelle, Mencken confided that nothing in the world agitated him more than Christian Science. "The thing is pishposh. Its fundamental ideas are idiotic. I can't imagine Marion taking such stuff seriously." If Mencken were hoping that Marion would blossom into a woman of sophistication and taste, her conversion to the teachings of Mary Baker Eddy ended the dream.

Chances are, though, that Mencken had already seen how hollow some of his aspirations for Marion were, and would have terminated the romance no matter what her faith. In fact, he was always ambivalent about Marion's social status. Her decision to cast her eternal lot with a denial of worldly pain confirmed what Mencken had painfully observed. On the one hand, as Mencken explained again to Estelle in a letter from 1921, "Christian Science is the one thing I can't abide. . . . My complaint is that she concealed her belief in it for a long while, and came near fooling me." Mencken credited Marion with "good acting" that "lost her a good beau." On the other hand, in a revealing letter written later in life, Marion described a poignant scene in Baltimore's Union Station when Mencken "swatted [her] cold" with his verdict on her prospects. He explained to her that if she had a different "background, financial security," their romance might continue. But he was a "high-born German" who needed his wife to "make a fine showing before his world." To Mencken, Marion was "unlucky" and "unfortunate," and he could not bear such people. After the trauma of war, Marion was not strong enough to take such a blow. She wrote to her sister that Mencken was "a shallow man who judges a woman by what she possesses." Writing "famous books" did not make Mencken a "gentleman." But Mencken was open about his aversion to poverty and people down on their luck. In a piece he wrote for the *Smart Set* soon after his breakup with Marion, he confessed to "one ineradicable prejudice," one against poverty. "I never have anything to do, if it is possible, with anyone who is in financial difficulties. . . . Such persons do not excite my compassion; they excite my aversion." In this respect, the romance with Marion was doomed from the start. Its longevity may indicate a patience on Mencken's part that surprised even him.

Perhaps Mencken's pursuit of a woman from the wrong side of the tracks, aside from the realities of sexual desire, stemmed from frustrations with the roles assigned to men and women. During the years that Mencken carried on with Marion, he wrote a book about men and women, *In Defense of Women* (1918), a volume that mocked traditional sex roles while confirming their ongoing legitimacy, and more to the point for the author, their genuine humor. Readers could describe it as either a brief on behalf of women's rights or an expression of one of the nation's most outspoken misogynists. It was one part Charles Darwin, the other James Thurber.

Instead of merely complaining about the inequities that women faced in a Victorian Protestant world or hyping abstract ideals about human equality, Mencken reveled in the contradictions of American women, taking their side while at the same time reinforcing stereotypes. For instance, Mencken contended that women were actually smarter than men (their brains were smaller in size but represented a greater percentage of body mass), and for this reason were too smart for the trivial tasks they were consigned to in the home. At the same time, he believed that the liberation of women had compromised the American dinner table. "Nowhere else in the world have women more leisure and freedom to improve their minds, and nowhere else do they show a higher level of intelligence," Mencken intoned, but "nowhere else is there worse cooking in the home, or a more inept handling of the whole domestic economy." That the United States was both "the land of the emancipated and enthroned woman" and the home of "canned soup, of canned pork and beans, of whole meals in cans, and of everything else ready-made" was no "mere coincidence." The same result—women as bad cooks—emerged from the way women thought about duty and the dynamics of courting and marriage. On the one hand, women were superior to men because they lacked "the dog-like fidelity to duty which is one of the shining marks of men." Instead of taking pride in what is "inherently disagreeable," women "always go to the galleys under protest," with "vows of sabotage," and a philosophy almost identical to socialism. On the other hand, once a woman had "caught a man," even if it came at a stage where she had not acquired "a fourth of the culinary subtleties that are commonplace even to the chefs on dining cars," she had no reason to concern herself with cooking. The woman's husband needed to eat, "in the last analysis, whatever she sets before him, and his lack of intelligence makes it easy for her to shut off his academic criticisms by bald appeals to his emotions." The husband thus turns the wife's indolence into proof "of her fineness of soul." The man is "abashed" in the presence of "her lofty incompetence."

The craftiness of women compared to the gullibility of men was another way for Mencken to point out the proportions of female vanity. He may have been speaking for himself when he wrote, "Men do not demand beauty, even in the most modest doses," since Marion herself lacked the physical appeal that Mencken saw in Aileen Pringle. Even so, men compensated for a beautiful form or face by "emotional suggestibility," a "herculean capacity for illusion," and an almost "total absence of critical sense."

> A film of face powder skilfully applied, is as satisfying to [men] as an epidermis of damask. The hair of a dead Chinaman, artfully dressed and dyed, gives them as much delight as the authentic tresses of Venus. . . . In brief, they estimate women, and hence acquire their wives, by reckoning up purely superficial aspects, which is just as intelligent as estimating an egg by purely superficial aspects. . . . The result is that many a man, deceived by such paltry sophistications, never really sees his wife—that is, as God is supposed to see her, and as the embalmer will see her—until they have been married for years.

This technique dominates the book. Mencken takes the female stereotype and turns it into a point that proves her superiority to man. In this case, a little makeup or the right frock could deceive even the most civilized of men "as readily as a yokel fresh from the cabbage-field."

The one class of women whom Mencken judged to be inferior because they were more like men than women was the suffragettes. These reformers drew upon envy rooted in the double-standard afforded men in sexual relations and their own inability "to ensnare males sufficiently under the present system." Women, he contended, were rich in a history of hard-won battles with men. These victories came despite traditional male privilege and allowed women great freedom and even power. But the suffragettes were not content with such advantages and sought instead for formal recognition of their equality, if not superiority. Most women, Mencken contended, regard suffrage of "small value" since they know they could "get what they want without going to the actual polls for it." The majority of women were also out of sympathy with the suffragist platform, "with its long list of quack sure-cures for all the sorrows of the world." Meanwhile, when women did obtain the vote, they used it decidedly against Woodrow Wilson, who while campaigning for James M. Cox "made an inept effort to fetch the girls by tear-squeezing." Such an obvious attempt to play to female empathy was doomed because every woman "has been vastly disappointed, either by failing to nab some pretty fellow," or worse, "by actually nabbing him, and then discovering him to be a bounder or an imbecile, or both." Once having experienced a broken heart, women knew the injury to be slight. Consequently, when Wilson "began sobbing and snuffling and blowing his nose tragically, the learned doctor simply drove all the women voters into the arms of the Hon. Warren Gamaliel Harding." In fact, once women become familiar with the mechanics of democratic politics "and get rid of the preposterous harridans who got it for them and who now seek to tell them what to do with it," they will abandon the political idealism that was the curse of the average man. Prohibition was one reason for this prediction. It had passed without the votes of women. The reason: "Every normal woman believes, and quite accurately, that the average man is very much like her husband, John, and she knows very well that John is a weak, silly, and knavish fellow, and that any effort to convert him into an archangel overnight is bound to come to grief."

That same estimate of men was at odds, Mencken conceded, with the delusion that the average man "who doesn't believe that Jonah swallowed the whale spends his whole leisure leaping through the seventh hoop of the Decalogue." In fact, the "secret scandal of Christendom," at least among Protestants, was that "most men are faithful to their wives." Deep down, and Mencken may have been writing from personal experience, men were too timid to engage in "overt acts of ribaldry." They may "conjure up the charms of carnality" even to the point of taking "actual peeps at it." But as for "taking a forthright header into the sulphur," most men did not have the courage.

> [F]or one husband of the Nordic race who maintains a blonde chorus girl in oriental luxury around the corner, there are ten thousand who are as true to their wives, year in and year out, as so many convicts in the death-house, and would be no more capable of any such loathsome malpractice, even in the face of free opportunity, than they would be of cutting off the ears of their young.

If the influence of Christianity was responsible for male restraint, Mencken admitted that it also accounted for a degree of women's liberation. He was aware of the psychological literature that concluded that women in Christian civilizations lived lives "heavy with repression and dissimulation" that in the long run produced "effects . . . indistinguishable from disease." The result was, at one end of the spectrum, the suffragette, "with her grotesque adoption of the male belief in laws, phrases and talismans, and her hysterical demand for a sexual libertarianism that she could not put to use if she had it," and at the other, "the snuffling and neurotic woman, with her bogus martyrdom, her extravagant pruderies and her pathological delusions." But Mencken saw through the Freudian challenge to Victorian conventions and recognized that "the glad tidings preached by Christ were obviously highly favorable to women." As presented in the Gospels, Jesus lifted women "to equality before the Lord when their very possession of souls was still doubted by the majority of rival theologians." Mariolatry was, therefore, biblical. What the medieval popes "actually invented . . . was the doctrine of women's inferiority." The influence of Christianity on women's status was on the whole a mixed bag. Christianity both "libelled women and flattered them."

Mencken even claimed that by nature women were "not naturally religious." Women's "ordinary" devotion was little more than a convention imposed by "the masculine notion that an appearance of holiness is proper to their lowly station." If the ladies ever displayed inordinate levels of piety—if they were "driven to frenzies by the merits of the saints," or found "weeping over the sorrows of the heathen," or "spending hours on their knees in hysterical abasement before the heavenly throne"—the reason was likely a "fair and toothsome" ecclesiastic who was likely "a good deal more aphrodisiacal than learned." Henry Ward Beecher was one such minister "of suave and ingratiating habit" whose antics were "far more suitable to the boudoir than to the footstool of the Almighty." On the flip side was the evangelist Billy Sunday, "the celebrated American pulpit-clown," whose appeal was predominantly to men. At one of Sunday's revival services, Mencken observed that men "in enormous numbers" came "swarming to the altar, loudly bawling for help against their sins." For six nights running, Mencken did not see a single female convert walk up front to the anxious bench. They had too much good sense, what Mencken called a "cynical view of religious emotionalism." And this outlook was responsible for women's avoidance of the ministry.

To be sure, some churches were beginning to ordain women, but the number of female ministers around the country could fit into "one small room." The idea that female pastors would drive men out of the ministry was likewise silly. Women, Mencken claimed, were "far too intelligent to make effective ecclesiastics." Their "sharp sense of reality" cut through the "whole sacerdotal masquerade" while their "cynical humor" prevented "the snorting that is inseparable from pulpit oratory."

If the distaff traits that Mencken lauded sounded a lot like those of the author himself, if in fact Mencken was really praising women for being simply another version of himself, the resemblance was complicated, if not confusing. On the one hand, his intellectual guideposts such as Darwin and Nietzsche did not exactly supply arguments for female superiority. Even Mencken had to concede at several points in *In Defense of Women* that women were biologically weaker than men. Furthermore, Nietzsche's own views on women hardly qualified as egalitarian or progressive—"let women be a toy, pure and delicate as a jewel." On the other hand, in Mencken's private correspondence he was not the champion of feminine virtues that he was in the book. He opined that he opposed executive jobs for women in publishing and observed that women with "a masculinized mentality" were inevitably "hard on the eyes." To another friend he wrote about wanting a social gathering to be free of women. "There are so many things to talk of I'd begrudge the attention [women] demand."

Even if Mencken preferred the company of men, he did admire strong and independently minded women, which might explain his restrained estimate of the joys of sex. In fact, for all of his opposition to the moralism and naïveté of Puritanism and Christian moralists, Mencken opposed the open flouting of conventional morality and even challenged, not so much on Christian grounds as on the basis of good taste, the mini–sexual revolution of the 1920s led by the psychologists, flappers, and sex educationists. For instance, he complained in the first series of *Prejudices* (1919) that the literature on "sex hygiene," once "timorous," was now spouting titles such as "What Every Child of Ten Should Know." The problem with the movement to make sex scientific was that it took the mystery away from its real referent, namely, sex. Sex manuals assumed one significant pedagogical error:

> [T]hey are founded upon an attempt to explain a romantic mystery in terms of an exact science. Nothing could be more absurd: as well

attempt to interpret Beethoven in terms of mathematical physics—as many a fatuous contrapuntist, indeed, has tried to do. The mystery of sex presents itself to the young, not as a scientific problem to be solved, but as a romantic emotion to be accounted for. The only result of the current endeavor to explain its phenomena by seeking parallels in botany is to make botany obscene.

The loss of mystery also resulted—and here Mencken echoed a point made by the witty Philadelphia essayist Agnes Repplier—in marriages where the bride "knows as much as the midwife of 1885," an awareness that was highly embarrassing to the sector of romantic men of which Mencken confessed to belong. His objection to the loss of romance in the pursuit of sexual fulfillment was not moral but aesthetic.

In the relations between the sexes all beauty is founded upon romance, all romance is founded upon mystery, and all mystery is founded upon ignorance, or, failing that, upon the deliberate denial of the known truth. To be in love is merely to be in a state of perpetual anaesthesia. . . . But how can this condition of mind survive the deadly matter-of-factness which sex hygiene and the new science of eugenics impose? How can a woman continue to believe in the honor, courage, and loving tenderness of a man after she has learned, perhaps by affidavit, that his haemoglobin count is 117%, that he is free from sugar and albumen, that his blood pressure is 112/79 and that his Wassermann reaction is negative? . . . What is neither hidden nor forbidden is seldom very charming.

Despite the candor that demystified sex, Mencken detected an important tie between the Comstocks, those who banned dirty books, and the sex hygienists—namely, that both believed that "virtue and ignorance were identical" or that the "slightest knowledge of sin was fatal to virtue." Anthony Comstock, Mencken asserted, fundamentally distrusted women. "The instant [a woman] was allowed to peek over the fence she was off to the Bad Lands." Consequently, a good woman was one "efficiently policed." The sex hygienists altered the logic by concluding that "sin was often caused by ignorance," and that women, being less experienced than men, were vulnerable to male sexual advances without sufficient knowledge. So along came the books of enlightenment: "If all girls of sixteen . . . knew as much about the dreadful consequences of sin as the average police lieutenant or midwife, there would be no more seductions." Comstock opposed the educational scheme but could not overcome "the impeccable respectability of the sex hygienists." Most of the latter were Puritans, and some were "towering figures of Christian rectitude." Mencken was not sure whether books on sex had corrupted American youth as Comstock feared. But he was certain that frankness had transformed American novels. The old stories "glossed over" the "Facts of Life." But after the revelations about sex from the realm of scientific education, old-time novelists seemed mild compared to the new crop of authors who told "it all." Consequently, when Mencken opened a novel and found nothing about Freudian suppressions, he assumed it was a book from the 1880s. He confessed that he used to send his review copies of such specimens, after he had "sweated through them," to the YMCA. "Now I send them to the medical college."

For all the mystery and romance surrounding sex, Mencken thought that men were far less interested than women in knowing or talking about the subject. Except for a "few earnest men whose mental processes . . . are essentially womanish," men think "they know all about it that is worth knowing." But women were different, especially ladies with economic independence. Once "women of the Western world" began "to plunge heroically into all of the old professions" and even invented labor "unimagined by men," they began to run amok in the previously forbidden field of "sexual knowledge and experiment." Mencken contended that women were mainly responsible for "all the current gabbling about sex, and proposing all the new-fangled modifications of the rules and regulations ordained by God." The reason was that the subject was new to them. "The whole order of human females," Mencken wrote, "is passing through a sort of intellectual adolescence, and it is disturbed as greatly as biological adolescents are by the spouting of the hormones." He believed that women's new interest in sex was charming but erroneous because they assumed the matter to be of first-rate importance.

Indeed, sex for men was simply "an afterthought and a recreation." Here Mencken was speaking more from his own perspective, as a man with a declining libido, than from his experience as a cub reporter twenty years earlier. For him, work was more important than finding the praise and rewards of women, and Mencken believed this was true for all genuine men:

Men work because they want to eat, because they want to feel secure, because they long to shine among their fellows, and for no other reason. A man may crave his wife's approbation, or some other woman's approbation, of his social graces, of his taste, of his generosity and courage, of his general dignity in the world, but long before he ever gives thought to such things and long after he has forgotten them he craves the approbation of his fellow men. Above all, he craves the approbation of his fellow craftsmen—the men who understand exactly what he is trying to do, and are expertly competent to judge his doing of it.

Mencken did not mean to discount the enjoyment husbands received from their wives' respect and admiration. But an intelligent man discovered that a wife's esteem did not "run in direct ratio to his intrinsic worth, that the qualities and acts that please her are not always the qualities and acts that are most satisfactory to the censor within him." At bottom, Mencken confessed, sex belonged "to comedy and the cool of the evening and not to the sober business that goes on in the heat of the day."

"As Easy as a Yale Sophomore"

Mencken thought that if marriage attracted a "first-rate" man, it needed to come later rather than earlier in life. "He may succumb in the end," but the superior man was "almost always able to postpone the disaster a good deal longer than the average poor clodpate." His friends concurred, though their reasons had less to do with Mencken's cultivation and more with his dependence on Anna Mencken, his mother. One of those friends observed, "as long as you have a mother, you won't get yourself a wife." Both of these circumstances coincided in the latter half of the 1920s, a time when Mencken was approaching fifty and coping with the death of his beloved mother. Marion Bloom was no longer available. Even though Christian Science almost killed their romance, they continued to see each other, and Mencken continued to challenge Marion's newfound faith, until 1922, when Marion began to see another suitor, Lou Maritzer, a Romanian historian. By the summer of 1923 Bloom and Maritzer were married, and Mencken resigned himself to the news. When he heard about the nuptials from Marion's sister,

Estelle, Mencken even wept, and the tears were bitter: "Well, such is human destiny in a world run by a jackass," Mencken joked to Estelle. "Little will that gal ever suspect how near she came to cooking, washing and ironing for the next President of the United States." Mencken was almost forty-three when his romance with Marion finally ended. This was midway between the age when a man is "woman proof"—thirty-five to thirty-eight—and the stage of life—fifty years old—when "he is quite as easy as a Yale sophomore." The trouble was that Mencken looked for a woman "rascally enough to deserve the fate of being put to living with [him]."

After his mother's death in 1925, he was still only forty-five but appeared to be in need of someone to replace Anna. During those hectic days of covering the Scopes trial and battling the New England Watch and Ward Society in Boston and the Washington courts, Mencken lured and entertained the affections of a series of women. In addition to the Hollywood celebrity Aileen Pringle, who was willing to give up her career and husband to marry Mencken, the press reported on Mencken's associations with two other movie stars, Anita Loos, who was also the author of *Gentlemen Prefer Blondes*, and Lillian Gish, who wound up becoming involved with Mencken's old colleague George Jean Nathan. Pringle was the most serious of those romances despite the rumors that gossip columnists circulated. But she was not the only woman that Mencken considered as he approached the ripe age of fifty. Mencken had great affection for a short time in 1925 for Beatrice Wilson, a New York journalist. He also carried on during 1927 with Gretchen Hood, an opera singer who also wrote on the side. In late 1927 Mencken even considered rekindling his old romance with Marion Bloom, who by then was divorced and living in Paris. Mencken concocted ways to travel to Paris to see her. In one of his letters to Marion he wrote, "if I come to Paris I would neck you so violently that the chastity of both of us would be in grave danger." But the trip never materialized. When Marion broached the subject of marriage in one letter, Mencken replied, "If I ever marry, it will be on a sudden impulse, as a man shoots himself."

Such hostility to marriage may have been the simple product of certain male stereotypes that, had Mencken written a book such as *In Defense of Men*, he may have leavened with good-natured ridicule. In his fourth set of *Prejudices*, published in 1924, Mencken complained about the disparity between female expectations of men and his own habits:

I am by nature one of the most orderly of mortals. I have a place for every article of my personal property, whether a Bible or a cocktail-shaker, an undershirt or an eye-dropper, and I always keep it where it belongs. I never drop cigar-ashes on the floor. I never upset a waste-basket. I am never late for trains. I never run short of collars. I never go out with a purple necktie on a blue shirt. I never fail to appear in time for dinner without telephoning or telegraphing. Yet the women who are cursed by God with the care of me maintain and cherish the fiction that I am an extremely careless and even hoggish fellow— that I have to be elaborately nursed, supervised and policed—that the slightest relaxation of vigilance over my everyday conduct would reduce me to a state of helplessness and chaos, with all my clothes mislaid, half my books in the ash-can, my mail unanswered, my face unshaven.

Mencken's theory was that men generally acted like slobs out of fear of becoming unpopular because "nothing is more obnoxious than a human being who is always challenging and correcting the prevailing view of him." But the thought of living constantly with someone whose understanding of him was so different from his own helped Mencken avoid settling down.

At the same time, he continued to date and consider marriage. He even seemed to take a special interest in a woman who was the dark horse during this flurry of romantic activity if only because of the disparity between them. Sara Powell Haardt, a writer from Montgomery, Alabama, whom Mencken had met in 1923, then a twenty-five-year-old instructor of English at Baltimore's Goucher College, was not only eighteen years younger than Mencken but was also only a few years out of her undergraduate studies, while Mencken was at the peak of his professional responsibilities. His habit was to give a couple of lectures a year at Goucher, an all-girls Methodist institution. The premise was to talk to the "appetizing cuties in the audience" about the life of a writer, but he usually resorted to talks about "how to catch a husband." Haardt accompanied the group that went out to dinner with Mencken after one talk, and her dignified manner and literary interests captured his attention. For the next several years they corresponded and saw each other frequently. Mencken mixed flirtation with literary advice, a reflection of the eighteen-year gap between them. Sara's health became another bond. Doctors diagnosed a lesion on her lung as a symptom of tuberculosis. Mencken, who knew Baltimore's medical establishment well, made recommendations and negotiated her care. Trips took Sara away from Baltimore and hindered deeper ties. Aside from traveling back to Montgomery for her health, by 1927 Sara was working in Hollywood as a screenwriter.

But, as Fred Hobson observes, distance was usually the great aphrodisiac for Mencken. During her sojourn in California, he corresponded more than previously, and when Sara announced her decision to return to Baltimore, Mencken was delighted: "The news that you are coming back at last is glorious. I have missed you horribly." He met her at Baltimore's Union Station when she arrived on New Year's Eve of 1927 and began to see her regularly. By the spring of 1928, even though Mencken had continued to correspond flirtatiously with Hood, Pringle, and Bloom, Sara was the chief object of his affection. A further incentive to Mencken's crush on Sara came in the fall of 1928 when doctors diagnosed the source of a new round of her physical affliction—an ovarian tumor that required surgery. Again, Mencken functioned as a chief consultant for Sara's health, even to the point of approving the removal of both ovaries without Sara's knowledge. During recovery, Mencken lavished her with attention by supplying all manner of beverages and reading excerpts from Baptist and Methodist newspapers that were part of his coverage of anti-Catholicism in the run-up to the 1928 presidential election. After she was released from the hospital, Sara's health continued to be spotty. Only eight months after her initial surgery, physicians discovered a tubercular infection on Sara's left kidney, which required another operation to remove the diseased organ. It was a vicious procedure that had surgeons wondering whether she would survive. When she did, doctors informed Mencken and Sara that she likely had only three years to live. At that point, Mencken determined to marry her and make the remainder of her life the happiest possible. After that resolution, he himself had the unhappy work of letting Pringle, Hood, and Bloom know that he was no longer an eligible bachelor. At the same time that he was finishing the book he considered to be his magnum opus, *Treatise on the Gods*, and planning for a trip to Europe to cover a military conference, Mencken had the unenviable task of letting down his female admirers. According to Pringle, the news "finished" her.

Marion Bloom later speculated that Mencken chose Sara out of a sense of pity for a woman in dire health, an opinion shared by some of Mencken's friends and colleagues. Sara's illnesses did bring out sides of her future husband that cemented their union. For instance, Mencken enjoyed controlling and managing situations and had pursued relationships with women with ambitions for writing whom he could encourage and oversee. Sara's physical condition added to Mencken's desire for a measure of gallantry. Even more, her courage in the face of death was a sign to Mencken of Sara's strength of character and even independence of spirit. He called her valor "magnificent." In contrast to the other women with whom Mencken flirted, Sara was, in the words of Terry Teachout, "shrewd and detached." When she read the gossip about Mencken's dalliances, Sara did not respond in ways that gave the slightest hint of desperation but held back and waited. In addition, Sara and Mencken shared sensibilities about superiority, whether of people, ideas, or civilization, that added to their mutual regard. According to Fred Hobson, their romance represented a meeting of backgrounds—"partly German and partly southern (for Mencken never relinquished the illusion that he was, in part, a southerner)"—as well as a meeting of the minds—"skeptical and freethinking." It did not hurt that as a fifty-year-old bachelor, Mencken also thought he was beyond passion. "Romance is for passionate love," he observed, "and passionate love has no more enduring place in marriage than the moon has in the broad, hard light of day."

After Mencken's return from London, he and Sara began planning their wedding but did not announce the news to friends until the summer of 1930. A few years before the wedding Mencken wrote an essay for the *Mercury* in which he complained about the lack of ceremonial or liturgical forms for the life events of "the damned." He was particularly vexed by a variety of burials he had observed for non-Christians. In one, the deceased left instructions that no words be said at the grave. The silence was "gruesome," and the whole event struck Mencken as "somehow unnatural and even a shade indecent"; to "dispatch so charming a fellow in so cavalier a fashion" was "brutal." In the same piece, Mencken expressed a need for a marriage service for infidels. He knew that a few "Radicals" had made the effort, but the product displayed a "characteristic lack of humor," which was a major defect because "humor is as necessary to a marriage service as poetry is to a funeral service." The problem for the damned was easily fixed, Mencken thought, because in most states of the Union a civil marriage was legitimate. Four years later he would be acutely aware that Maryland was not one of those polities. In 1930 the state of Maryland still required church marriages. Mencken and Sara complied with the law and were married at an Episcopal church in Baltimore, Saint Stephen the Martyr. Newspapers had announced a September 3 ceremony. Mencken had used this date as a ruse to keep the press away. The ceremony took place a week earlier on August 27, 1930.

The minister the couple secured was a relatively old friend of Mencken's, Herbert Parrish. He was an Episcopal priest from New Jersey who had written roughly half a dozen pieces for the *Mercury*. His iconoclasm surely endeared him to Mencken. In one of Parrish's first articles for Mencken, he proposed the idea of a "new" God for America. The existing gods were either inadequate or too numerous. The United States needed a single god who was sufficiently grand to compel reverence and powerful enough to unify the people. Other than such dabbling in alternative theology, Parrish stuck to what he knew best in the pages of the *Mercury*—namely, the Episcopal Church. In one article he complained about the lay popes that dominated American Protestantism, namely, the wealthy men who ran church finances, from approving the pastor's salary to having final say in a congregation's physical plant. In another piece about the plight of ecclesiastical hierarchy, Parrish tried to explain the high regard that Episcopalians had for bishops, the "only valid nobility" in America. When the Anglican Communion at its 1928 Lambeth Conference came out with resolutions that approved contraception, Parrish was quick to supply Mencken with a piece on the history of married clergy and church teaching on sex and concupiscence. Parrish was by no means someone who merely stood in for Mencken and Sara's nuptials. He was a thoughtful member of the American clergy, and at the very least held a literary friendship with the groom.

The ceremony was a quiet affair held at 4:00 p.m. on a hot summer day. Guests were almost exclusively immediate family members on both sides—about ten in all—along with a handful of Mencken's professional colleagues. After the wedding, the couple and attendants posed for pictures before being driven to Baltimore's Pennsylvania Station, where Mencken and Sara boarded a train headed for Canada, their honeymoon destination. At the first stop in Montreal, Mencken wrote to a friend that he and Sara were having a "swell time." From Montreal they traveled to Quebec City, which was too hot for the couple and provoked a detour to Nova Scotia and New Brunswick. After little more than a week in Canada, Mencken and Sara returned to Baltimore—with stops in Vermont and New York to see literary friends. Their home was an elegant third-floor apartment on Cathedral Street in Baltimore's Mount

Vernon neighborhood, a spot Henry James called the city's parlor. It was the first time Mencken, now two weeks shy of his fiftieth birthday, had ever resided somewhere other than 1524 Hollins Street.

As a couple, the Menckens pursued a social calendar that was much more ambitious than either had maintained when flying solo. Some of this socializing—which included visits from Clarence Darrow and Edgar Lee Masters and their wives—came about because friends wanted to meet Sara. Even so, the pace continued to be brisk when they traveled to New York City and there regularly dined or drank with Mencken's publishing associates, or when they took trips for pleasure such as a 1931 outing to Vermont to visit Sinclair Lewis and Dorothy Thompson (which turned out to be less than delightful, thanks to Lewis's dipso-maniacal disposition). Sometimes Sara's health limited the couple's social life, even if a fascination with disease—owing to Mencken's own hypochondria and Sara's string of maladies—further cemented their ties. At the same time, he remained a family man and functioned as the head of the extended Mencken family. They regularly entertained Mencken's brother and sister, and Mencken himself visited the family homestead almost weekly to ensure a degree of maintenance, both structural and physical. When his sister Gertrude and brother August mentioned a desire to move out of the house at 1524 Hollins Street and find an apartment, Mencken could not bear the thought "of strangers living in it." But such consternation could not keep Mencken from reflecting, about the time of his first wedding anniversary, that he had feared being "homesick for Hollins street," but "nothing of the sort ensued." "I am far more comfortable than I was in Hollins street," he confessed. For her part, Sara admitted to a friend, "I have the one perfect husband." That was an estimate delivered from the vantage of their honeymoon. But even if Sara needed to adjust to some of Mencken's friends back in Baltimore, along with negotiating his family and her husband's garrulity when socializing, she was more happy than content with the marriage.

Mencken's delight in marriage was a good thing for him, since he regarded the estate as a permanent arrangement, not one from which he could be easily extricated. To be sure, the physicians attending to Sara were not optimistic about her long-term prospects. But not long before their marriage, Mencken went into print with an understanding about divorce that he considered quite reasonable. The reason was that he had considered the matter without the aid of theologians who "make a mess of everything they touch." Consulting the Bible or theology about marriage was, in fact, like asking "members of the W.C.T.U. about the mixing of drinks," because everyone knew that theologians and pastors regarded "even the most decorous kind of marriage with lubricous suspicion." Mencken's interpretation of Paul's instruction about marriage and celibacy went like this:

> The really virtuous man avoids [marriage] like the plague—his ideal is complete chastity. If, tempted by Satan, he finds that chastity is unbearable, he may take a wife to escape something worse, but that is only a poor compromise with his baser nature.

This left residents of Christendom with only adultery as grounds for divorce. A man could beat his wife "all he pleases" and escape divorce. Likewise, a wife could "waste her husband's money, insult him in public and chase his friends out of the house" and leave her husband without recourse.

Instead of consulting theology, Mencken recommended a "realistic" view of marriage. What Americans needed was knowledge of why men and women married and what factors held husbands and wives together. Reformers who recommended the abandonment of marriage or the substitution of half-measures were clueless. They forgot that "the real essence of marriage [was] not the nature of the relation but the permanence of that relation." Marriage was essentially a "device" built for the long haul, like every other human institution. "Its one indomitable purpose is to endure." The solution to the problem of unhappy marriages was not to lessen the stakes but to dissuade people for whom marriage was "a sheer psychic impossibility" from entering it. The majority, the people who liked marriage and wanted it to endure, needed help "in making it endurable." Mencken had no solutions except to say that romantic, scientific, and theological proposals would not fix it. The subject still awaited "hard, patient, impartial study."

Aside from Mencken's conviction that marriage was permanent, the success of his own experience with the institution depended less on sex than on conversation, a hierarchy of values appropriate to a fifty-year-old, perhaps. He considered Sara the most "rational woman" he had met and enjoyed her company and talk. To Sinclair Lewis Mencken once wrote, "I protest that frigging is much less important in marriage than you seem to make it out." "The main thing," he explained, "is simply talk." But even a full eight years before his wedding, Mencken thought about the ideal marriage in terms that would characterize his own life with Sara. In one of the most poignant sections in *In Defense of Women*, he described the heaven that marriage might be:

> Every man, I daresay, has his own notion of what constitutes perfect peace and contentment, but all of those notions, despite the fundamental conflict of the sexes, revolve around women. As for me—and I hope I may be pardoned, at this late stage in my inquiry, for intruding my own personality—I reject the two commonest of them: passion, at least in its more adventurous and melodramatic aspects, is too exciting and alarming for so indolent a man, and I am too egoistic to have much desire to be mothered. What, then, remains for me? Let me try to describe it to you.
>
> It is the close of a busy and vexatious day—say half past five or six o'clock of a winter afternoon. I have had a cocktail or two, and am stretched out on a divan in front of a fire, smoking. At the edge of the divan, close enough for me to reach her with my hand, sits a woman not too young, but still good-looking and well-dressed—above all, a woman with a soft, low-pitched, agreeable voice. As I snooze she talks—of anything, everything, all the things that women talk of: books, music, the play, men, other women. No politics. No business. No religion. No metaphysics. Nothing challenging and vexatious— but remember, she is intelligent; what she says is clearly expressed, and often picturesquely. I observe the fine sheen of her hair, the pretty cut of her frock, the glint of her white teeth, the arch of her eye-brow, the graceful curve of her arm. I listen to the exquisite murmur of her voice. Gradually I fall asleep—but only for an instant. At once, observing it, she raises her voice ever so little, and I am awake. Then to sleep again—slowly and charmingly down that slippery hill of dreams. And then awake again, and then asleep again, and so on.
>
> I ask you seriously: could anything be more unutterably beautiful?

In print, Mencken was indefatigably the rabble-rouser. At home, whether with his mother or his wife, he was thoroughly domesticated.

CHAPTER EIGHT

Finding Meaning and Losing Readers

In 1931 Will Durant, the often acquired but seldom read chronicler of civilization, solicited from a number of writers their thoughts on the meaning of human existence. The published volume included writers and academics such as Theodore Dreiser and Charles Beard, as well as celebrities or world leaders such as Will Rogers and M. K. Gandhi. H. L. Mencken was an obvious choice since he was an author and editor with whom most people in the publishing world had to reckon—the church world was obviously a different matter. But Durant likely did not have a churchgoing readership in mind, since the book was designed to be "an anthology of doubt." That Mencken would accept Durant's invitation was perhaps not so obvious given the Baltimore native's aversion to idealism, philosophy, and religion. But Mencken, who seldom missed an opportunity to sit at his typewriter, accepted Durant's offer and composed an eight-paragraph personal reflection on, of all things, "the meaning of life." The fact that Mencken was completing two treatises, as he called them, on morality and divinity, may explain his philosophical state of mind.

As a Darwinian naturalist, Mencken was not squeamish in expressing his low aspirational horizons. He compared himself to both a chicken and a cow. "I go on working for the same reason that a hen goes on laying eggs," he wrote, because in every living creature there existed "an obscure but powerful impulse to active functioning." Without it, life, which "demands to be lived," was "painful and dangerous." The specific activity of writing was determined by heredity. "I do not lay eggs, as a hen does," Mencken also admitted, "because I was born without any equipment for it." The work he found that came "easiest to [his] hand" was writing, because he was born with "an intense and insatiable interest in ideas." It was also something of an accident of existence that Mencken was "born with rather more than the average facility for putting [ideas] into words." His likeness to a cow owed to the almost necessary or predestined nature of Mencken's output. "What I do was ordained by the inscrutable fates, not chosen by me." In fact, Mencken believed he would remain a writer "until the end of the chapter," the way "a cow goes on giving milk all her life, even though what appears to be her self-interest urges her to give gin." Even the pleasure Mencken derived from writing—he believed he had lived "an extraordinarily pleasant life"—was comparable to bovine joys. "I have not written and published to please other people," he explained, "but to satisfy myself, just as a cow gives milk, not to profit the dairyman, but to satisfy herself." Such a rationale for Mencken's work ethic may have alarmed America's Protestants, but his output made his logic hard to deny.

For Mencken work had to share space in his box of delights with family and friends but not with religion or metaphysics. Behind professional duties Mencken placed "the day to day intercourse with family and friends" as the other source of great happiness. The womenfolk he mentioned were his mother, sister, and wife, with whom he was "completely happy." His male friendships extended to associates of "very old standing." He confessed that he seldom spent extended time with someone he had known for less than a decade. "These friends delight me," Mencken wrote, and he turned to them "when work is done with unfailing eagerness." He was thinking of the members of the Saturday Night Club, the band of professional and amateur musicians that gathered weekly to perform symphonic music, eat, drink, and carouse. Mencken said this group had "given me more pleasure in this life than any external thing." "I love it more every year." But religion was not so pleasant. Christian worship, Mencken huffed, "seems to me to be debasing rather than ennobling" since it involved "groveling before a Being who, if He really exists, deserves to be denounced instead of respected." He concluded that life had no ultimate meaning. What he did know was that for as long as his life lasted, human existence was entertaining. "Even its troubles, indeed, can be amusing"; these troubles in turn fostered "human qualities that I admire most—courage and its analogues." Mencken did not believe he excelled in these virtues, but here, echoing Nietzsche, the noblest of men was the one who "fights God, and triumphs over Him."

Mencken's philosophical turn did not result in much of a theory about the whys of human existence, but he had reached a stage of life when he was stock full of ideas about humanity's search for meaning. In fact, Mencken spent a great measure of time during his generally hectic schedule of editing, book reviewing, column writing, and Sara courting to produce two intellectually ambitious treatises, the final rounds of his projected trilogy. The word "treatise" connotes a study of a systematic and comprehensive kind, and it was the one Mencken chose for the two books he considered his greatest achievements: *Treatise on the Gods* (1930) and *Treatise on Right and Wrong* (1932). To some of his readers, these books lacked the humorous bounce of his wider output and must have seemed a departure from his forays into ordinary life. They were unmistakably destructive of received verities but also indicated a willingness to grapple with the big questions. For Mencken himself, these books may have been indicative of a personal resolve that he needed to summon in the face of the woes that the 1930s brought to him. For the first three decades of his career, Mencken had been a fresh—in both senses—voice in American letters and opinion. In middle age, however, his antics looked much less inviting, even unforgivable. That Mencken wrote only to delight himself, as he explained to Will Durant, was a good thing, because, as a writer in his fifties, fewer readers found his provocations delightful.

The Origins of Meaning

Between falling in love with a woman whose days were numbered and approaching a birthday that underscored the limits of his own mortal frame, Mencken turned philosophical and hoped to produce books that could match his outlook. In 1927 he confessed that he was no longer an "artless youth" "chiefly interested in the gaudy spectacle of life" or the "superficial effects of ideas." As an "ageing man," Mencken was increasingly interested in "the immemorial instincts and emotions" that supported human thought and aspirations. His original contribution to the trilogy on politics, religion, and morality, *Notes on Democracy*, was by all accounts a failure. In fact, by the late 1920s Mencken understood that most of what he had written was "transient and trivial," words and arguments that "will be forgotten in twenty-five years." Whether he also grasped that his desire for an intellectual output of some permanence appeared to be disproportionate to his own abilities or training is unclear. Had Mencken forgotten that twenty-five years earlier he had simply wanted to be a newspaper reporter? Or had he not remembered how he had excelled in observing the follies and ironies of American life? Where did he get the idea that he could give a lasting account of the universe's mysteries?

Whatever the source, Mencken's interest in what he called "high and ghostly matters" was not a recent development. As he explained to Will Durant in his reflections on life, Mencken had been a lifelong student of theology beginning with his childhood experience in Sunday school. He even suspected that he knew more of the Bible and theology than the average American pastor. Even Mencken's letters, as catalogued by Fred Hobson, contained pious phrases that, although mocking Christian devotion, also showed a firsthand acquaintance with the disciplines of mainstream Protestant piety: "I have spent the whole day in prayer and soul-searching"; "I shall spend the day searching the Scriptures"; "I begin to believe seriously that the Second Coming may be at hand"; "The marvels of God constantly astonish me"; "Let us praise God from whom all blessings flow"; and "God will reward you." Hobson also notes that sometimes Mencken closed his letters to close friends with "Yours in Christ."

His fans could readily attribute Mencken's remarks about religion to his penchant for ridicule, but the sustained attention he gave religion even aside from his treatises suggests a different story. To say that Mencken was haunted by religion would be simplistic. He was, nevertheless, surrounded by religious people, institutions, and expectations, could not escape the effect they had on American life, and so reported (and mocked) them as part of his chronicle of the United States. Before he started the *Mercury*, Mencken's writing about religion was spotty. For instance, in S. T. Joshi's collection of Mencken's writings on religion, only three of the sixty-plus articles come from before 1920, and these follow predictably Nietzschean themes or provide an outlet for objecting to Marion Bloom's attraction to Christian Science. When Mencken went to the *Mercury* and started to notice the broad spectrum of national life, however, he not only included articles by the likes of Herbert Parrish—the priest who married Mencken and Sara—on the affairs of the churches or featured snippets of folk life in the Americana section of the magazine, but the editor himself wrote repeatedly on national religious developments. And his point was not simply to ridicule but to observe the tensions that afflicted believers as they tried to make straight the way of the Lord in the crooked place of the American republic. Among the items that Mencken featured in the *Mercury*, these two are representative:

Mississippi
From an address to the Kiwanis Club of Columbus, a rising town on the Tombigbee river, by the Rev. W. F. Powell, a gifted exhorter of those parts.
>*God was the first Kiwanian.*

Pennsylvania
Counter offensive against the Pope in Chester County, as revealed by the distinguished West Chester *Daily Local News*:
>*MILK from a Holstein cow; Protestants only. Reba Marie Jacons, New Centreville.*

In other words, the religion of Americans was just one of the people's many foibles, right alongside political titles, manners, and travel. In a whimsical piece for his fourth collection of *Prejudices* (1924), Mencken set down a stream-of-consciousness list of memories and observations on "people and things":

The Capital of a Great Republic
The brother to the wife of the brother-in-law of the Vice-President . . . The aunt to the sister of the wife of the officer in charge of ceremonials, State Department . . . The neighbor of the cousin of the step-father of the sister-in-law of the President's pastor . . .

Ambassadors of Christ
Irish priests denouncing the Ku Klux Klan . . . Rabbis denouncing Henry Ford . . . Presbyterians denouncing Flo Ziegfeld . . . Missionaries collecting money from the mill children in Raleigh, N.C., to convert the Spaniards and Italians to Calvinism . . . Polish clergymen leaping out of the windows at Polish weddings in Johnstown, Pa., hoping that the next half-dozen beer-bottles won't hit them . . .

Bilder aus schoener Zeit
The burgundy from the Cresta Blanca vineyards in California . . . Michelob on warm Summer evenings with the crowd singing "Throw

Out the Lifeline!" . . . A wild night drinking Swedish punch and hot water . . . Two or three hot Scotch nights . . . Twenty or thirty Bass' ale nights. Five or six hundred Pilsner nights . . .

The High Seas
The buxom stewardess who comes in and inquires archly if one rang . . . The discovery that one forgot to pack enough undershirts . . . This wilting flowers standing in ice-pitchers and spittoons in the hallways . . .

The Shrine of Mnemosyne
The first inauguration of Woodrow Wilson, and the pretty suffragette who drank beer with me at the Raleigh . . . A dull night in a Buffalo hotel, reading the American Revised Version of the New Testament . . . The day I receive the proofs of my first book . . . A good-bye on an Hoboken pier . . . The Palace Hotel in Madrid.

The mind boggles at Mencken hoisting mugs of beer while singing the gospel hymn "Throw Out the Lifeline." The religious life of the United States was part of the fabric of his existence. Mencken's attitude more often than not was that taking offense was pointless since the ideas and ways of believers were simply the price of doing business in his homeland.

That attitude gave Mencken a perspective on religious develop-ments that few insiders could muster, since as an outsider he was criti-cal but as a chronicler of human folly he was amused. Three significant articles from the 1920s on Protestantism revealed that Mencken was capable of great insight precisely because he was not merely mocking but reading between the lines and underscoring unintended conse-quences. In a 1925 piece for the *Mercury*, "The Decline of Protestant-ism," Mencken had the sense to look beyond the fundamentalist con-troversy as the source for the division among the nation's Protestants and look instead at liturgy. He argued that at opposite ends of the spectrum Protestants were going in antagonistic directions, one "in the direction of Rome," the other "down into voodooism." Mencken admitted that he had been unaware of the former tendency until he noticed reports from local congregations about their midnight services on Christmas Eve. Perhaps an Episcopal church calling worshipers to "no less than three Christmas masses . . . two low and one high" was not altogether surprising given the trajectory of Anglo-Catholicism, but

Wesleyans sponsoring a "medieval carol service"? Since Mencken dated the end of the Middle Ages to the Ottoman conquest of Constantinople, he was certain that a medieval service was not Protestant. He thought it especially significant that even the Methodists were employing such tactics:

> Tiring of the dreadful din that goes with orthodox Wesleyan demon-ology, they take to ceremonials that grow more and more stately and voluptuous. The sermon ceases to be a cavalry charge and becomes soft and *pizzicato*. The choir abandons "Throw Out the Life-Line" and "Are You Ready for the Judgment Day?" and toys with Handel. . . . [W]hat would the old-time circuit-riders say of it, imagining them miraculously brought back from hell?

On the other side of the Protestant aisle, the faithful were descending rapidly into "barbaric devil-chasing." "In all those parts of the Republic where Beelzebub is still as real as Babe Ruth or Dr. Coolidge, and men drink raw fusel oil hot from the still," Mencken explained, Protestants had thrown overboard the New Testament and "gone back to the Old, particularly to the bloodiest parts of it." He had in mind the Anti-Saloon League and the Ku Klux Klan. Of course, this divide within Protestant-ism correlated to the modernist-fundamentalist contest, but Mencken sensed a dimension that transcended debates either about human ori-gins (evolution) or about history's end (the second coming).

Three years later, during the 1928 presidential election that saw Protestants come out in force against Al Smith, Mencken sensed that the lower end of the Protestant spectrum was gaining ground. Protes-tant dignitaries, he observed, were agitated about the political polem-ics and called for a return to the simple faith of Christ who "preached no complicated mysteries and demanded no pedantic allegiance." As much as Mencken, a man who "loved peace and deplored the uproars now going on," preferred this approach, he concluded that the religion of Jesus was as unworkable in 1920s America as it was in first-century Palestine. The Sermon on the Mount was a "sweet dream," but with "no more reality than a young man's hallucination of the damsel who has snared him." For that reason, to argue that the politicization of Prot-estantism had damaged the evangelical sects was "the most palpable nonsense." As long as a pastor in the Bible Belt confined himself "to dunning his customers in the interest of the heathen he dunned deaf and flapping ears." But as soon as he "leaped into his night-shirt and began chasing Jews, Unitarians, Aframericans, fancy women, bootleggers and the Pope, they followed him as ecstatically as the peasants of the Eleventh Century Rhineland followed Peter the Hermit." The revival of evangelical Protestantism was comparable, Mencken argued, to the "Great Awakening of 1740." "The Old Time Religion, *i.e.*, the Religion With Teeth In It and hair on those teeth, is triumphant again. . . . The Holy Spirit walks the land, armed with a pitchfork and carrying a bucket of tar."

By 1930, roughly the same time that *Treatise on the Gods* appeared, Mencken sensed a distinctly different mood in American Christianity, one that not only mellowed antagonisms among Protestants but was also dissolving differences between Protestants and Roman Catholics. In a review essay for the *Mercury* encompassing fourteen books on religion, from Ernest R. Trattner's *As a Jew Sees Jesus* to Shirley Jackson Case's *Jesus through the Centuries*, Mencken assessed the American tendency toward progressive uplift and its consequences for Christianity.

> All decent Americans believe that it is better to boost than to knock, that the radio is a wonderful invention, that all communists come from Russia and ought to be sent back there, that the public schools do a great work, and that the best cure for anything that happens to ail one is a dose of aspirin.

Such optimism, Mencken believed, was dissolving differences between Protestants and Roman Catholics. He predicted a "common" American religion, one part Wesleyan, the other "borrowing a great deal from Latin practices." Mencken already detected signs of the "Methodization of Holy Church in the Republic." The differences between the American and Roman Catholic theories of government animated opposition to Al Smith in 1928, but most Roman Catholics in the United States, especially Smith himself, could not understand the contrast. In fact, Mencken pointed to a time when public utterances by clergy easily came in either Protestant or Roman Catholic cadences. But that time was no more. "With one cardinal archbishop damning Einstein as a corruptor of youth and another entering into an alliance with Methodists and Presbyterians . . . it becomes increasingly difficult to mark the point where John Wesley ceases to be a heretic and becomes a saint." The changes were equally evident among the Methodists, whose services used to be "indistinguishable from an auction sale." But the popularity of ritual among Methodists not only meant that pastors were "pining publicly for the Book of Common Prayer as it was revised by Wesley in 1784," but in worship "they go through ceremonies almost as stately as a hanging." Some even lit candles. None of this reflected a growing ecumenical spirit among American Christians. Instead, it was merely "the function of the general standardization now going on in the United States."

With a keen eye on religious developments in the United States, Mencken's *Treatise on the Gods* provided a large canvas to develop such observations, but his approach was more analytic than journalistic, more a system of classification akin to his investigation into American language than a debunking of belief. To be sure, Mencken's disregard of revelation left all religions on the even playing field of human constructions—thus leaving himself the advantage of the superior man who had no need for religion. All religions, whether "the artless mumbo-jumbo of a Winnebago Indian" or the "elaborately refined and metaphysical rites of a Christian archbishop," boiled down to an attempt to gain access to the higher powers in the universe that controlled human destiny. From there it was a short step to the rise of priests or persons particularly adept at placating or manipulating the higher powers. The first man who successfully propitiated "the inimical and impenetrable powers of the air" became the spiritual figure upon whom his neighbors could rely. The average man was incapable of the psychological and intellectual demands required for dealing with the gods. His concerns were transient; "he has all he can do to face the policeman on the beat and his own wife." So he entrusted the "business of wrestling with Omnipotence" to the specialist, a person "who by habit and training" was "subnormally god-shy" and had "a natural talent for remonstrance and persuasion." Mencken's evolutionary and anthropological account of religion's origins lacked the humor that characterized his other writing, though the colloquial nature of his prose and his choice of images made *Treatise*'s prose lively. On occasion Mencken let his characteristic sarcasm creep in, such as when commenting on Mississippi Baptists "who, in fear that even unfermented grape-juice might deliver them to the Rum Demon, used coca-cola" but never "soda-pop" for the Lord's Supper. But *Treatise* was chiefly serious.

Mencken's main point about religion as a function of fearful primitives negotiating with higher powers for "more blackberries," "fewer

185

mosquitoes," a "dead wife to come back, or a living wife to die" recurred throughout the book. Even so, his discussion of the origins, evolution, varieties, Christian form, and contemporary features of religion, as reductionistic as it was, failed to become repetitive or labored if only because Mencken covered so much ground. In fact, his bibliographical essay ran for ten pages; mentioned over one hundred either scholarly or institutional works, from Hastings's *Encyclopedia of Religion and Ethics* to *The Doctrines and Discipline of the Methodist Episcopal Church*; and concluded with "*Soli Deo gloria!*" Even though the book featured Christianity—which Mencken attributed to his own upbringing and social location—he tried to account for religion in its sundry developments. When, for instance, he explained the triumph of the Earth Mother over the Sun God, Mencken invoked observations about male-female relations that had served him well in *In Defense of Women*. Primitive man faced a sorry fate. Instead of a glorious hunter, he was more likely coming home with rabbits instead of "sabre-toothed tigers." The rise of agriculture was no remedy for man's poor status since it was a "feminine discovery," monopolized by women for centuries. "No wonder the Earth Mother was the earliest really first-rate divinity!" She stood for the high position of women. Only after men asserted their position as *paterfamilias* did the Sun God return to its preeminence as "maker and guardian of Heaven and earth."

Mencken's account of Christianity was the largest part of the book and displayed consistently a skeptic's reading. The New Testament was "a miscellaneous collection of historical records, theological speculations, pontifical bulls and moral homilies in sharp conflict." Even so, this was not simply the disdain of the village atheist who would hardly have known, as Mencken did, that baptizing Jesus, the Son of God, could be a theological challenge. Mencken relied on the answer in the Letter to the Hebrews, which he paraphrased as "Jesus, though He felt that He was sinless, was yet sufficiently humble to admit that He might be mistaken." Mencken was much more dismissive of the Old Testament. While the New Testament bore the marks of a "remote and innocent age"—if "there are some palpable stretchers in it, then stretchers of the same sort are to be found" in other contemporary histories—the Old Testament "reeks with irreconcilable contradictions and patent imbecilities." Mencken knew and used the literary analysis—so-called JEDP—that broke the Pentateuch down into sources that reflected distinct periods in Israel's history. What did capture his imagination, though, was the Old Testament's poetry. "The Bible is," he asserted, "unquestionably the most beautiful book in the world." Considering that Mencken disliked poetry, this was not terribly high praise. But for Christian or Jewish readers of *Treatise*, Mencken did show a respect for the Scriptures:

> Allow everything you please for the barbaric history in the Old Testament and the decadent Little Bethel theology in the New, and there remains a series of poems so overwhelmingly voluptuous and disarming that no other literature, old or new, can offer a match for it.

The rise of Christianity with Jesus at its core was not, for Mencken, as beautiful as Hebrew verse, but it was almost as unintelligible. The teachings and life of Jesus were undoubtedly crucial to the origins and spread of Christianity. Even so, Mencken thought the circumstances surrounding Jesus's appeal as cultic figure were obscure. Jesus may have come from an "elite rank" ("the tribe of Judah") and pursued a common trade, but his early religious practices were hardly unusual. "If," Mencken speculated, Jesus "abandoned His work as a carpenter and went up to Jerusalem for the holy days, then He did only what thousands of other good Jews did." Mencken also thought it improbable that Jesus considered himself to be the Messiah. In fact, the great contradiction at the core of the Gospel narratives, for Mencken, was Matthew's recording of Jesus's acknowledgment of his divine status over against Mark's and Luke's accounts where Jesus commanded silence about his person. Even Jesus's death was inconsequential on the face of the Gospel narratives. But instead of retreating into the desert once he recognized that his teachings had failed to gain a hearing, Jesus, according to Mencken, decided to submit to his opponents and be executed. "He could testify to the truth of what He taught by dying for it, publicly and brilliantly." What tipped the balance in Christianity's emergence as a religion of influence was the resurrection. "Upon that theory, though it wears upon every rationality that enlightened men cherish," Mencken wrote, "the most civilized section of the human race has erected a structure of ideas and practices so vast in scope and powerful in effect that the whole range of history showeth nothing parallel." The rest was history. "The simple, childlike faith that sustained the first believers in the face of contumely and persecution," Mencken announced, "oozed out of their successors, and in its place there arose a complicated dogmatic structure, bristling with metaphysical refinements and logical impossibilities." Here Mencken cued the Council of Nicea.

Mencken gave scant attention to Christian developments after the ante-Nicene era. Constantine made a cameo appearance by stopping the theological and ecclesiastical "free-for-all" that had characterized the ante-Nicene church. With the decline of the Roman Empire, the papacy "fell heir to most of [the imperial] authority and all of its prestige." Although the pope "became an Asiatic despot, responsible to no one," the papacy itself received vigorous infusions of competency because it was not a hereditary office. The Reformation owed its vigor to economic and political developments in Europe, even as Protestant theology was "quite as silly as the old." In fact, Mencken opined that Protestantism, for all its numerical strength, remained a "feeble force in the world, and has very little influence upon the main stream of human thought." Of course, here was a section of *Treatise* where Mencken could have worked in his feud with Puritanism, but silence about his old nemesis may have been an indication of secular sanctification. As it was, Luther and Calvin provided ample targets for his disdain. The former was the typical theologian—"cocksure, dictatorial, grasping, self-indulgent, vulgar and ignorant." Calvin "was even worse," a man of "gloomy and nonsensical ideas." Still, Mencken could not resist one jab at Puritanism. Calvin was Puritanism's "true" father.

In the concluding chapter, Mencken took stock of modern religion. Here the author indulged a Whiggish outlook that contradicted his general affirmation of purposelessness and human folly. Mencken believed that science had knocked religion from its intellectual pedestal, and this reality was obvious:

> There was a time when a man laid low by the ague sent for a priest and made a votive offering; now he sends for a physician and takes quinine. There was a time when it took a miracle to fling him through the air; now he proceeds by airplane. There was a time when he bore all his burdens with resignation, fearing to offend the gods that sent them; now he rises and tries to throw them off. There is no longer any resignation among enlightened men; there is only resolute patience.

Things were not so intelligent among the theologians or the mob. Christian reconcilers of theology and science tried to find room for God in the "gaps in knowledge." Meanwhile, most people clung to faith out of fear and a need for an "answer to the intolerable riddle of existence." These were inferior sorts of people who could not even appreciate what Mencken did in the gods—the beauty of religion. Once again, he admitted that the biblical narrative, for instance, the story of Jesus as told in the Synoptic Gospels, was "the most lovely story that the human fancy has ever devised." Lest believers take too much encouragement, Mencken qualified his assessment by comparing the life of Christ to "the sempiternal Cinderella story, lifted to cosmic dimensions." As for the claim that religion was generally responsible for inculcating virtue, Mencken demurred. "The devotee, believing that he will escape the pains and penalties that his god will visit upon other men," he explained, "almost inevitably develops the attitude of mind denounced by Jesus in the Pharisees."

Mencken's own estimate of *Treatise* was high even if the book had a short shelf life. He regarded it as his "best book," "smooth," "good-tempered," "adroitly written," "a model of condensation." But what was it? Scholarship? Journalism? Theory? Terry Teachout observes that Mencken was constantly torn between "the journalistic desire to say it at once and have done with it, and the more scholarly desire to say it carefully and with some regard to fundamental ideas and permanent values." Mencken himself thought *Treatise* a scholarly treatment. Sales indicated that the public was inclined to receive it as journalism—it went through seven printings and sold 13,000 copies within its first year in print; within a decade Mencken admitted that "it is seldom discussed, or even alluded to." The problem of the book's reception might have resided elsewhere, however. Instead of offering readers Mencken's usual assortment of swipes at convention or sober reflection on serious matters—some objected that the combination defanged the author's incisive perspective—*Treatise* may have been far more personal than anything else. In fact, if someone reads the book as Mencken's own attempt to make sense of a land where so many people of apparent intellect and sense continued to place their hopes and destiny in religious teachings and practices, *Treatise* becomes plausible. Call the book a warm-up for Mencken's highly personal memoirs a decade later.

The beginning and end of the book invite this interpretation. In the preface Mencken explained that he was writing as neither a fanatic nor an abuser of religion. He described himself as an "amiable" skeptic. "I am quite devoid of the religious impulse, and have no belief in any of the current theologies," he explained. "But neither have I any active antipathy to them, save, of course, in so far as they ordain the harassing of persons who do not believe in them." Some religious teachings actually had "a considerable plausibility," and Mencken could imagine "more or less rational persons believing in them." Aside from the plausibility of religion's claims, Mencken could not deny that faith had "conditioned the thinking of mankind since the infancy of the race." Consequently, dismissing religion was "a proceeding that is far more lofty than sensible." Call this respect for religion begrudging, but it nevertheless showed an attitude that was much more complicated than the one that reduced religion to imbecility.

The closing scene of *Treatise* suggests as much. Mencken reached back into old newspaper clippings—his own—to demonstrate the ongoing power of religion. He introduced the account of a hanging with reassurances that the truly superior man did not need religion. He invoked Nietzsche's admonition "Be Hard!" along with William James's claim that the advance of the race depended as much on a "hardness of mind" as on a hardness of fist. Civilized men did not need to find meaning in life for it to be interesting. Satisfaction came not from "a childish confidence that some vague and gaseous god, hidden away in some impossible sky, made [man] for a lofty purpose." Instead, simply exercising one's mind, the way animals exercise their muscles, was sufficient for a small range of advanced men. Not the soul but a way of thinking was what separated man from beast, and what gave man a "way of facing the impenetrable dark that must engulf him in the end." And then there were the men who needed religion, such as one "poor fellow" who had with "the Seventh Commandment in mind" killed his wife and so needed to pay his "debt to the Sixth." Accompanied on the gallows with a Baptist pastor, the convict "broke into a loud, confident recitation of the Twenty-Third Psalm." Mencken quoted from his news story:

The Condemned—(Loudly) *The Lord is my shepherd; I shall not want. He maketh me to lie down in green pastures.* (They reach the foot of the gallows.) *He leadeth me beside the still waters. He restoreth my soul.* (They mount the steps.) *He leadeth me in the paths of righteousness for his name's sake. Yea, though I walk through the valley of the shadow of death* (The sheriff binds his legs) *I will fear no evil: for thou art with me; thy rod and thy staff they comfort me.* (The sheriff adjusts the noose.) *Thou preparest a table before me in the presence of mine enemies; thou anointest my head with oil; my cup runneth over.* (The sheriff signals to

the hangman). *Surely goodness and mercy shall follow me all the days of my life; and I will dwell in the house of—*
    The drop falls.

As this account stood, readers could either find a tribute to this man's faith and the apparent comfort of the psalm, or notice the large disparity between religion's fairy-tale promises and sin, justice, and death. Mencken helped readers through the ambiguity by adding, "As an American I naturally spend most of my time laughing, but that time I did not laugh." That last sentence of the book captured its larger effect: sober respect for religion, combined with deep-seated incredulity.

Reviews of the book were mixed, but none of them addressed why this topic would be of such significance to a man who was an avowed skeptic, why Mencken would consider this his most important book. All people are likely prone to self-delusion and so incapable of properly evaluating themselves. But even if Mencken was wrong about *Treatise*, the book did reveal the importance of religion to him, not captured by simply chalking the entire business up to yet another version of sophomoric disdain or Nietzschean conceit. Granville Hicks heaped praise on Mencken's achievement. He complimented the book for its learning and Mencken himself for treating the subject as a "tolerant and not utterly sympathetic skeptic." Hicks was on to something, though, when he wondered about the audience for the book. He suspected that Mencken was writing primarily for the *American Mercury* readership, which was fine, but that market had "either reached Mencken's conclusions long since" or had rejected religion altogether. Hicks understood that Mencken was better read in religion than the "average intelligent man" but did not ask why. He did wish that Mencken had written about more than the religion of the masses, say, about the piety or devotion of an Augustine or Aquinas, the type of faith that might interest a learned reader.

Reinhold Niebuhr was not so sympathetic or instructive. In his short review for the *Atlantic*, Niebuhr assumed a knowing—even condescending—air and found *Treatise* to be predictably Menckenian:

The gleam of fanaticism is in Mr. Mencken's eye while he inveighs against the bigotry of the priests and the stupidity of their followers. It is only when dealing with moral and social issues that he achieves the heights of complete detachment, and in this case the detachment is that of the cynic rather than that of the scientist.

That Niebuhr could not resist taking a personal jab at the book—that it revealed more "how one fanatic feels about other fanatics" than about religion—was not necessarily surprising. But that Niebuhr did not see the ground he conceded in his defense of a better class of religion than the magical kind that *Treatise* featured must have left Mencken feeling victorious. A difference between magic and religious rites led Niebuhr to think his faith was superior to the kind that Mencken depicted. Mencken knew "nothing" about mystics who saw in life's mysteries the "grace of God," or the prophets who contributed to "the advancement of the race." In fact, Mencken doubted divine revelation as the source of religion as much as Niebuhr assumed the better sort of religion could persist without too much attention to the origins of revealed truth. If the reviewer had wanted to extricate the social justice exhortations of the prophet Amos from the Bible's less believable parts—whether the conquest of Palestine or the virgin birth—Niebuhr would have to do more than render Mencken a cultured despiser of religion.

Really Contra Mundum

If *Treatise on the Gods* was in Mencken's estimate his best work, it may have also marked a turning point in his career and public reception. That he wrote a book on religion while courting and planning to marry a woman whose days were numbered may have been merely coincidental. But that he showed no signs of interest in religion's comforts even while pondering human mortality displayed remarkable determination to live life independently of the gods' aid. One way to look at the book's timing is that Mencken needed to intensify his resolve about not needing religion at precisely the moment when circumstances made faith look plausible. However the book functioned therapeutically for him as he determined to make a life with Sara, *Treatise* was an indication, along with marriage, of Mencken's willingness to settle down. Most biographers readily pigeonhole the book in Mencken's collection of human folly specimens, with religion occupying the biggest closet. As much merit as that assessment has, the book, both in content and in form, reflected a seriousness that Mencken may have lacked as he rattled the cages of the nation's cultural guardians. He attempted to treat systematically and thoroughly a subject that had long fascinated and repelled him. *Treatise* was not meant to be funny; it was meant to be serious. It was just like hypocrisy, the tribute that virtue pays to vice, or his way of unbelief paying respect to belief.

That maturity of thought and manner was a reservoir on which he would need to rely during the 1930s as he endured a number of setbacks both professional and personal. Ironically, Mencken's development as a writer who addressed life's big questions may have also been responsible for the larger trajectory of his career after he turned fifty—his decline in popularity among the nation's educated readers. The reception of *Treatise on the Gods* was itself no indication of this development, since it sold well. But its sequel, *Treatise on Right and Wrong*, did indicate that Mencken's regular audience was unprepared for such serious inquiry.

The volume on ethics was in many respects derivative of the one on religion even if at times Mencken showed genuine insight. Like *Gods*, *Right and Wrong* followed the formula of "origins," "evolution," "varieties," "Christian form," and the contemporary state of ethics. He grouped ethical systems around three sources—reason, revelation, and instinct—on the way to discussing all manner of difficult material such as freedom and determinism and the problem of evil, as well as major theologians from Gregory of Nyssa to Thomas Aquinas, "a man of supple, enterprising and highly original mind." As competent and matter of fact (because he was mainly reporting) as his discussions of the major questions in ethics were, Mencken's powers of observation were keenest when he described the problems facing contemporary Christians. On the subject of Roman Catholics and sex, Mencken was downright prophetic:

> On the one hand there is the draconian mandate of *Casti connubii* [a 1930 encyclical from Pius XI that restricted the end of sex to reproduction], and on the other hand there is the disconcerting fact that a great many Catholics are now practicing birth control, and that the more intelligent, opulent and influential they are, the more likely they are to do so. If they are actually guilty of mortal sin, and persist in it contumaciously, then it must be assumed that all of them will go to Hell *post mortem*, which is a doom which no humane confessor, I take it, wants to contemplate for the flower of his flock.

Mencken similarly regarded the church's teaching on divorce "so preposterous" that the bishops had to resort to evasions in declaring

annulments that in secular courts judges would have "flatly called divorce." Protestants may not have faced the tortured logic that followed
from papal pronouncements, but Mencken was equally adept at pointing out the ironies and inconsistencies among the descendants of
Martin Luther. Protestants' "moral mandates [were] no longer taken
seriously by any intelligent person." Ministers might thunder against
war, but then listeners might remember "the sadistic furies of . . . chief
ecclesiastics in 1917." Meanwhile, Protestants' moral crusades placed
them "on friendly terms with the lowest sort of politicians." The old
Puritanism, furthermore, had degenerated into a "kind of voodooism."
"Repelled by the cold rigors of Puritan ecclesiasticism" in the Northeast, those in the lower ranks of the faithful in the South and West "rebounded into the arms of the Methodists." Along the way, the "Calvinis-
tic doctrine of grace resolved into an imbecile theory that the sanctified
are actually purged of sin." The only New Englanders left to carry on the
old Puritan moral system and support police in their efforts to rid the
city of "naughty books and wicked plays" were "Irish Catholics."

What prevented these astute observations about American Christianity from propelling *Right and Wrong* into a vigorous critique of conventional morality was Mencken's fairly predictable and Whiggish reading
of the history of morals. He stated confidently that the Renaissance and
scientific revolution had evacuated the older ethical systems of their primary motivation—fear. His chief intellectual heroes were Montaigne,
Francis Bacon, René Descartes, Spinoza, and Leibniz, who led a double
revolt against Christian and Greek dogma. Grotius, Hobbes, Kant, and
Bentham put the icing on the cake of the modern "ethical revolution,"
and left the civilized man with an adequate moral foundation. This more
or less progressive account, however, did not fit with Mencken's assessment of Bolshevism and fascism, both of which rejected older moral
systems, only to replace them with even more oppressive norms.

Indeed, his optimism about modern ethical theories conflicted
with his general outlook that humans were fundamentally foolish and
flawed, a reality especially evident in the inability of civilization to produce good government. Rather than performing basic social services,
government invariably became a device for exploiting William Graham
Sumner's "forgotten man," that "obscure, decent, uncomplaining good
citizen who works hard, obeys the laws, cares for his family, and pays his
own way." The forgotten man did not sound like a reader of Nietzsche
or Bentham, but Mencken's identification with him did put Mencken in

opposition to every "New Freedom" or "New Deal," that is, every scheme "to set up new virtues by law and inculcate them by force." Instead of going all the way and recognizing a measure of solidarity with the average Americans who avoided *American Mercury* and still went to church, Mencken construed this battle between the forgotten man and bad government as the old conspiracy of "inferior men against their betters." And rather than recognizing that better men like himself might have similar concerns as their inferiors, Mencken decided to conclude the book by praising "such a thing as progress" and the values it produced as "authentic and durable," truths to be discovered by "honest and sensible men." That ending left *Right and Wrong* some distance from the closing scene of *Treatise on the Gods*. It sounded more like Rotarian uplift than the typically sober estimate of human limitations that Mencken understood.

The optimistic tone of *Right and Wrong* certainly was out of sync with Mencken's own experience of middle age. He had written his two treatises with a Republican, Herbert Hoover, in the White House and an economy in free fall. But that did not bring him to admire Franklin Delano Roosevelt or his New Deal. Mencken did vote for FDR in 1932, even though he had predicted Hoover's victory. By 1936 he was adamantly opposed to FDR and hoped for the thirty-second president's defeat to the Republican candidate, Alf Landon, a desire based much more on animus than on any realistic assessment, since Landon won only two states (New Hampshire and Maine). The consequences of the crash of 1929 caught Mencken completely off guard. During the years running up to the 1932 election, he refused to acknowledge the economic devastation even as he noticed homeless men sleeping outside his hotel in Chicago as he covered the Republican National Convention. When his brother Charlie lost his railroad job, Mencken still thought "the effects of depression [were] greatly exaggerated." When FDR took office and started to implement his variety of economic remedies, Mencken only saw a bloated federal government that was taking on socialist proportions. His belief in small government, free markets, and even states' rights was partly responsible for such blinders. But as Fred Hobson observes, the antagonism was also personal. Mencken's sense of civilized men collided directly with FDR's abandonment of his own class while pandering to the average man. The disparity between Roosevelt's own background and the policies of his administration led Mencken to conclude that the president was a charlatan with a messiah complex. At least FDR confirmed Mencken's estimate of democracy—"the theory that the common people know what they want, and deserve to get it good and hard."

Hobson also wonders if Mencken's opposition to Roosevelt owed to envy, the one sin the journalist could not abide because it came with a sense of inferiority. Mencken observed that the Depression had thrown the college "boys and gals into the arms of Roosevelt II." Mencken added that he was "relieved to get rid of them." But his relief over losing the younger set may have also hidden his sense that he was losing a generation of educated Americans. The nation's intellectuals and their avid readers had flocked to the Baltimore writer and editor during the 1920s; Mencken's prime was the age of flappers, jazz, and illegal liquor. But the economy, combined with Mencken's flippancy about it, prompted America's intellectuals to look elsewhere either for a laugh or a poke. The Depression had exposed Mencken's weakness to the Left; he was good for mocking the cultural and political establishment but had no use for prescribing a better society. The literary Right now had grounds to make plausible the contention that Mencken's antics were "nearer to intellectual vaudeville than to serious criticism." Edmund Wilson, literary critic for the *New Republic*, complained that Mencken was incapable of adaptation. Once the "civilized consciousness of America," the Baltimorean had shown himself to be "stuck in the same intellectual jam, content to rage and complain without hope." Could Mencken have lost his edge because, as an op-ed writer in the *Omaha World-Herald* put it, life had grown "sweeter," "with a happy marriage, with a plumper middle age, with a more sedentary existence"? Whether Mencken was finally settling down or incapable of adjusting to the realities of economic woe and political uncertainty, he had lost his once avid audience.

This loss took its toll on the *American Mercury*. The peak of the magazine's popularity was 1928, perhaps because of the publicity surrounding "Hatrack" and the ensuing legal proceedings, with a circulation of roughly 88,000. From there it was downhill, and the causes were multiple. Mencken blamed the business manager, Samuel Knopf, Alfred's father, for favoring a plan of large circulation that the magazine itself could not sustain without equivalent advertising. He still wanted the magazine to be not an imitation of the *Atlantic* or *Harper's* but "the voice of that eager and unconventional minority." Mencken did not consider his own faults. Some of these were accidental such as distractions from domestic life and work on books like *Right and Wrong*. But Mencken's own limits as an editor were also a factor. One contributor to the *Mer-*

cury complained that writers needed to conform to Mencken's style. Terry Teachout remarks sensibly that Harold Ross at the *New Yorker*, who was not himself a writer, gave his contributors freedom to develop their own prose. Mencken, in contrast, was a great writer with a unique style, and "such writers rarely make good editors." With the magazine increasingly mirroring Mencken's outlook and manner and with his inability to provoke and rile in an environment of austerity and fear, the *Mercury*'s edge turned caustic.

As early as 1931 Mencken informed Knopf of his plans to retire. It took two years for that information to take effect, and Mencken expressed willingness to contribute while advising that the magazine should be more literary than political. His last issue as editor was December 1933, and even then Mencken did not exit peacefully. He commented on *Mein Kampf* in ways that did not register the alarm that Knopf felt appropriate. Mencken thought Hitler's anti-Semitism was absurd, along with any number of other Nazi Party ideas. But as a long-time German sympathizer, Mencken did not condemn Hitler's aims to expand Germany's influence or his anticommunism sufficiently for Knopf's tastes. This was an ominous foreshadowing of yet another Mencken character tic that would further alienate him from American intellectuals. The kerfuffle ended amicably and closed Mencken's tenure at the *Mercury* at the round number of a decade. Mencken accepted the revisions, and Knopf retained Mencken as a friend and author. In fact, reduced editorial duties left time for the *Mercury*'s founder to complete the *Treatise on Right and Wrong*, which was published by Knopf. Even that book, however, marked Mencken's decline in popularity. The reviewer for the *Saturday Review*, for instance, complained that the "routine patter of the now blowzy Menckenese invective" was little more than a patina for serious learning.

The one reader he cared most about was his wife, Sara, and Mencken would even have to confront losing her soon after deciding to leave the magazine. The couple had wanted to travel to Germany, but in the winter of 1934 settled for a cruise in the Mediterranean with, at least for the husband, Mark Twain's *Innocents Abroad* in mind. Naples and Palestine were particularly impressive to Mencken, the former because it was now, under Mussolini, "orderly, precise, soldierly," the latter because the Jews who had settled in the desert, "skeptics of a somewhat extreme wing," had made it bloom. During the trip Sara's health, always hanging in the balance, declined. She ran a high fever that confined her to their hotel room for five days in Cairo and that Mencken attributed to tuberculosis. For the remainder of the calendar year Sara experienced bouts of high fever that prompted physicians to examine her lungs. The results were always better than Sara's general condition. By the end of the year, when her mother died, Sara was unfit to travel to Montgomery. The next month, January 1935, Sara was back to writing stories. But she continued to suffer a variety of afflictions that led finally on May 26 to the diagnosis of tubercular meningitis, a determination that Mencken knew to be a death sentence. Three days later he saw her at the Johns Hopkins Hospital for the last time. For the next two days Mencken reflected on Sara's mortality, partly surprised that he, "her senior by 18 years" and never in great health, would outlive her. When she finally succumbed to tuberculosis on May 31, Mencken dutifully notified family and friends, received callers at their Cathedral Street flat, and later mused, "I can well understand why the more naive sort of people cling to the hope of a reunion after death" but "I do not share it."

The funeral service was held on June 3 at a local funeral home with family and close friends attending, and a young Episcopal priest officiating. Mencken described the day as "the most dreadful" of his life. He refused to accompany his brothers, who took Sara's remains to the crematory. Her ashes were eventually buried at the foot of Mencken's mother's grave at Loudon Park Cemetery. A year later, Mencken paid tribute by assembling a collection of Sara's stories in which he wrote a biographical sketch:

> I find it hard, even so soon after her death, to recall her as ill. It is much easier to remember her on those days when things were going well with her, and she was full of projects, and busy with her friends and the house, and merry with her easy laughter.

Five years later in his private notes, Mencken indicated that his anguish was still fresh: "I was fifty-five years old before I ever envied anyone and then it was not so much for what others had as for what I had lost."

Between the Times

When Mencken turned fifty in 1930, he was arguably at the peak of his fame and notoriety. Indicative of that was Sinclair Lewis's speech at the ceremonies where he received the Nobel Prize for Literature. In a talk that heaped a measure of scorn on the arbiters of American letters, the novelist went out of his way to praise Mencken as "our most vivid critic" and for cultivating and advocating a host of writers. Four years later at the annual Gridiron Club dinner, where the nation's best journalists engaged in humor and satire, sometimes directing their remarks at the sitting president, with the latter having the last word, Mencken was scheduled to speak first and planned to take aim at FDR. He did in ways that Interior Secretary Harold Ickes later recalled were "cleverly cynical," not "particularly ill-natured." When the president had his chance for rebuttal, he went after Mencken, but perhaps in an even more clever way. FDR denounced American journalists as unlearned, uncivilized, "pathetically feeble and vulgar, and so generally disreputable." At some point during his remarks, the audience recognized that FDR was simply quoting Mencken's own assessment of the press corps from his essay "Journalism in America." Biographers disagree about the degree to which FDR humiliated Mencken. Even if, as Fred Hobson observes, he was able to brush off the president's effort to alienate Mencken from his peers, the evening was a sure indication that the Baltimore writer was no longer the icon of irreverence and iconoclasm but the odd man out. Once the writer whom knowing Americans quoted to indicate sophistication and awareness, now Mencken was the man of fringe and even unacceptable opinions.

Not to be missed in this exchange with FDR was the fact that the president of the United States was reading, preparing for battle with, and quoting a man who thirty years earlier, with only a high school degree under his belt, was working as a cub reporter for a second-tier city newspaper. As much as the incident gauged Mencken's decline in popularity, it was also evidence of his remarkable career and success. That was small comfort, though, for a widower who understood that the lasting consolations in life had less to do with publicity and were more fleeting than celebrity. His only real comfort was the company of people.

CHAPTER NINE

Delivered from Anonymity

Mencken's popularity may have declined during the 1930s, but his prosperity did not. Within months of Sara's death, he accepted an of-fer from *Sunpapers* to take a more active role in its affairs than he had for some time. Mencken agreed to serve as an adviser at first, which required him to go to the office five afternoons a week rather than fol-low his relaxed schedule of recent years. As a member of the board of directors and owner of stock in the Baltimore newspapers, Mencken had financial incentives for his decision. Nor did it hurt that Paul Pat-terson, president of the company, increased Mencken's salary from $5,000 to $12,000 a year. In addition to royalties and dividends from investments—he boasted at one point that he owned stock in fifty-eight different corporations—Mencken enjoyed a side of newspaper work far removed from his days as a beat reporter when he was much more skeptical about management. Formerly wary of the WASP cul-tural institutions where Baltimore's business elite socialized, in his late fifties Mencken found himself joining the Maryland Club, the Uni-versity Club, and the Baltimore Club, where he was on familiar terms with the city's professionals and business owners and where he enter-tained out-of-town guests. Although he was engaged with the paper at a different level, the return to the world of journalism may well have been a safe haven for him after Sara's death and during his declining popularity. In 1938 Mencken agreed to serve as a transition editor for the *Evening Sun* and remarked that it was "fatiguing but certainly very amusing."

As much as newspaper work may have reinvigorated him—Mencken worked from 9:00 a.m. to 4:00 p.m. each day—he was not up to it physically. A lifelong hypochondriac, Mencken's frame increasingly matched his fears. Flu, bronchitis, tracheitis, and a vasectomy were just some of the ailments or procedures that took him to the hospital. Soon after leaving the *Sunpapers*, he checked into the hospital worried about his condition. His physician recommended "complete rest." Mencken used that as a reason for a trip in the summer of 1938 to Germany. He declined to write up his observations for the paper. He was merely "eager to take a look before the coroner calls."

Mencken's failure to show concern about conditions in Germany, especially the Nazis' treatment of Jews, has indicated for many either his anti-Semitism or his stubbornness about German superiority (the flip side of his Anglophobia). As correct as those assessments are, Mencken's sights were set less on the conditions of Hitler's Germany than on paying his respects to the Mencken clan. To his cousin in Oldenburg, Anne, the matriarch of the family in that part of the country, with whom Mencken corresponded regularly, he had expressed regrets that his grandfather, Burkardt, had ever left Germany. Now he was struck by the reality that the Menckens were becoming extinct. He visited the big cities—Berlin, Bremen, Halle, Wittenberg—plus Oldenburg, where he noted the memorials to family members and paid respects at the graves of previous generations of the family. Mencken experienced a sense of completeness and finality:

> I started for home feeling that a chapter had ended—that I'd probably never visit Germany again. I was already 58 years old, and my state of health was showing it: moreover, another great European war was certain, and it would be a long while before peaceful travel would again be possible.

Back in New York, he commented to a reporter that Germany—Hitler's Germany, no less—"looked like a church to me, it was so quiet."

That Germany turned Mencken from a default setting of skepticism to nostalgia undoubtedly reflected the grief he still experienced over Sara's death as well as his own sense of coming to the end (even though he would live for another eighteen years). A trip that was supposed to improve his health did not. Back in the United States in late 1938, Mencken had little energy for work. His condition continued to be "rocky." The following summer, when out for an errand on foot on a hot July afternoon, he experienced symptoms of a minor stroke—numbness in the back of his head and tingling on the left side of his face. The condition persisted, and he went to his doctor the next morning. It was Mencken's first stroke. He self-diagnosed it as a "spastic cerebral episode" and was hospitalized for a week. Mencken recovered quickly, but the incident shook him. He confided in close friends and swore them to secrecy. He did not want people to know that he was seriously ill. Even so, he knew it. To a friend he wrote, "I believe that I'll have to look forward to being disabled more or less for the rest of my life." This was the beginning of the end, and the stroke confirmed his "life-long feeling that I would probably not live much beyond sixty."

By any measure Mencken was a hypochondriac, and so remarkably sensitive to physical discomfort. He regularly mentioned ailments to colleagues and included lists of discomforts in his writings. The irritations ranged from hemorrhoids and tonsillitis to "a sour stomach" and "burning in the gospel pipe" (a reference to symptoms associated with hay fever). By the 1920s Mencken had created an "Illnesses" file in which he placed copies of letters and notes in order to monitor and fend off sickness. Fred Hobson observes that these records were Mencken's equivalent of Walt Whitman's "Song of Myself," a "catalogue, a virtual poetry of affliction, boasting, and chanting of pain and illness." Hobson speculates that it was Mencken's way of proving, like Job, that he was still alive. To one of his lady friends, he wrote, "Hay fever has me by the ear." To his friend Ernest Boyd, he proclaimed, "God has me by the balls." Aside from proving his ongoing vigor (at least in the sense of enduring suffering), Mencken also monitored illness as a way of trying to impose order upon a chaotic world. As Hobson also observes, that Mencken lived in a city with a first-rate hospital (Johns Hopkins University) added to his obsessive tendencies. In fact, Mencken regularly functioned as a medical broker who oversaw visits by family and friends to Baltimore and arranged for meetings with physicians, many of whom he knew either professionally or as friends.

The most important reason for monitoring health so closely, though, was to maintain literary output. If it is true that Mencken wrote over 10 million words—and there is no reason to doubt that claim—attention to low-level discomforts and high-octane illnesses made perfect sense. His work depended on a measure of good health, and the slightest threats to that productivity were noteworthy. Hypochondria may have been the flip side of Mencken's unparalleled work ethic. That assertion certainly looks plausible in the case of Mencken's stroke. His brush with mortality stimulated Mencken's last barrage of prose.

The Days Recollected and Counted

A fear of running out of time added a sense of urgency to Mencken's efforts, begun after Sara's death, to arrange his affairs, from manuscripts and notes to financial and domestic records. He had a mountain of effects to sort through since he had saved everything, from hotel menus and receipts to random notes for ideas—not to mention the mounds of articles sent from clipping services whenever his name appeared in newspapers and magazines. Mencken also functioned as the family archivist, an office that required him to dispose of the Mencken family Bible in which births and deaths had been recorded by his mother. He cut the registry out of the Bible and pasted it in a separate book. The Bible itself, "a nuisance," he consigned to a fire. Archival work even prompted Mencken to find the old family home on Lexington Street, then occupied by an African American, "a very intelligent and decent fellow," who was engaged in renovations.

Such a retrospective mood, ironically, gave Mencken a new lease on life and was responsible for a trilogy of memoirs that arguably showed off his wit and style as no other assignment had. The first of these books, *Happy Days*, appeared in 1939 but had been brewing for some time. As early as the 1920s Mencken had written columns about his boyhood on the streets of Baltimore. Sara's death and his move from the Cathedral Street apartment back to Hollins Street stimulated Mencken's reminiscences further and led to a 1936 essay, originally published in the *New Yorker*, "The Ordeal of a Philosopher," that described his boyhood encounters with blacks in the alleys behind the family house in West Baltimore. The success of that piece and the editors' interest in additional reminiscences led to a second article, "Innocence in a Wicked World," which described an elderly African American woman from the neighborhood who specialized in showing up at funerals. Both articles survived in *Happy Days*, a book that owed its existence to the encouragement of Harold Ross at the *New Yorker*. Mencken had hoped to replicate a work like Ben Franklin's *Essays to Do Good*, something like *Advice to Young Men*. But the memoirs got in the way, and Mencken never started the book of advice. Despite his ministroke in July, Mencken completed the manuscript in the months that sandwiched his hospitalization.

Bitterness and even misanthropy were evident in Mencken's perceptions of American life during the period when he completed his memoirs. For instance, in 1941 he wrote in his diary a stinging assessment of his West Baltimore neighborhood. The place was "slowly going downhill" thanks to the "filthy poor whites from Appalachia and the Southern tidewater" migrating there. The women were "squatty and hideous creatures," the men caroused and deflowered young women, sometimes even their own daughters. His neighbors lived like "animals" and were "next-door to animals in their habits and ideas." Mencken's vitriol was not reserved for his nearby inferiors. It also extended to colleagues at the *Sunpapers*. His closest friend at the paper, Paul Patterson, was guilty of lacking courage and harboring suspicion of "men with ideas." Hamilton Owens, another *Sunpapers* colleague with whom Mencken socialized and carried on friendly relations, was "a time-server with no more principle than a privy-rat." In fact, Owens had become increasingly "the Southern cracker—dogmatic, unreliable, and incapable of learning anything new." Even Gerald Johnson, a columnist who would follow Mencken from Baltimore's readers to a national audience and whom Mencken had championed throughout the 1920s, was "practically useless" as a writer.

But when it came to *Happy Days*, Mencken resisted any temptation to settle scores or hurl condemnations, even though he had little to lose and seemed to care about others' perceptions even less. The book's conclusion illustrates a generous spirit and sense of irony, the qualities that so often characterized his best writing. The last chapter was a story about a trip with his grandfather Abhau to relatives—the Almroths—in Ohio's Western Reserve. Mencken remembered having a roaring good time with his cousins, cracking walnuts, fetching apples from the cellar, hauling firewood, and of course, consuming "enormous country dinners and suppers, with their pyramids of fried chicken and their huge platters of white home-cured hog-meat, swimming in grease." Only on Sunday, however, did Mencken learn of his extended family's Christian devotion. He and his grandfather arrived late for the Lutheran service and sat in the back in hopes of avoiding "the glare of notoriety." But at the end of the service the pastor reported that two visitors were in their midst and asked the Baltimoreans to rise:

As we were passing out afterward [my grandfather] was introduced to the pastor and all the notables of the congregation, including many who welcomed him in German, for the whole Lake Erie littoral was full of Germans. The pastor eyed me speculatively and seemed about to try me out on the Catechism, but just then a female customer began to whoop up his sermon in high, astounding terms, and I escaped under cover of his grateful thanks.

On the way home Mencken and his grandfather received word of his other grandfather's (Mencken) death. He recalled seeing for the first time a piece of black crepe on the handle of the doorbell at his grandfather's home, a sight that made him "feel creepy." At the same time, Mencken admitted having wicked thoughts and chalked them up to his only being ten years old, an age when boys' emotions are "not those of philosophers." His untoward thought was the result of calculating the sequence of days involved in his grandfather's death: "The day was Thursday—and they'd certainly not bury the old man until Sunday." In other words, "No school tomorrow!" With those two lines, Mencken closed his reflections on his boyhood. They were clearly in sync with his lifelong encounter with the dilemmas, mysteries, and annoyances of death and religion. Those parts of human existence might be uncomfortable, especially in the way that Mencken's neighbors sought to observe human mortality and the promise of immortality. But he did not sneer. With the subtext of a twinkle in his eye, he observed the ironies and folly that generally attended attempts to express or capture the higher truths. Mencken mixed sarcasm and respect for religion in ways unrivaled by other debunkers, iconoclasts, or skeptics.

The reception of *Happy Days* was warm. The book ascended the best-seller lists, and reviewers, such as the writer for the *Atlantic Monthly*, opined that it was a "book to be read twice a year by young and old, as long as life lasts." The writer for London's *Times Literary Supplement* compared Mencken to Mark Twain in ways that had to please the former: "it is no accident that this book . . . should exude a Mark-Twainish robustness, even earthiness." *Happy Days* in the end lacked the "magic" of *Huckleberry Finn*, "but it may well stand on the same shelf." Terry Teachout likely put it best when he wrote that *Happy Days* is "unsentimentally affectionate" and a "masterpiece of pure style, offering those readers who recoil from Mencken's politics an opportunity to wander without guilt along the long, looping arcs of [Mencken's] cun-

ningly poised sentences." So successful was *Happy Days* and so solici-
tous were the editors at the *New Yorker* for autobiographical sketches,
that Mencken devoted another volume of memoirs to his early work as
a journalist, *Newspaper Days*, published in 1941.

If the young man who had escaped the cigar business for newspaper
work had experienced obstacles because of the wider Christian society
surrounding him, Mencken's reflections on his days as a journalist did
not dig them up. He was too beguiled by the world of "normalcy" that
he encountered as a newspaperman, one that ran from presidents and
vice presidents, bishops and archbishops, movie stars and heavyweight
champions, to millionaires and "labor goons." But Mencken was not
going to turn his memoir into an excuse to recount "astounding tales
of journalistic derring-do" that dotted the landscape of reporters' auto-
biographies. Sure, he might write about the 1912 scheme to put him on
the Democratic ticket as vice president, or the offer of $30,000 by mem-
bers of Congress for him to write anti-Prohibition speeches, or even the
solicitation from an Episcopal bishop "to throw a nascent convert, female and rich, who had thrice slipped out of his hands at the very brink
of the font." Instead, what stood out in hindsight was the ordinariness
and folly of a trade that gave him a front-row seat at the world's stage
but was hardly cut out to improve the race.

In the newsroom and editorial offices, he did not have to worry
about too much sanctimony or spiritual uplift, but sometimes his duties unearthed both sides of the question of Christianity's truth. As a
reporter who covered Baltimore's city council, Mencken became acquainted with Major Richard M. Venable, a bachelor with a "belly so
vast that his waistcoat looked like a segment of balloon." Locals knew
Venable to be the local atheist, with Christianity occupying half of his
two great hates—the other was women. Mencken recalled that Venable
had a large library that consisted chiefly of works on theology that he
read "constantly" and damned "violently." So opposed to the Christian
religion was the city magistrate that he desired his body be cremated
and the ashes dumped in "any convenient ashcan." Venable left little
impression other than providing proof "that honest and competent
men could sometimes get on the public payroll." His usefulness for
proving Christianity wrong or foolish was not so obvious.

On the other side of Christian truth that Mencken remembered was
an evangelist that he had encountered during his 1900 trip to Cuba.
While awaiting return passage, Mencken ran into a Methodist mission-

ary who ran a local chapel. Mencken thought he was fit for a match with the evangelist but escaped only on a technicality:

> Being sober at the time, I resisted, and inasmuch as I was already something of an amateur theologian, and hence familiar with all the classical grips and grapples, I resisted to some effect. But I am glad to testify today after so many years, that never in this life have I gone to the mat with a tougher evangelist. He beat any Christian Scientists ever heard of, or any Presbyterian, however ferocious, or any footwash Baptist. I have been tackled in my day by virtuosi ranging from mitred abbots to the kitchen police of the Salvation Army, but never have I had to fight harder to preserve my doctrinal chastity. Over and over again the old boy got to my chin or midriff with scriptural texts that had the impact of a mule's hoof, and when he turned from upbraiding to cajolery, and began to argue that my sufferings in Hell would be upon his head, I almost threw up the sponge. Indeed, if it had not been for the audience lying in wait . . . I'd have gone down to his gospel mill with him, if only to get rid of him, but as it was I was in honor bound to resist, and in the end he gave up in despair.

Despair was the theme of another episode that Mencken recalled from his days as city editor, though in this case he was on the side (in a way) of the evangelist who had battered him so fiercely. The story involved a young woman from Red Lion, Pennsylvania, "of four-square Pennsylvania Dutch stock, and as sturdy as the cows she serviced," who had engaged in premarital sex with her beau and thought her only alternative was to join the world's oldest profession. Her reasons had to do with the moralistic novels she had been reading and the point that the authors drove home about the consequences of illicit sex. The domino theory of chastity was that once a young girl lost hers, she inevitably lived a life of promiscuity. Characters making cameo appearances in this narrative were Peebles, a Scotsman who had served twelve years in prison for killing his wife but now drove a team of horses around Baltimore and possessed a reputation for pristine honesty, and Miss Nellie d'Alembert, the owner of a brothel who stayed on the good side of journalists by acting as a source of news about city gossip (learned from customers). These were the sorts of people that initially drew Mencken into the world of journalism and that colored his own outlook about the follies of reformers and believers.

But as much as he was willing to overlook the peccadilloes of fellow travelers, Mencken was not content to let the girl from Red Lion become a professional harlot. When Nellie notified him about the girl, Mencken first dispatched his Sunday editor. But the latter wanted Mencken to hear the story also. After hearing Nellie describe the girl's reasons for coming to Baltimore, Mencken's newspaper colleague explained that the old penalties for moral lapses were no longer in place and that the stories she had read were so dated that even "a newspaper editorial writer [would] cough and scratch himself" while reading one. "The world is much more humane than it used to be," he explained. "Just as it no longer burns men for heresy or women for witchcraft, so it has ceased to condemn girls to lives of shame and death in the gutter for the trivial dereliction you acknowledge." The advice from the sage counsel of Baltimore's journalists was for the girl to return home, make up an excuse to her father for her mysterious disappearance, take her lover to their pastor, and join the young man "in indissoluble love." The plan brought Nellie to tears. Mencken and his colleague chipped in for the girl's return train fare. The owner of the bordello contributed a boxed lunch, and Peebles, the buggy driver, returned the girl from Pennsylvania to the train station. The story acquired legendary status among the local cops and even prompted the Sunday newspaper editor, according to Mencken, to write up the incident as a screenplay, one the censors "always vetoed." But Mencken never heard more about the girl from Red Lion who lived on only in his recorded memories.

Those recollections also included an unusual bit of service that Mencken provided to a Baptist congregation on the eastern shore of the Chesapeake Bay in Virginia. This good deed emerged from his memories about difficulties he endured while trying to manage the "fantastic Crocodilidae," also known as newspaper artists. These "jitney Dürers" had certain traits that were certain to annoy editors. They invariably looked down on journalists as philistines "almost comparable to bartenders or policemen." When fires broke out and editors needed "illustrative art," artists displayed a "supernatural talent for getting out of the way." They also had a knack for sneaking something scandalous at the last moment into artwork approved for publication, "to the delight . . . of every soul in town save what we then called the Moral Element." For all of their unreliability, one artist did come to Mencken's aid when a Baptist pastor and former acquaintance solicited help in producing a mural for a new church that would adorn the baptismal tank. Mencken remembered one particular illustrator whom he had fired—for reasons unremembered—and who left the newspaper to paint sideshow fronts for a circus. The image that the artist produced was "the most splendiferous work of ecclesiastical art since the days of Michelangelo":

> On a canvas fifteen feet high and nearly forty feet long the artist shot the whole works, from the Creation as described in Genesis I to the revolting events set forth in Revelation XIII. Noah was there with his ark, and so was Solomon in all his glory. No less than ten New Testament miracles were depicted in detail, with the one at Cana given the natural place of honor. . . . The Tower of Babel was made so high that it bled out of the top of the painting, and there were three separate views of Jerusalem. The sky showed a dozen rainbows, and as many flashes of lightning, and from a very red Red Sea in the foreground was thrust the maw of Jonah's whale, with Jonah himself shinning out of it to join Moses and the children of Israel on the beach.

Properly adorned, the church became a stop for Baptist pilgrims from as far away as Cleveland, Tennessee, and Gainesville, Florida, and "it wrecked all the other evangelical filling-stations of the lower Atlantic littoral" as locals transferred their allegiance to the congregation with the spectacular baptismal tank.

As comical as the practices of believers may have appeared, Mencken's reactions, even after a life of opposition, showed good-natured bemusement. Whether chronicling cops who "laughed at reformers" and knew that most women "who sold their persons" wound up at the "altar of God" with better husbands than they would have gotten had they "kept their virtue," or comparing Sunday school superintendents' capacity for beer to that of expert drinkers like the Baltimore *Herald*'s printer, a man named Bill, Mencken let the religious and moral tide of everyday life wash over him. His disarming style managed to reduce even the most serious of religious claims to ordinary foibles of human existence, such as his recollection of a Methodist pastor who believed that "Jews, unless they consented to be baptized, would all go to Hell." The minister established a mission in one of the city's poor neighborhoods, was unsuccessful with adults, but attracted boys to his services "by showing them magic-lantern pictures of the Buffalo Bill country and the Holy Land." Outraged Jewish parents, who knew "it was a mortal sin in those days for an orthodox Jew to enter a *Goy Schul*," complained to the police district captain, who in turn looked for a plausible charge to bring against the evangelist. The cop eventually detained the pastor for "disorderly conduct, making loud and unseemly noises, and disturbing religious worship." The police knew the charges would not stick, but the tactic worked because "talk of the penitentiary" so scared the Methodist that "he shut down his mission forthwith, and left the Jews to their post-mortem sufferings." Incidents like this still occur in the United States—consider evangelists among Muslim Americans—but few writers or observers see as well as Mencken did how ordinary a situation ripe with conflict was.

Even when Mencken proceeded to the third installment of his memoirs, *Heathen Days*, a title that suggested an open identification with unbelief, he was loath, even as an older man prone to bitterness, to settle scores. This installment of memories was the least unified of the three *Days* books. With several essays left over from *Newspaper Days*, Mencken wondered about putting them in another volume of memoirs. Again, Harold Ross encouraged him to go forward. During the war years of 1941 and 1942 Mencken added chapters, and the result was another book of reminiscences that enjoyed a warm reception. *Heathen Days* sold close to ten thousand copies in its first year of publication. Mencken himself admitted in the preface that the book's contents were "random." But even as he explained that this book was going to be his last stroll down memory lane, he also admitted that he had lived a charmed life: "Like any other man I have had my disasters and my miseries, and like any other author I have suffered from recurrent depressions and despairs, but taking one year with another I have had a fine time of it in this vale of sorrow, and no call to envy any man." The knack for such contentment was to stick "always" to what you could do "with reasonable comfort" and so avoid "begrudging the other man his competence." Self-awareness even pushed Mencken to wax philosophical. The output of memoirs had led him to think that "every man given over professionally to hearing and seeing things ought to be allowed two lives—one to hear and see and the other to set down what he has heard and seen." Since he could not be two selves, Mencken settled for alternating between seeing and hearing and writing about the acquisition of sights and sounds.

Once again, Mencken could not help but notice the Christian circumstances that had surrounded him. Those aspects of American society were generally pleasant and amusing, hardly rising to the level of annoyance. Part of his self-chosen identity as a heathen was his liberation from the moral uplift of the local YMCA. His involvement with the Y had occurred when he was fourteen and his father, though atheistic, turned once again to the institutions of Protestantism for help with his son in nonspiritual matters. As a teenager Mencken was becoming a bookworm and acquiring a posture that went with reading—"round-shouldered." To cure his "scholarly stoop," the elder Mencken saw the YMCA's "wooden horse and flying rings" as a quick remedy. What rescued the boy was the unwelcome presence of an older teen who gathered other boys around him as he read platitudinous pieties from one of the popular manuals of virtue—with lines like "It is never too late to mend." Mencken at first thought the lad ironical but discovered that the "poor ass" was "enchanted" and wanted to "spread his joy." Of all Mencken's recollections about religion in his life, his account of this "pimply, officious fellow" turned him once for all:

> It was easy to recognize in him the anti-social animus of a born evangelist, but there was also something else—a kind of voluptuous delight in the shabby and preposterous, a perverted aestheticism like that of a latter-day movie or radio fan, a wild will to roll in and snuffle balderdash as a cat rolls in and snuffles catnip. I was, as I have said, less than fifteen years old, but I had already got an overdose of such blah in the McGuffey Readers and penmanship copybooks of the time.

Moralism was one thing, but a promise of forgiveness was something that fascinated Mencken, at least in his accounts about death row and the spiritual counsel of African American pastors to convicts (since "the great majority of culprits hanged below the Mason and Dixon Line were of that great race"). The challenge that awaited these "smart and snappy fellows" was to convince a black man, "taken red-handed in some brutal and deliberate atrocity, usually freely admitted," that he would escape the fires of hell and "become an angel in Heaven, white in color and of the highest repute." Every convict knew, having listened to preachers his entire life, that the wages of sin was death and eternal damnation. "But now, having yielded the last measure of devotion to those propensities, he was asked to believe that he would escape Hell altogether, and even meet with what amounted to special handling in Heaven." Mencken observed that the convicts struggled with this irrationality for months, if only because it seemed to turn hell into a myth and upset the whole system of cosmic justice. But invariably the preachers were successful, even though Mencken could not explain their answers "with definiteness" after having listened to their explanations "for hours." The outcome of such pastoral care was a "client" who "still retained his full faith in Hell, along with the utmost confidence in its system of justice," and yet was "completely convinced that he would escape its fires." In fact, Mencken observed convicts-turned-converts who approached the gallows "jauntily as if they were going to the barbershop" thanks to a certain confidence that they would, "like a butterfly from a caterpillar . . . emerge a celestial creature with large, snowy wings and a complexion to match that of any white lady in the land."

When Mencken recalled his trips to lands venerated by the faithful, he was no less charmed and amused by the disparity between holy aspirations and ordinary life. During his 1914 trip to Rome, Mencken had a formal meeting with Pope Pius X. It was not an appointment he had arranged but an experience he merited by speaking German. After a tour of Saint Peter's Basilica, Mencken and his fellow tourists were deciding on a spot for lunch when they heard a German priest hectoring a group of pilgrims, about to be received by the pope, about Vatican etiquette:

> Over and over again he explained to them the stage management of a papal audience, and cautioned them to behave in a seemly and Christian manner. They would be lined up on their knees . . . and his Holiness would walk down the line, blessing them as he went and offering them his ring to kiss. Under no circumstances were they to attempt to kiss his hand, but only the ring. "Nicht die Hand!" he kept on repeating. "Kuesst den Ring!" . . . What a scandal it would be . . . if the illustrious Pope of Rome, the spiritual father of the whole universe, were exposed in his own almost sacred person to the lewd osculation of the vulgar!

With his homily complete, the Germans gathered to enter the Vatican, and Mencken and his friends decided, "Why not, indeed?" The immediate effect was disappointing:

> I expected to see a large hall elegantly turned out, with maybe a couple of pictures by Raphael or Leonardo on its walls, but the priest actually led us into a series of modest rooms that looked like parlors

in a bourgeois home . . . arranged *en suite*, and the Pope . . . would traverse them one after another.

When the order came to kneel, Mencken and his companions did but worried about being detected by the Swiss Guards. What impressed Mencken about Pius X was his frailty: "He looked immensely old as he passed so slowly before us, and pretty well worn out. But he walked without help, and in less than two minutes he was gone." Mencken speculated that his career had taken its toll on the pope:

> He had been Pope, by now for eleven years, and was close to eighty years old. A man of deep piety and simple tastes, he had resisted, back in 1880, an effort to make him Bishop of Treviso, but a few years later he had been caught by the cogs of the Roman escalator and by 1893 he was the Cardinal and Patriarch of Venice and ten years later he was Pope. His reign, alas, had not been any too peaceful: there had been struggles with France, turmoils among the Italian bishops, and all sorts of vexatious disputes.

Mencken's visit was in May. The assassination that began World War I came on August 2, 1914. By August 20 Pope Pius was dead. Mencken and his friends managed to escape through the Sistine Chapel, which was empty, and in which they hid for ten minutes before finding a door that led outside the Vatican.

Back among a larger party of American tourists, Mencken had trouble convincing the devout Roman Catholics of his audience with the pope. But when he did, they became indignant and interpreted the uninvited and unscheduled visit as "an insult to the Pope" and a "carnal and blasphemous attack upon the Holy Church itself." Some even wondered if Protestants should be barred from the capital of Christendom. Mencken defended his honor by noting that Teddy Roosevelt, William Jennings Bryan, and Thomas Jefferson had all visited the pope. Over time the argument cooled and the discussion returned to "the discomforts of boiled shirts and long sleeves in hot weather."

Twenty years later Mencken made a pilgrimage to Jerusalem, and by then, at least if he had accurately calibrated his memories, his skepticism about holy artifacts had matured. At the Church of the Holy Sepulchre, for instance, he encountered the hole, ten-by-twenty-by-twelve feet, where Jesus was buried. Mencken was underwhelmed. "Obviously enough, at least to anyone familiar with John xix, 41, as I was, it was bogus; indeed it was bogus by the Synoptic Gospels also, for unless Joseph of Arimathea was a reincarnation of Samson no one could imagine him rolling a stone large enough to close it." Still, Mencken remained quiet and paid his respects to the Coptic priest monitoring the crowd. In Bethlehem Mencken was annoyed by the small opening at one end to the Church of the Nativity, and even more so upon learning that the door at the rear of the church was large enough "to let in a Fifth avenue bus." He heard that the reason for bringing pilgrims in through a "hole in the wall" that forced the faithful "to bend almost double," was "to make the pious sweat a bit, lest pride consume them." But again, Mencken had trouble squaring "the elaborate marble grotto" in the church "with the manger described in Luke ii, 7, 12, and 16." The piece of Holy Land sightseeing that made the deepest impression was a visit to the battlefield of Armageddon:

> Here the Hittites met the Egyptians, the Egyptians met the Persians, the Persians met the Greeks, and the Jews were slaughtered by one and all. . . . There is probably no more likely battlefield on earth; it seems to have been made for marching and counter-marching of infantry, and dashing cavalry charges. As we rolled over it, I could not help thinking of the hundreds of thousands of miserable John Does who had watered it, over so many ages, with their blood.

Mencken could also not resist the thought of what Americans would do with such a battlefield:

> [I]t would be dotted with hideous monuments to the Fifth Pennsylvania and the Tenth Wisconsin, and there would be guides to carry tourists over it, and plenty of hot-dog and Coca-Cola stands to stoke them. But at Armageddon I couldn't find so much as a marker or a flag.

Ironically enough, Mencken may have displayed more annoyance with American customs overseas than at home. His chapter on Prohibition overstated its inconvenience for obvious effect: "It seemed almost a geological epoch while it was going on, and the human suffering that it entailed must have been a fair match for that of the Black Death or the Thirty Years War." Mencken himself escaped the torments of the "noble experiment" by brewing his own beer. He even claimed to be the "first man south of the Mason and Dixon line" to make a home brew. He also distributed his recipe "on a sort of chain-letter plan," but only to those trustworthy, "anyone save a few abandoned Methodists, Baptists, and Presbyterians." Mencken explained that he was not dependent on his own brewing skills for the dozen or so years of dryness. Among the incidents of discovering speakeasies, he recalled his 1924 visit to Bethlehem, Pennsylvania, with Alfred Knopf, for the annual Bach festival. Mencken claimed that every musicologist knew that "the divine music of Johann Sebastian cannot be digested without the aid of its natural solvent." But to his surprise and distress, none of the local establishments had any beer on tap. While in the process of boarding a train to New Jersey, where a friend would escort Mencken and Knopf to a tavern, they heard from a taxi driver about a place that served beer in Bethlehem. The hitch was gaining the confidence of the doorman. He needed to know that the two guests were not Prohibition agents in disguise. Nothing was persuasive until Mencken remembered that he had the piano score for the Mass in B Minor under his arm. Once inside, the Bach enthusiasts had five steins of beer between them (three for Mencken) and two sandwiches. The bill—sixty-five cents total—left more of an impression on Mencken than the pilsner's quality.

Mencken's good-natured recollections of Protestantism's annoyance were even evident in his chapter on the Scopes trial. Here he tried to correct several impressions that lingered from the summer of 1925. The first was that Mencken so offended the residents of Dayton that they "formed a posse and ran [him] out of town." This had become such a part of Scopes folklore that some of the "yahoos" themselves still claimed to "have taken pot shots" at Mencken as he ran from town. In fact, Mencken recalled only one Daytonian who objected to his reporting, and even then "he was extremely polite." Mencken also wondered, if he had been so offensive, why the founders of "Bryan 'Fundamentalist' University" had invited him to attend its "consecration" in 1926. The only visitors for the trial who "suffered any menace to their lives and limbs" were Clarence Darrow, a reporter for the Hearst papers, a YMCA secretary, and an itinerant atheist. The journalist's brush with the law came when he outfoxed the judge by reporting that the move to quash the indictment would be defeated before the official word was announced. He escaped jail time through the "magnificent forensic powers" of Richard J. Beamish, a reporter from the *Philadelphia Inquirer*.

The atheist's offense was to prove that humans were similar to apes by carrying around a "mangy chimpanzee." The YMCA secretary suffered the humiliation of being arrested thanks to a story that Mencken and a colleague had circulated, through a local evangelist, that a report from Cincinnati included word that communists were planning to travel to Dayton to assassinate Bryan. The news reached the police, who dispatched a unit to meet the next train from Cincinnati. The only passenger that disembarked the passenger cars was the YMCA worker, who "looked innocent enough." But the cops took no chances and "rushed him to the hoosegow." With Mencken's help, the local evangelist convinced the police that the YMCA worker was just that, not a Bolshevik.

In Darrow's case, the locals obviously "had no taste" for someone who "derided the Good Book." Still, they felt no obligation to punish him because they were confident that God would. As a result, "they kept away from him, for they didn't want to be present when the lightnings from Heaven began to fall." Darrow's treatment was the opposite of that of Bryan, who was "the star of the show." The prosecutor always had a large following because he liked country people and "he was as thoroughly soaked in the Holy Scriptures as many another aspirant to the Presidency has been in alcohol." Even so, Mencken refused to unload another round of calumny on Bryan. He simply acknowledged that many in Dayton and across the United States believed Bryan "no longer merely human" but had "lifted himself to some level or other of the celestial angels, archangels, principalities, powers, virtues, dominations, thrones, cherubim and seraphim." In fact, no one would have been surprised "if he had suddenly begun to perform miracles." Perhaps Mencken's obituary from 1925 had emptied him of the grudge he had held against the Great Commoner since 1900.

Mencken was not finished with Bryan, however. The final chapter in *Heathen Days* included reminiscences of four American politicians, "Beaters of Breasts," who gained a hearing thanks in large measure to Christianity. Bryan was one of them. The others were Al Smith, Gerald L. K. Smith, and Father Charles E. Coughlin. On Bryan Mencken almost sounded sheepish about his 1925 obituary:

> After the death of William Jennings Bryan, in 1926 [*sic*], I printed an estimate of his life and public services which dismissed him as a quack pure and unadulterated, but in the years since I have come to wonder if that was really just. When, under the prodding of Clarence

Darrow, he made his immortal declaration that man is not a mammal, it seemed to me to be a mere bravura piece by a quack sure that his customers would take anything. But I am now more than half convinced that Jennings really believed it, just as he believed that Jonah swallowed the whale. . . . I find myself convinced, nevertheless, that his support of the Good Book against Darwin and company was quite sincere—that is, as sincerity runs among politicoes.

Of the other "political mountebanks," Al Smith was the "most amusing" and "most attractive." The New York governor's "most effective harangues . . . were probably more or less unintelligible to himself." But he knew his audience, that crowds in Tennessee, or Michigan, or Missouri did not differ "more than four per cent from a New York crowd," and so he delivered "all the old stuff," and it "went down again with a roar." Compared to Bryan, as an orator Smith was a "BB shot to a twelve inch-shell," but neither could match Gerald L. K. Smith:

> I have heard all the really first-chop American breast-beaters since 1900, and included among them have been not only the statesmen but also the divine, for example, Sam Jones, Gipsy Smith, Father Coughlin and Billy Sunday, but among them all I have encountered none worthy of being put in the same species or even in the same genus, as Gerald. His own early training was gained at the sacred desk but in maturity he switched to the hustings, so that he now has a double grip upon the diaphragms and short hairs of the *Anthropoidea.* Add to these advantages of nurture the natural gifts of an imposing person, a flashing eye, a hairy chest, a rubescent complexion, large fists, a voice both loud and mellow, terrifying and reassuring *sforzando* and *pizzicato*, and finally an unearthly capacity for distending the superficial blood-vessels of his temple and neck, as if they were biceps—and you have the makings of a boob-bumper worth going miles to see and hear, then worth writing home about.

Coughlin, in comparison, was "a much inferior performer," good for the radio but ineffective "face to face." Mencken had heard that the priest was experimenting with a "mike fixed to his shoulders" so that he could "gesture normally without any risk of roaring futilely into space."

And with that, Mencken concluded his last set of memoirs to appear while he lived. Readers hoping for reflections on his career must have been disappointed by the conclusion. But for a man who devoted many of his waking moments to words, remarks about the rhetorical abilities of the nation's leading orators were entirely fitting. For over forty years Mencken had concocted and dissected the American language in most of its expressions. From the slang of the street that had absorbed his attention as a young reporter, to the exhortations of inspired preachers, to his prolonged study of the American usage of English, to his analysis of the upper reaches of the nation's letters, Mencken lived for language. The person using words did not matter as much as the actual usage. Consequently, his estimate of language did not depend on whether a speaker or writer were religious or paraded foolish ideas. Even in the case of Bryan, a person who brought out the worst in Mencken almost as much as Stuart Sherman, the Illinois professor who defended the Puritans, Mencken still listened and found the words enlivening, even exhilarating. Among American writers of the first half of the twentieth century, Mencken was arguably one of the greatest—he was certainly unique. Yet, his own high standards and sense of literary craftsmanship did not lead him to regard himself as a linguistic guardian. That at the close of his memoirs Mencken acknowledged the genius of reformers and evangelists who put the language to compelling effect was not odd but appropriate. His own immersion in language swamped his incredulity over the doctrines or morals for which his Christian fellow Americans used their speech.

More Tragic Than Comic

Mencken's *Days* books were partly responsible for a recovery of his reputation, even though privately the recognition that his life, friends, and work were coming to an end haunted him. In 1941 he retired from work at the *Sunpapers* as an editor (he was still on the board of directors), thanks in part to disagreements again over United States involvement in a war against Germany. But as was his wont, Mencken kept busy with any number of writing and editing projects. In 1941 Knopf published his 1,300-page compilation, *New Dictionary of Quotations*, a massive work that ran to more than 800,000 words and 40,000 separate quotations.[1]

---

1. Trying to detect Mencken's biases in his selection of quotations is difficult. Here is a sample:

Two years later he completed a supplement to *The American Language*, a volume that updated his fellow countrymen's usage since 1936; it ran to more than 700 pages and 350,000 words. He also had ideas for another ten books. Mencken's ongoing vigor and activity led him to comment that he was "in an almost ideal situation for an aging man." He did whatever he wanted, dropped in on old newspaper colleagues "to gossip," wrote without constraint on any subject, and had a peaceful domestic situation with "two good servants" who made "the best lunches I ever get in Baltimore." But so much reminiscing also aroused the specter of gloom. His entries in his diary about his family during holidays showed greater awareness of decline than usual. Meanwhile, the anniversary of Sara's death could summon up despair. In 1942 he admitted that he faced "hard years" without his wife, "even supposing that I live at all." Mencken's sense of the end of things extended to the Menckens more generally. "In a few years," he wrote, "the Mencken family will be at an end." He wondered if he would have had an easier life in Germany, and concluded that he still found "it impossible to fit myself into the accepted patterns of American life and thought." He confessed that he remained "a foreigner."

Of the affairs that gave Mencken's dark soul solace, his work had to be high on the list. Not only was he a consistently diligent author, editor, reader, and correspondent, but Mencken's work also afforded him a measure of material comfort that kept him from adding worries about finances to the thoughts that hounded his awareness of death's proximity. For instance, his income during the war years of 1941 and 1942 was $23,500 per annum. He estimated in 1943 that his net worth was $185,000, and this did not include assets such as life insurance, book rights, and stock in the *Sunpapers* and Alfred A. Knopf, Inc. To top off his prosperity, in 1945 Mencken received the largest six-month royalty payment of his career—$14,547, chiefly for *The American Language* supplement. In his preface to *Happy Days*, Mencken wrote that

---

"I believe the Bible as it is." William Jennings Bryan, p. 102.

"The Bible only is the religion of Protestants." William Chillingworth, p. 100.

"I am a Catholic, but not a papist." Daniel O'Connell, p. 147.

"The Catholic religion is the only one that is true." Pope Leo XIII, p. 146.

"Light for all." Motto of the *Baltimore Sun*, p. 850.

"I read but one newspaper and that . . . more for its advertisements than its news." Thomas Jefferson, p. 850.

"It is a newspaper's duty to print the news, and raise hell." Wilbur F. Story, p. 851.

he had entered the world "a larva of the comfortable and complacent bourgeoisie." Nothing he had done threatened his place within "that great order of mankind." If anything, his status was so secure that not even another world war could shake it.

Still, money did not matter (though earning it did) as much as people. He continued to maintain friendships near and far. When in New York City he associated with friends and colleagues in the publishing world—Harold Ross at the *New Yorker*, Edgar Lee Masters, Sinclair Lewis—and even overcame old antagonisms with George Jean Nathan to make the former colleague a regular companion. In New York he often spent a night with Alfred and Blanche Knopf at their suburban home in Purchase, where Mencken gave free marriage counseling. Women were also a prominent part in Mencken's social life. As much as he mourned the loss of Sara, he resumed a corresponding relationship with Aileen Pringle and encouraged her marriage in 1944 to his old friend Jim Cain. His admission to Pringle that he had not "looked at a gal for years" may have been true, but it did not work the other way. A number of women pursued him, including Clare Leighton, an Englishwoman who visited Baltimore with letters of introduction. At first, she thought Mencken looked like "an English pork butcher or an old-time barber." Over time his charms broke through and she judged Mencken "the most sentimental of creatures." Another woman who attracted his affections and minor intimacies was Marcella du Pont, the wife of Alfred du Pont. Mencken was a regular at the du Ponts' homes in Delaware and Washington, DC, and accompanied Marcella, who had remarkable independence from her husband, on jaunts to visit with mutual friends. Fred Hobson suggests that Marcella would have liked to leave Alfred for Mencken—the du Ponts were eventually divorced. But Mencken enjoyed the relationship as it was—with a pretty, younger, charming woman who could light up a room but without the challenges of marriage.

Women may have intrigued Mencken, but the men with whom he played music were arguably his closest companions. As early as 1903 he began to play serious music—Mencken on the piano—in off-hours with newspaper associates and city residents; Emmanuel Daniel, a writer at the *Herald*, and Albert Hildebrandt, a violin maker, were his first musical comrades. Gradually this group absorbed others who gathered to perform symphonic music as a form of socializing. They took the name Saturday Night Club, even though the group met originally on weeknights. High-minded though this mix of amateur and professional musicians was (it included members of the Baltimore Symphony and teachers at the Peabody Conservatory of Music as well as the US Naval Academy's bandmaster), its members also consumed large quantities of food and beer. In *Heathen Days*, Mencken described a meeting in 1922 when one of the club's members had the idea to perform all of Beethoven's symphonies (minus the Ninth, "because the club's singing section, at the time, lacked castrati") in one evening:

> The First Symphony was child's play to us, and we turned it off in record time, with a pause of only ten minutes afterward. By six o'clock we had also finished the Second, and then we stopped for cocktails and dinner. After dinner there was some relaxation, and we dallied a bit with some excellent malt liquor, so that it was eight o'clock before we tackled the Eroica. It began so badly that we played the first movement twice, but after that it picked up momentum, and by 9:30 we had finished it. Then we paused again, this time for sandwiches, a walk in the woods—it was a lovely moonlit night—and another resort to the malt, but at 11:30 or maybe a little later we were back in the trenches, and the Fourth was begun. For some reason or other it went even worse than the Eroica . . . so we decided to knock off for an hour and find out what the malt had to offer in the way of encouragement.

Over the next four hours, as the club continued to struggle through Beethoven's symphonies and members left quietly, survivors started the Seventh. What happened next is a matter of dispute. The official account claimed that performers finished all eight symphonies in the light of the next morning. The other story has it that they started the Seventh, "blew up in the middle," and proceeded to the Eighth, where again the remaining three performers "blew up" before being "chased out by our host, assisted by his hunting dogs."

Meeting as he did with these fellows once a week for four decades, Mencken established a group that could sustain him as a bachelor and then a widower. His closest friends in Baltimore were invariably linked to the Saturday Night Club. He regularly had lunch with Hildebrandt and Heinrich Buchholz, the director of a publishing company that produced educational material. He shared four-hand piano duties with Max Broedel, an anatomical artist at Johns Hopkins. He was also fond of Carl Schon, a local craftsman, and Willie Woolcott, brother of Alexander Woolcott, the *New York Herald* drama critic. Fred Hobson observes that the qualities Mencken most appreciated in his friends were not "brilliance and flamboyance" but "steadiness, modesty, generosity, and humor." Mencken described Hildebrandt as the happiest man he had ever known. Schon was a "man of great charm . . . and courtly manners." Woolcott had "less malice" and "more charm" than anyone Mencken knew. Woolcott himself did not play an instrument. He participated in the Saturday Night Club as an audience member. Food, drink, and friendship were obvious additional attractions for listening to music that at times must have sounded rough. Louis Cheslock, a regular and longtime member who taught at Peabody, once observed of Mencken's performances that his "humming as he plays [the piano] sounds like the groaning man in agony who tried to stifle the sounds to keep face." (Had Mencken lived to hear recordings of Glenn Gould, he may have taken that as a compliment.) The loss of several of these friends during World War II was another stage in Mencken's reckoning with mortality. Raymond Pearl's and Max Broedel's deaths were "stupendous" blows. Of Broedel Mencken wrote, "I had sat beside Max every Saturday night for exactly thirty years" and "we were naturally on the most intimate terms."

If human companionship was a great solace to Mencken's perseverance, the disappointments that came from family added to his sense of declension. His survey of his life also led him to assess his family and their progress in the United States. His five cousins, children of his uncle Henry, had suffered unhappy fates. The three daughters either suffered from hard marriages or had made a "dreadful mess" of their lives; that two of them had married Roman Catholics was cause for bewilderment. The two male cousins had not done much better. One married a Seventh-Day Adventist; the other moved West to learn mining and died in a hunting accident. His family in Ohio also provided no consolation. The Almroths, the ones he had visited at the close of *Happy Days*, had lost the family farm, and his cousin, "the lovely Mary of 1891," had led "a hard and dismal life." Even closer to home among the Baltimore wing of the family, Mencken's niece Virginia proved to be a disappointment. He approved of her wedding to a prosperous Pennsylvanian and paid for the proceedings. But she was generally distant from her uncle and lacked the professional ambition that he thought she should have had given her breeding and advantages.

That Germany was in the process of losing all its former glory only added to Mencken's gloom. He rarely spoke about Hitler or Germany's execution of the war, perhaps because it was too painful. Although the war rarely affected his routines or writing projects, it was likely responsible for many of Mencken's harsh judgments of friends and family. Germany had been a source of his sense of superiority—a civilized nation of superior men—that provided a world historical perch from which Mencken could look down on Anglo-American moralism and progressivism. But to contemplate Germany's disgrace, either in defeat or owing to its contemporary enormities, was to lose his privileged standing. Only occasionally did the war grant him a chance to preen, such as after the atomic bomb was dropped on Hiroshima, when Mencken opined that the act "crowns our Christian civilization." He added that "the firing of Japanese women and children was specifically ordained by our Redeemer." Such cynicism let up once the war was over. For several years after the Allies' victory he sent care packages to distant relatives and friends in Germany, and a few in England. One of Mencken's cousins wrote to him that his assistance was solely responsible for her survival.

Such expressions of gratitude may have helped to offset Mencken's somber mood, but the process of remembering his life and accomplishments produced more sorrow than joy. The irony should have been apparent even to Mencken himself. A trilogy of books, perhaps his best sustained writing, had restored Mencken's reputation as one of the nation's literary treasures. *Life* magazine produced a cover story on him that speculated that "something in the air of this second postwar period" had reinvigorated "the appeal of the Sage of Baltimore." Biographers like Edgar Kemler and William Manchester also began to arrive at Mencken's West Baltimore home to seek his assistance and approval for their assessments. But that same set of memoirs was also responsible for a host of reflections on the end of life. One of the greatest burdens was the thought of Sara's passing, a person whom he esteemed and by whom he marked his own quality of life. In his diary for August 27, 1942, Mencken wrote:

> Today is the twelfth anniversary of my marriage to Sara. She is now dead for more than seven years, and she begins inevitably to recede into the shadows. Never a day passes that I do not think of her, but my life has been reorganized to do without her, and so it will continue to the end. Despite her frequent illnesses, and the cruel anxieties that

went with them, my scant five years with her were completely happy, and I look back upon them with the utmost satisfaction. But sometimes I wonder if her death wasn't for the best. If she had lived longer it would have been as an invalid, uncomfortable and unhappy. When she died I was still in full vigor, but a year later I began to break up, and the spectacle would have given her dreadful distress.

Mencken remained unwilling to consider the consolations that faith or an afterlife might bring. But as an older man, his refusal of religion's comforts stemmed not from the cockiness or sense of superiority that he had cultivated while making his mark as an author. Instead, his unbelief was simply who he was. As he explained to Aileen Pringle in 1940 as a reason for not pursuing romance, "you have invented a fellow who doesn't exist, and maybe never could exist. . . . I only wish he were real." Mencken's unbelief was genuine, but he did not appear to consider it heroic.

CHAPTER TEN

What Could Be More Preposterous Than Keeping Alive?

If Mencken needed reasons for contemplating suicide, the circumstances of his last two decades provided many. His most powerful reflections on the subject came in his late forties and appeared in *Prejudices: Sixth Series* (1927); this was a time when he was doing battle with censors and fighting off prospective designing women. Even so, despite the energy he still possessed and the ambition that fueled him, Mencken was sufficiently self-aware to understand where agnosticism led. If Nietzsche was right, if immortality were an illusion, if religion were simply a function of humanity's immaturity, and if morality were a convenience, then why go on? Mencken might have answered in a manner similar to his response to questions about why go on living in the United States when the place was filled with a people that constituted "the most timorous, sniveling, poltroonish, ignominious mob of serfs and goose-steppers ever gathered under one flag in Christendom since the end of the Middle Ages." He explained that he lived in America for the same reason that people went to zoos.

Here the general average of intelligence, of knowledge, of competence, of integrity, of self-respect, of honor is so low that any man who knows his trade, does not fear ghosts, has read fifty good books, and practices the common decencies stands out as brilliantly as a wart on a bald head, and is thrown willy-nilly into a meager and exclusive aristocracy. And here, more than anywhere else that I know of or have heard of, the daily panorama of human existence, of private and communal folly—the unending procession of governmental extortions and chicaneries, of commercial brigandages and throat-slittings, of

225

theological buffooneries, of aesthetic ribaldries, of legal swindles and harlotries, of miscellaneous rogueries, villainies, imbecilities, grotesqueries, and extravagances—is so inordinately gross and preposterous, so perfectly brought up to the highest conceivable amperage, so steadily enriched with an almost fabulous daring and originality, that only the man who was born with a petrified diaphragm can fail to laugh himself to sleep every night, and to wake every morning with all the eager, unflagging expectation of a Sunday-school superintendent touring the Paris peep-shows.

But staying alive in the face of cosmic futility was a different question from deciding whether to live in the United States or join the nation's literary exiles in Paris or London. In his mid–1920s' reflections on mortality, Mencken asked, "What could be more logical than suicide? What could be more preposterous than keeping alive?" In fact, people had "no more intelligible reason for hanging on than a cow has for mooing." The human imagination might conceive of death as "dreadful" and "grotesque," but suicide was much more likely to be messy than natural death. But with the aid of science, suicide could be "safe, sure, easy, and sanitary." Theological objections to self-extinction were pointless. "From the earliest days Christianity has depicted life on this earth as so sad and vain that its value is indistinguishable from that of a damn." So why go on? "[V]anity and unpleasantness are parts of the will of a Creator whose love for His creatures takes the form of torturing them." Even so, Mencken conceded that human wisdom could not do much better than Christian doctrine: "Disappointment is the lot of man. We are born in pain and die in sorrow . . . human existence is a painful futility. Out, out, brief candle!" No good reason for persisting existed, and Mencken conceded that if he knew one, he would be "sitting in a hall of crystal and gold, and people would be paying $10 a head to gape at [him] through peep-holes."

The best response Mencken could muster against the hole at the center of human life was to emulate the industrious Protestants that surrounded him. Work! Any kind of activity, in fact, was essential to distracting from life's purposelessness:

Man cannot sit still, contemplating his destiny in this world without going frantic. So he invents ways to take his mind off the horror. He works. He plays. He accumulates the preposterous nothing called property. He strives for the coy eyewink called fame. He founds a family, and spreads his curse over others. All the while the thing that moves him is simply the yearning to lose himself, to forget himself, to escape the tragi-comedy that is himself.

Mencken somehow still admitted that his life was "happy." "I work a great deal," he explained, "but working is more agreeable to me than anything else I can imagine." He even conceded that he had no "vast, overwhelming and unattainable desires." Yet his conclusion, "at the gate of senility," was that life was "a grandiose futility, and not even amusing." Work and play were merely the means of postponing "suicide for at least another day."

A decade later, Mencken might have added marriage to the list of distractions. But nothing could have prepared him for the last eight years of his life. During the summer of 1948 Mencken returned to form as a journalist and visited Philadelphia three times to cover the national political conventions. His health prevented following the Republicans for the duration, but he rebounded to take in the Democrats and the Progressives. He was hardly fit and even started to decline speaking invitations with a sense of an imminent disability. Yet his vigor throughout the summer and fall of 1948 was as impressive as he was in demand. On November 24 he had an appointment to lunch with Evelyn Waugh and William Manchester at the Maryland Club. The night before, Mencken dropped off work to his typist, Rosalind Lohrfinck. During the meeting, Mencken began to talk incoherently. Lohrfinck called Mencken's physician, Dr. Benjamin Baker, who upon his arrival determined that the patient had suffered a major stroke, the one Mencken had feared for the better part of a decade. Recollections of that night vary. Mencken's brother August later said the doctor told him that Mencken was "practically dead on arrival" at the hospital. Physicians close at hand said that Mencken's life was not in danger. Alfred Knopf said Dr. Baker told him that Mencken had suffered a stroke. Baker added, "I am sorry to say he is recovering from it." The meeting between Mencken and Waugh never happened.

The reason for Baker's regret over his patient's recovery had little to do with Mencken's lack of cooperation but everything to do with the severity of the stroke. At first, all but those closest to Mencken—his brother August and Alfred Knopf—thought the stroke was slight. A news story by the Associated Press on November 30 reported that Mencken had experienced a "small stroke" and that his condition was improving. But anyone connecting the medical dots, even the most hopeful, should have concluded otherwise. Mencken was in the hospital for a full six weeks—until January 6, 1949. Louis Cheslock, a Saturday Night Club member, was one of the first to visit. His description was telling:

> [Mencken's] first few sentences were among his best. His speech at times became quite confused and irrelevant. . . . There were flashes of his old penetrating wit and also lapses into vagaries. Almost always he called days, weeks or months "years"—being gently corrected by August. His chief complaint was about his eyes—not being able to read—but frequently referred to his eyes as his "ears"—window as "wind," alien words & stray fragmentary phrases kept cropping up despite his intense effort to steer a straight course in his thinking & speech.

For a few months after returning home, not even Mencken knew how bad his condition was. He managed to dictate some letters and tried to type some himself. He believed he would recover his full ability to read and write. But by the spring of 1949, after a trip to Florida with his brother that was meant to bring additional healing, Mencken realized the full extent of his state. He could not read or write. He described 1948 as the year he "died." As Fred Hobson observes, the irony of Mencken's situation, given the way he had described Friedrich Nietzsche at the end of his life, was breathtaking: "There he would sit day after day, receiving old friends but saying little." Like Nietzsche, Mencken's mind "never became clear enough for him to resume work, or even to read." Like Nietzsche, Mencken had to "grope for words" and struggled to remember his books. "His chief delight was in music." If Nietzsche was a "pathetic" figure as "this foe of men, gods and devils—being nursed and coddled like a little child," how much more Mencken as he sat in the parlor of 1524 Hollins Street.

Suicide returned as an option. Without work, Mencken was not the person he had been for almost five decades. His physicians recalled him saying, "My life is so hideous. . . . I believe I'd commit suicide if it weren't for my brother." Another time he said, "I don't have any children," so why "should I be kept alive"? He also communicated to friends that he wished he were dead. But once spring weather made gardening possible, Mencken found an outlet for his limited abilities. In fact,

Fred Hobson points out a poignant symmetry in Mencken's life. His poststroke work in the garden and befriending of neighborhood children—Butch and Alvin—to whom he gave candy, was a resumption of the Hollins Street gang about which Mencken had written in *Happy Days*. In warm weather he lived a boy's life, playing (actually, sorting out sticks and mulch) in the backyard and going to the local grocer. The problem, as Hobson adds, was that a remarkable life of writing, editing, and business deals had come between Mencken's existence in the alley behind 1524 Hollins Street and his current situation. He could not "return to the simpler pleasures of the boy." But in the warmer months the world behind the Mencken home offered a measure of solace.

Additional comforts came from the regular companions in his life, though part of Mencken's misery in his final years was to witness even more of them pass from the scene. He still went to the Saturday Night Club—which persisted until 1950—but only to listen. Louis Cheslock, a composer who taught at the Peabody Institute and belonged to the group, became a weekly guest in Mencken's home for lunch. But on the whole, Mencken was too embarrassed by his condition to go out or receive visitors. Women with whom he had flirted and corresponded wanted to see him, and he invariably refused. The person he saw the most was his brother August. He monitored access to Mencken even to the point of warning brother Charlie what to say to avoid upsetting the patient and threatening his fragile condition. Arguably, the greatest challenge was how to kill time. Mencken and August found only limited outlets. For one period soon after the stroke, the Mencken men went to the movies, sometimes seeing two or three in one evening. Over time the novelty of cinema wore off, and Mencken was reduced to sitting at home. August arranged for select visitors to read to Mencken when it became apparent that he would not recover his own ability to read. The list of authors included the old favorites. After going through the morning papers, readers opened the novels of Mark Twain and Joseph Conrad.

Medical treatment and the hope of recovery was another diversion from the monotony. In fact, once Mencken grew tired of movies and listening to the radio, August convinced physicians at Johns Hopkins to use Mencken for research into stroke victims. He explained, "if [Mencken] could be convinced that he was being used in part as a guinea pig and that the information derived from the work . . . was of interest and value to the medical profession . . . he would look at things in a different light." Philip Wagley was the physician who took up the challenge, and even though he was not able to do much to reverse the stroke's effects, he became a close companion to the patient, and that in turn improved Mencken's spirits. Hamilton Owens noted the change: Mencken was "no longer gloomy" but "quite philosophical." That difference could not, however, prevent the ravages of time. In the fall of 1950 Mencken suffered a major heart attack that returned him to the hospital for several months and left him in an even weaker condition. Although Mencken appreciated Wagley's attention and friendship, he began finally to have second thoughts about the powers of modern medicine. He even regretted their capacity to keep him alive. August observed that Mencken had for most of his life viewed physicians as "sacred cows" with powers to perform miracles—almost the scientific equivalent of priests. Now it looked like they could merely prolong a miserable form of life.

Despite such a weakened and despondent state, Mencken still maintained a public profile through his writings. When the stroke happened, he was in the last stages of preparing *A Mencken Chrestomathy*, a title itself that revealed Mencken's fascination with words as well as his sense of self-importance; "anthology" would not do when a collection of his out-of-print writings needed to say something different about *him*. Soon after his stroke in 1949, Mencken became aware of how incapacitated he was when he attempted to read proofs for the book. He could not and turned the task over to his assistant, Mrs. Lohrfinck. The book followed the topics he had established in *Prejudices*; he included thirty different subjects, from "Homo Sapiens" to "Sententiae." "Religion" and "Morals" were the fourth and fifth sections, with the former rivaling "Women" and "Literati" for the winner of the largest section. But even in the parts not devoted to religion, Christianity was prominent. In the "Statesmen" section was his savaging of William Jennings Bryan. In "Odd Fish" was Mencken's account of the Los Angeles evangelist Aimee Semple McPherson, along with Rudolph Valentino and Charles Joseph Bonaparte, attorney general under "Roosevelt I." In "Music" was one of Mencken's reports on his visits to Bethlehem, Pennsylvania, for the Bach festival. The book's final section, "Sententiae," included five sections, one entitled "Arcana Coelestia." It reprinted some of Mencken's finest summaries of Christian folly:

> Archbishop—A Christian ecclesiastic of a rank superior to that attained by Christ.

Christian—One who is willing to serve three Gods, but draws the line at one wife.

Creator—A comedian whose audience is afraid to laugh.

Hymn of Hate, with Coda—If I hate any class of men in this world, it is evangelical Christians, with their bellicose stupidity, their childish belief in devils, their barbarous hoofing of all beauty, dignity and decency. But even evangelical Christians I do not hate when I see their wives.

Show me a Puritan and I'll show you a son-of-a-bitch.

The book received high praise in most quarters. No one noticed that the book had been largely prepared before the stroke and that it signaled the end of Mencken's career. Some readers even thought *Chrestomathy* indicated that the author was on the mend.

Another book on which Mencken worked with his remaining powers was *Minority Report*, a collection of notes he had begun to assemble in the years before his stroke. Mencken had consulted with Alfred Knopf while collecting what Mencken himself described as a "small book of very short essays *a la* Bacon and Montaigne." It consisted of 432 different entries, the longest taking up three pages, the shortest two lines. The subjects covered were the same ones Mencken had written about over the course of his life. If *Minority Report* is representative of his interests, then the 65 separate entries on Christianity or related subjects suggest that roughly one-seventh of Mencken's writings covered religion, which might also indicate how much he thought about matters of dogma and faith. Readers of a particularly skeptical bent might applaud the ridicule that Mencken vented, and which likely resonated as much during the religious revival of the 1950s led by the likes of Billy Graham, Reinhold Niebuhr, and Fulton Sheen as those observations had during the era of Billy Sunday and William Jennings Bryan. On the one hand, Mencken debunked Christianity by saying the claim that "Christianity brought charity into the world" was false. It did not, he retorted. All Christianity and Judaism did was to convert "charity into a sort of pious racket" where philanthropists received eternal rewards for doing good. On the other hand, Mencken displayed a sensitivity to matters of faith that his skeptical fans often overlooked:

The loss of faith, to many minds, involves a stupendous upset—indeed, that upset goes so far in some cases that it results in something hard to distinguish from temporary insanity. It takes a long while for a naturally trustful person to reconcile himself to the idea that after all God will not help him. He feels like a child thrown among wolves. For this reason I have always been chary about attempting to shake religious faith. It seems to me that the gain to truth that it involves is trivial when set beside the damage to the individual. To be sure, he is also improved, but he is almost wrecked in the process.

Minority Report sold well—over twenty thousand copies in several months—and was an indication that Mencken had not lost his touch even in his enfeebled state. Ironically, his physical condition was responsible for the one literary award he accepted. Mencken was always skeptical about the prizes bestowed on writers. He had, for instance, advised Sinclair Lewis to refuse both the Pulitzer Prize and the Nobel Prize. Mencken had also criticized Theodore Dreiser for accepting an award from the Academy of Arts and Letters. Mencken believed such honors were simply political and had little to do with actual merit. But in 1950 Mencken accepted the Gold Medal for Essays and Criticism from the Academy of Arts and Letters. His secretary, Mrs. Lohrfinck, had read the letter of notification to Mencken and interpreted his reaction as an indication of "great pleasure" at the news. But Mencken had not understood the letter, nor had Mrs. Lohrfinck rightly constructed Mencken's garbled words. When Alfred Knopf saw a news story about the award and asked Mencken about it, the latter was "greatly disturbed and upset," and wanted the prize revoked. But it was too late. Mencken received it in absentia and, as Fred Hobson well observed, was "ushered into that realm of institutional respectability he had fought all his life to avoid."

By 1954 Mencken's speech had improved sufficiently—though he never recovered the ability to read or write—to grant interviews. He had his last public appearances through reporters such as William Manchester and R. P. Harriss, who interviewed him for the *Baltimore Sun* and *Gardens, Houses and People*. Mencken spoke about current events and gave passing marks to Truman and Eisenhower. He said little about his own condition but did indicate that he wished "it were all over" and expressed frustration that he had not written "all I wanted." His most candid assessment of his condition for the last years of his life came four years after his stroke when physicians asked him for it and he dictated his response to Mrs. Lohrfinck:

> My description is now so bad that it is completely impossible for me to talk. When I start on a subject I lose it very quickly and in a little while it is gone altogether. It is not general to most people that I am so difficult. They imagine that I can understand what everybody says, but actually I see very little and it doesn't last any time. My whole time is half dead. I am like a man who is half awake. I don't wake up sometimes for an hour. When I am working on stuff here I do nothing whatever and think of nothing whatsoever. My mind is completely dead. . . .
>
> My hope is that I'll go very quickly, because this thing is something awful. I feel all the time rotten. If anyone talks to me I am pretty well done. Oh, well, what the hell! I don't give a damn. I can't see anything at all, you see. Everything is bad. I am going to hell. I'll never finish this job. I can't talk about my illness and I can't think of it in detail. It just doesn't come to my mind. I don't know what I am talking about. It is really an outrage to be sick like this. I should die and get it done with.

It took four more years for Mencken to have his wish granted. On January 28, 1956, a Saturday, he spent the afternoon listening to the Metropolitan Opera's matinee broadcast of Wagner's *Meistersinger*. After dinner Louis Cheslock stopped by, and while Mencken downed three martinis and discussed the release of *Minority Report*, he complained about chest pains. He told Cheslock, "this is the last time you'll see me." He went to bed earlier than usual—at 9:00 p.m.—and listened to more music on the radio, his alternate to bedtime reading. The next morning at 8:30 Mencken's orderly found him still in bed. When physicians arrived at 10:00 they determined that Mencken had died in his sleep between 3:00 and 4:00 a.m. The cause of death was a coronary.

In the reverse of the evangelical custom of being born again, Mencken died again. His first death had been the stroke of 1948 that took his livelihood of work, writing, and ideas. The second was the heart attack that took the rest of his living remains. For whatever reason, Mencken decided not to play God with his death. In the end, he let forces greater than himself determine his exit from the carnival that his talents had made even more entertaining than it was in itself.

CONCLUSION

Learning from H. L. Mencken

Mencken contrived a way of continuing to speak even from the urn that contained his ashes (which was buried with his family at Baltimore's Loudon Park Cemetery). In 1989 he was back in the news thanks to publication of his diaries, a collection of reflections begun in 1930 that turned especially dark in the 1940s as his career petered out. Mencken had specified that the diary, after being sealed for twenty-five years, should be available only to "students engaged in critical or historical investigation." Some letters suggested the possibility for a wider inspection. Attorneys decided the diary's fate and ruled that it could be published, which it was, though by then it reached a sensitive public that had little acquaintance with the full range of Mencken's opinions. Then came to light two more manuscripts that Mencken had left unpublished and wanted to remain so for a generation or so after his death. The first was another memoir, *My Life as an Author and Editor* (1991), and the second a recollection of his career as a journalist, *Thirty-Five Years of Newspaper Work* (1993).

Although Mencken's attitude toward Jews attracted the most attention—in a dozen or so instances, he identified various persons unflatteringly as "Jew"—the newly published material once again revealed his objections to Christianity. In his diaries, he described a number of exchanges and social engagements and so had less room for pontificating about ideas and institutions. For instance, he dined with Bishop James Cannon Jr. of the Methodist church, one of the chief proponents of Prohibition. By the 1930s they had become friends, and Mencken was helping Cannon gain access to the right physicians for "severe arthritis." They reminisced about politics and theology, and when Cannon

234

said that he agreed with J. Gresham Machen's theology but disagreed with his manner, Mencken observed that Cannon's "protest against an excess of vehemence . . . naturally amused me greatly." The diaries also described Mencken's "pleasant" times with J. B. Dudek, the Roman Catholic chancellor of the Oklahoma City Diocese, and a frequent consultant of Mencken's about matters linguistic. His "old friend" was on holiday, and over lunch and dinner Dudek talked to Mencken about the politics of the Roman Catholic hierarchy, the bishop's luxurious estate in Oklahoma, Dudek's manuscript on the Czech language, and the cleric's stamp collection.

In the other posthumous works, Mencken resorted to typical disparagement of Christian inanities. *My Life as an Author and Editor* had less directly provocative material about religion in the United States since it covered primarily Mencken's magazine work as a literary editor. Jonathan Yardley, who wrote the introduction, opined that Mencken's "impregnable self-confidence" was his "least appealing" trait. Mencken's recollection of his relationship to F. Scott Fitzgerald may have proved Yardley's point, though condescension comes to mind more than self-confidence. *The Great Gatsby* was for Mencken not much of a story, but at least as a "piece of writing" it was "sound and laudable." But in *Thirty-Five Years of Newspaper Work*, Mencken recalled his wider social circles and so accorded brief attention to Howard Kelly, one of the prize physicians at Johns Hopkins medical school and hospital who was also an evangelical Protestant, or as Mencken put it, "Bible Christian." Kelly annoyed Mencken because he "spent a large part of his time and even more of his money promoting all sorts of Pecksniffian causes—Prohibition, vice crusading, Sabbath observance, and so on." When Mencken began to "maul" such crusades, Mencken wrote, Kelly "remonstrated earnestly, and told me that he proposed to pray for me." Mencken reported that "I bade him do his damnedest, but predicted that he would never fetch me." When Mencken added to his list of buffooneries such "medical quackery" as antivaccination, antivivisection, and Christian Science, Kelly had to allow that Mencken "was not altogether evil, but nevertheless . . . kept on protesting against my animosity to Christian endeavor." Even though they achieved a sort of friendship, Mencken still regarded Kelly, as he did many of his Christian contemporaries, "the easiest mark that the wowsers of Baltimore had ever encountered . . . good for a substantial contribution to any pseudo-moral cause." That form of put-down of Protestant moral activism published in 1994 might have upset the likes of Jerry Falwell or Pat Robertson, if they or any evangelical social conservative like them knew or cared about Howard Kelly. As for Mencken's verdicts on the nation's literary figures, what possible good could his criticism of *The Great Gatsby* do for returning prayer and Bible reading to public schools?

That practically no one among the Religious Right decided to use Mencken's unflattering reentry into public life for his or her advantage was an indication of how little one of the most prolific and pungent writers of the first half of the twentieth century mattered to the second half. With concerns about evolution in Kansas public schools again taking on Tennessee proportions, and with Christian objections to secularization fueling so much of the evangelical Protestant base for the Republican Party, some Americans must have been surprised that Mencken's tarnished reputation did not become at least a talking point in the so-called culture wars of the 1980s. James Davison Hunter, the sociologist of religion who was one of the first to try to diagram the battle lines in that conflict, identified Mencken as giving voice to the secular and progressive disdain for religious orthodoxy. In *Culture Wars: The Struggle to Control the Family, Art, Education, Law, and Politics in America* (1992), Hunter cited Mencken's obituary of William Jennings Bryan and his "venomous" depiction of fundamentalism at the Scopes trial as "the judgment of an entire generation of progressively oriented church people and secular intellectuals." In his recent discussion of the culture wars, *A War for the Soul of America: A History of the Culture Wars* (2015), Andrew Hartman also points to Mencken's role in the Scopes trial as the one responsible for depicting fundamentalists as "rubes." Hartman includes a line from Edith Schaeffer, the wife of Francis Schaeffer, the so-called intellectual father of the Christian Right, who believed that Mencken "would never have written" about fundamentalists the way he did if he had met her. (Her son Frank would likely disagree.)

Even so, as much as Mencken's writing about fundamentalism haunted conservative Protestants who struggled with a reputation for being enemies of free thought and progress, only Richard John Neuhaus in his influential book *The Naked Public Square: Religion and Democracy in America* (1984) decided to take on Mencken. "For most Americans blessed or blighted by higher education," Neuhaus wrote, "everything associated with fundamentalism has been indelibly poisoned by the acid brilliance of H. L. Mencken and his innumerable imitators." Had Neuhaus been writing after the publication of Mencken's diaries and additional memoirs, perhaps he might have used the Baltimorean's declining reputation to associate secular intellectuals with unbelief's own assortment of embarrassments.

That no one else on the conservative side of the nation's cultural battle lines rose to employ Mencken against religion's cultured despisers was an indication of how his challenge to American Christianity ended not with a bang but a fizzle. His early embrace of Nietzsche attracted attention and gave Mencken a pose of superiority but hardly made Nietzschean philosophy a going concern. Nor, thanks to Mencken, did American culture become particularly receptive to things German. Perhaps because of the deep ties that attend the language that Mencken catalogued, Anglophilia remains secure. Americans do not watch *Hannes und der Bürgermeister*, but they do *Downton Abbey*. Mencken's brief against Puritanism was also part of what made him such a noteworthy literary critic during the second and third decades of the twentieth century, but the academy would soon reject Mencken's critique, first with Perry Miller, and then with the phalanx of students and colleagues who flocked to the universities founded by Puritans, Harvard and Yale, to locate the nation's exceptionalism in English Calvinism. Again, Mencken's role at the Scopes trial looms largest in the American imagination, hence the character E. K. Hornbeck in the 1960 movie *Inherit the Wind*. But evolution hardly stands secure either in the public school classroom or in the wider Christian world thanks to the efforts of people who make a case for Intelligent Design, the excesses of Darwinism, or arguments that people cannot be good with a creator they call God. The greatest evidence of Mencken's failure to dent American attitudes comes from the realm of politics. His ridicule of faith-based political causes, whether Prohibition or censorship, was legendary. But the mixture of religion and politics only became more potent since Mencken's death, both through religiously inspired causes and candidates, and through repeated invocations, started by John F. Kennedy, of the United States as a city on a hill. As for Mencken's verdict on democracy, elitism and hierarchy are lost causes even in the US Senate.

Despite his failures, might Americans still have something to learn from Mencken's observations and criticisms of religion and its effects? One group that could benefit are the so-called new atheists. Sam Harris rarely mentions Mencken, nor did the late Christopher Hitchens, though in 2006 he did speak at the annual Mencken Day festivities at

Enoch Pratt Library in Baltimore. But people who write about the new atheism sometimes lump Mencken with the modern proponents of contempt for Christianity. The sociologist of religion Peter Berger, for instance, recently observed that what characterize the current popular expressions of atheism are "its aggressiveness and its attitude of absolute certainty (in that curiously mirroring conservative Christianity, its main antagonist)." Berger went on to link new atheism to the older varieties on tap in Friedrich Nietzsche, Albert Camus, and Mencken. Of Mencken, Berger wrote:

> [Camus's atheism] was a far cry from the flippant contempt for religion that characterized H. L. Mencken (I would see him as a precursor of the post–1960s intelligentsia). He once proposed that the universe is a gigantic ferris wheel, that man is a fly who happened to land on it, and who thinks that the whole contraption was created for his benefit.

Berger did concede that Mencken's shallow view of religion should not detract from his status as "one of America's great satirists."

Humor is one matter that distinguishes Mencken from the new atheism, but it is not the only one. Sam Harris, for instance, writes at the beginning of his *Letter to a Christian America* that his intention is "to demolish the intellectual and moral pretensions of Christianity in its most committed forms." He warns that liberal and moderate Christians may not recognize themselves in his demolition project, but they will certainly understand "one hundred and fifty million of their neighbors." Where Harris sees bogeys, Mencken saw amusing collections of human foibles; Harris's cockiness might even amuse Mencken. In *Treatise on the Gods*, Mencken took almost the opposite approach to Christianity. Of the people who wrote about religion and in contrast to those who were "fanatical, and believe in it too much," the new atheists qualify as "those who hate it, and abuse it too much." Mencken claimed to be an "amiable" skeptic, someone "quite devoid of the religious impulse." But that did not mean that Mencken was out to discredit religion or its adherents necessarily:

> [N]o matter what may be said against [religion] on evidential grounds, it must be manifest that [it has] conditioned the thinking of mankind since the infancy of the race. . . . Thus [it deserves] examination in a

fair and scientific spirit. . . . [D]ismissing the thing itself as a mere aberration is a proceeding that is far more lofty than sensible. What has been so powerful in its effects upon human history deserves sober study, whether it be an aberration or not.

Such begrudging respect also accounts for the difference between Mencken's and Harris's views of liberal Christianity. Where Harris seems to prefer liberal theology for its affinities to atheism, for Mencken modernism was "completely incompatible, not only with anything rationally describable as Christianity, but also with anything deserving to pass as religion in general." He added that religion, "if it is to retain any genuine significance, can never be reduced to a series of sweet attitudes, possible to anyone not actually in jail for felony." To see in Mencken nothing but disdain of religion is to read only a few sound bites and neglect the bulk of his comments, both pithy and elaborate, about Christianity.

Equally important is Mencken's commitment to offending everyone. Unlike the new atheists, Mencken could ridicule secular notions of salvation and progress as much as Christian varieties. Of course, he had a high estimate of reason, or at least his own faculties. But his opposition to the prosecution at the Scopes trial did not rest on some belief that humanity would only reach its final destiny of peace and justice if Darwin triumphed over Moses. Instead, Mencken's beef with Bryan boiled down to honesty. Rebranding the cosmology of the ancient Hebrews as biological instruction was simply dishonest. Still, Mencken had no hope that teaching evolutionary biology to America's youth would usher in a better world. In fact, Mencken was not altogether confident that even his own efforts amounted to anything meaningful. His own estimate of his work could be stunningly candid:

> The vanity of man is quite illimitable. In every act of his life, however trivial, and particularly in every act which pertains to his profession, he takes all the pride of a baby learning to walk. It may seem incredible but it is nevertheless a fact that I myself get great delight out of writing such banal paragraphs as this one. The physical business of writing is extremely unpleasant to me, as it is to most other human beings, but the psychic satisfaction of discharging bad ideas in worse English is enough to make me forget it entirely. I am almost as happy, writing, as a judge is on his bench, listening with one ear to

the obscene wrangles of two scoundrelly attorneys, or a bishop in his *cathedra*, proving non-sensically that God loves the assembled idiots.

That is vintage Mencken—a swipe at religion cheek by jowl with a shot at lawyers—as well as himself.

Not to turn Mencken into a sage, which is the wrong way to read him, but contemporary readers, especially the combatants on both sides of the culture wars, could well learn from the Aristotle of Baltimore the virtue of not taking themselves too seriously. Since my own credentials as a Christian who studies the history of Christianity will not go far among secularists, I will not presume to think that this book's positive estimate of Mencken will be persuasive among unbelievers. But if secularists were to read more Mencken, along with contemporary humorists like P. J. O'Rourke and Christopher Buckley, they might nurture in themselves Mencken's pervasive sense that humans suffer from folly as much as they excel at covering it up.

The tougher sell for Mencken's brand of self-skepticism is the believers whose convictions invariably apply a dose of divine blessing to most human activities in hopes of elevating the trivial and ordinary to levels sublime and sacred. What might help believers resonate with Mencken is a recognition that he echoed the sentiments of portions of Holy Writ, namely, the counsel of the wisest king in the history of redemption who was also struck by the pervasiveness of human folly and meaninglessness "under the sun." No doubt, Mencken would be uncomfortable with—even disdainful of—a comparison to Scripture. But when Mencken saw folly everywhere he looked, even in his own inability to make sense of the world, was he not echoing precisely Solomon's understanding of the follies and pleasures of human existence this side of death?

> For what happens to the children of man and what happens to the beasts is the same; as one dies, so dies the other. They all have the same breath, and man has no advantage over the beasts, for all is vanity. All go to one place. All are from the dust, and to dust all return. Who knows whether the spirit of man goes upward and the spirit of the beast goes down into the earth? So I saw that there is nothing better than that a man should rejoice in his work, for that is his lot. Who can bring him to see what will be after him? (Ecclesiastes 3:19–22 ESV)

Like Solomon, Mencken recognized the follies and pleasures of life. He understood the appeal of religion as one of "man's bold efforts . . . to penetrate the unknowable, to put down the intolerable, to refashion the universe nearer to his heart's desire." But in the end, religion was as much a testament to human "imbecility" as it was to man's "high striving." That left Mencken, like Solomon, with the consolation of work, food and drink, and friends. He did not try to inflate his own capacity to "put down the intolerable," his ability to go on with life in the face of its meaninglessness, into a program for psychological well-being, let alone a movement.

That kind of honesty should gain at least as much respect for Mencken from believers as he many times paid to Christianity. Still, his recognition of the limits of human existence, the race's inability to crawl out of its misery, let alone to immanentize the eschaton (bring heaven down to earth), the various ways that people (believers especially) deluded themselves into thinking that they were ushering in God's kingdom on earth—this pessimism about human endeavor is one that has generally been foreign to American Christianity. Perhaps one of the best illustrations of the congenital gullibility of American Christians is their propensity for civil religion. Could any average citizen imagine a pastor or priest or pious American ever writing what Mencken wrote about Abraham Lincoln?

> Lincoln becomes the American solar myth, the chief butt of American credulity and sentimentality. . . . All the popular pictures of him show him in his robes of state, and wearing an expression fit for a man about to be hanged. . . . Worse, there is an obvious effort to pump all his human weaknesses out of him, and so leave him a mere moral apparition, a sort of amalgam of John Wesley and the Holy Ghost. What could be more absurd? Lincoln, in point of fact, was a practical politician of long experience and high talents, and by no means cursed with idealistic superstitions.

When it came to the Gettysburg Address, Mencken was equally blunt about the gauze of idealism that clouded citizens' and saints' vision:

> But let us not forget that it is poetry, not logic; beauty, not sense. . . . The doctrine is simply this: that the Union soldiers who died at Gettysburg sacrificed their lives to the cause of self-determination—"that

government of the people, by the people, for the people," should not perish from the earth. It is difficult to imagine anything more untrue. The Union soldiers in that battle actually fought *against* self-determination; it was the Confederates who fought for the right of their people to govern themselves.

That sort of candor was also evident in Mencken's assessment of George Washington, another American statesman that Christians in the United States have turned into a model of sanctity:

> If George Washington were alive today, what a shining mark he would be for the whole camorra of uplifters, forward-lookers and professional patriots! He was the Rockefeller of his time, the richest man in the United States, a promoter of stock companies, a land-grabber, an exploiter of mines and timber. He was a bitter opponent of foreign entanglements, and denounced their evils in harsh, specific terms. He had a liking for all forthright and pugnacious men, and a contempt for lawyers, schoolmasters and all other such obscurantists. He was not pious. He drank whiskey whenever he felt chilly, and kept a jug of it handy. He knew far more profanity than Scripture, and used and enjoyed it more. He had no belief in the infallible wisdom of the common people, but regarded them as inflammatory dolts, and tried to save the Republic from them. He advocated no sure cure for all the sorrows of the world, and doubted that such a panacea existed. He took no interest in the private morals of his neighbors.

Whether Mencken was accurate in these comments is less important than what these observations say about his capacity to expose civil religion's pretense, idealism, and hollowness. Since Christians were (and still are) more prone to see only the best in people and situations, Mencken had more targets for his complaints about human gullibility in the believing sector of the population than among other groups. Even so, he objected to idealism wherever he found it—whether among Christians, Rotarians, politicians, or English literature professors. If Christians felt singled out, their sensitivity likely said more about an incapacity for troubling thoughts than it did about Mencken's prejudices.

Mencken acknowledged that his outlook was unappealing because it lacked hope. In one of his discussions of faith, the people he ridiculed were not Christians but socialists. Mencken followed Henry James and divided humanity into two groups, the tough- and the tender-minded. The former "demanded proofs before they will believe." The latter, like socialists, "are willing to believe anything that seems to be pleasant." He continued:

> [I]t is the tender-minded who keep the quacks of all sorts well-fed and active, and hence vastly augment the charm of this world. They find it wholly impossible to distinguish between what is subjectively agreeable and what is objectively true. Would it be nice if the whole world turned sober overnight, and even flappers put away the jug? If so, then there must be a quick and sure way to accomplish it. Does Prohibition promise to do so? If so, then Prohibition must be true.

The problem with Christianity for Mencken was that it nurtured tender-minded people, believers who in the face of enormous suffering and intractable wickedness thought such difficulties could be overcome, whether through right policies, education, or amusements, as if attendance at worship services would somehow reverse Christian Europe's endless pursuit of war.

To be sure, by placing himself in the camp of the tough-minded, Mencken separated himself from the rest of the herd. Still, he recognized that the skepticism he advocated had its own tender moments. It did not send a person down a one-way street of disillusionment or despair but simply made the tender-minded driver unhappy. Cynics themselves are "among the most comfortable and serene of mammals: perhaps only bishops, pet dogs and actors are happier." The reason was that cynics saw the truth, something "hard and harsh," but "solid under the feet":

> A cynic is chronically in the position of a wedding guest who has known the bride for nine years, and has had her confidence. He is a great deal less happy, theoretically, than the bridegroom. The bridegroom, beautifully barbered and arrayed, is about to launch into the honeymoon. But the cynic looks ahead two weeks, two months, two years. Such, to borrow a phrase from the late Dr. Eliot, are the durable satisfactions of life.

The irony was that the people who took hope from the Christian message were far worse equipped to deal with the hardships of human existence than was Mencken. For him, war, pestilence, hunger, misery were all part of the human predicament, never to be eradicated. For Christians (mostly), the adversity of human life usually came as a shock, possibly because a belief in the goodness of God had eliminated all recognition of human sinfulness and its relentless grip on human endeavor. Indeed, some Christians, those in the Augustinian tradition who conceded the depths of human depravity, could have given Mencken a run for his cynicism. Where they would have diverged was in placing the hope of the resurrection after a recognition of depravity. For Mencken, the peaceful and joyous hereafter was another ideal that lacked proof, simply a tender-minded idea to get through the hard night of human misery. But short of beliefs about human existence after death, Mencken could well have found more Christians to share his skepticism and iconoclasm had they taken seriously the very reason for the Christian gospel in the first place—human sinfulness and the concomitant incapacity of men and women to overcome its consequences. What happened to Christianity instead was that it morphed into a form of moralism and uplift, a sense that believers were more virtuous than unbelievers, and that the goal of the churches was to make more people ethical and thereby add to human flourishing. Mencken saw through that, both as an abandonment of historic Christianity and as laughably foolish. Christians interested in preserving the reasons for their hope might find in Mencken a surprising ally in diagnosing human existence this side of the new heavens and new earth.

But even if Mencken's despair about this world is too difficult a taste to acquire for contemporary believers, his outlook is at the very least a useful reminder of the antithetical character of Christianity. From George Washington to George W. Bush, American believers, with a few bumps in the road, have long asserted that religion is the proper basis for true community. Whether faith supplies a common morality or a shared purpose, whether this is a carryover from Constantinianism and European ecclesiastical establishments or simply a response to crime and licentiousness, the notion that religion unites has a long pedigree among Americans. That Christians would find this idea convincing is odd if only because the Bible and Christian doctrine highlight the fundamental difference between believers and unbelievers. Even more important, Scripture and theology generally recognize that Christians will be surrounded by people hostile to the faith until the day of Christ's second coming. Any Christian system that recognizes the fundamental antagonism between belief and unbelief, and that understands true faith as a minority position in a world dominated by falsehood and wickedness, should readily challenge the American assumption that religion unites.

If Christians want further support for questioning this American ideal, they need look no further than the unbelievers with whom they share space in the United States. Mencken is one among many useful resources for those who might consider how unbelievers live and move and have their being when surrounded by Christians. He was certainly aware of the way he differed from other Americans, and considering how deep those differences were, he was remarkably willing to live with them:

> My essential trouble, I sometimes suspect, is that I am quite devoid of what are called spiritual gifts. That is to say, I am incapable of religious experience, in any true sense. . . . I can no more understand a man praying than I can understand him carrying a rabbit's foot to bring him luck. This lack of understanding is a cause of enmities, and I believe that they are sound ones. I dislike any man who is pious, and all such men that I know dislike me.

As much as Mencken may have been unfriendly to the faithful, especially in the years his popularity was as high as his mockery of religion was acerbic, believers did not seem to consider the situation for a person, like Mencken, surrounded by believers (and their naïveté).

> [T]his deficiency is a handicap in a world peopled, in the overwhelming main, by men who are inherently religious. It sets me apart from my fellows and makes it difficult for me to understand many of their ideas and not a few of their acts. I see them responding constantly and robustly to impulses that to me are quite inexplicable. Worse, it causes these folks to misunderstand me, and often to do me serious injustice. They cannot rid themselves of the notion that because I am anesthetic to the ideas which move them most profoundly, I am, in some vague but nevertheless certain way, a man of aberrant morals, and hence one to be kept at a distance. I have never met a religious man who did not reveal this suspicion. No matter how earnestly he tried to grasp my point of view, he always ended by making an alarmed sort of retreat.

Part of the value of reading Mencken and his reactions to the very religious times in which he lived is to understand the limited appeal of religious and moral claims to people without faith. Christians should not need the jolt of reading Mencken to understand this. But if they do, they may at least be thankful that in Mencken's case, the reminder of faith's difference from unbelief comes with a chaser of laughter.

Notes on the Sources

Throughout this book I have relied on the exemplary cataloguing and interpretation of biographical minutiae, including quotations from primary and secondary sources, available in the most recent accounts of Mencken's life. Those include Fred Hobson's *Mencken: A Life* (New York: Random House, 1994), Terry Teachout's *The Skeptic: A Life of H. L. Mencken* (New York: HarperCollins, 2002), and Marion Elizabeth Rodgers's *Mencken: The American Iconoclast* (New York: Oxford University Press, 2005). Additional insights come from Joseph Epstein, "H. L. Mencken for Grownups," in *Partial Payments: Essays on Writers and Their Lives* (New York: Norton, 1989), 38–54; Joseph Epstein, "Mencken on Trial," in *Pertinent Players: Essays on the Literary Life* (New York: Norton, 1993), 222–45; Edward A. Martin, "H. L. Mencken," in *The Oxford Encyclopedia of American Literature*, ed. Jay Parini (New York: Oxford University Press, 2003), 99–111; Philip Wagner, *H. L. Mencken* (Minneapolis: University of Minnesota Press, 1966); Joseph Wood Krutch, "This Was Mencken, An Appreciation . . . ," *Nation*, February 11, 1956; Vincent Fitzpatrick, *H. L. Mencken* (Macon, GA: Mercer University Press, 1989); William Manchester, *H. L. Mencken: Disturber of the Peace* (New York: Collier Books, 1962); Charles A. Fecher, *Mencken: A Study of His Thought* (New York: Knopf, 1978); and Fred Hobson, *The Serpent in Eden: H. L. Mencken and the South* (Baton Rouge: Louisiana State University Press, 1995). One of the ironies of Mencken studies is the failure of the historical profession to turn its standards of judgment to the Baltimorean. Without a biography accepted as the norm among historians (as contested as those criteria sometimes are), Mencken studies remain a terrain where practically anyone with an interest in the subject and the stamina to wade through the vast sources can hoist his or her interpretive flag and watch it wave until the next invader arrives.

The best sources on Mencken's youth and early career remain his own memoirs. Library of America has recently produced a critical and expanded edition of *Happy Days*, *Newspaper Days*, and *Heathen Days* edited by Marion Elizabeth Rodgers: *H. L. Mencken: The Days Trilogy, Expanded Edition* (New York: Library Classics of the United States, 2014). Care must be applied, of course, in using Mencken as a source about himself and his motivations. Even so, these memoirs contain unrivaled insights into the nature of city life in Baltimore during the 1880s and the workings of a metropolitan daily in the early twentieth century. Even if Mencken sometimes looks better than he should—though he generally applied a healthy dose of self-deprecation—his eye for detail always reveals more (and possibly provides more accuracy) than even he realized.

His early efforts at nonjournalistic writing are available in a number of sources. *Menckeniana*, a quarterly magazine published by Enoch Pratt Free Library in Baltimore, regularly includes never-before-published fiction, poetry, and essays by Mencken along with articles about him. S. T. Joshi, *H. L. Mencken: An Annotated Bibliography* (Lanham, MD: Scarecrow Press, 2009), includes a comprehensive list of all of Mencken's writings, including his more than fifty books and all their editions, from *Ventures in Verse* (1903) to *Carnival of Buncombe* (1956). Among the collections of Mencken's essays and criticism, William H. Nolte's *H. L. Mencken's Smart Set Criticism* (Washington, DC: Regnery/Gateway, 1987) assembles a large sampling of the author's first efforts. Michael Schudson's *Discovering the News: A Social History of American Newspapers* (New York: Basic Books, 1981) provides a helpful perspective on the newsroom that Mencken encountered when he started as a reporter.

For insights on Mencken's work as a magazine editor, again the subject himself affords some of the best material. S. T. Joshi's *Mencken on Mencken: A New Collection of Autobiographical Writings* (Baton Rouge: Louisiana State University Press, 2010) presents several essays on the workings of the *Smart Set* and the *American Mercury*. Louis Hatchett's *Mencken's America* (Macon, GA: Mercer University Press, 2002) assembles the news stories that caught Mencken's eye while editing the *American Mercury*. The remarkable story of Mencken's brush with the law during the "Hatrack" incident again comes from his own telling in *The Editor, the Bluenose, and the Prostitute: H. L. Mencken's History of the "Hatrack" Censorship Case*, ed. Carl Bode (New York: R. Rinehart, 1988).

Paul S. Boyer, *Purity in Print: Book Censorship in America from the Gilded Age to the Computer Age* (Madison: University of Wisconsin Press, 2002), gives historical perspective to Mencken's struggle. Henry S. May, *The End of American Innocence: A Study of the First Years of Our Own Time, 1912–1917* (New York: Columbia University Press, 1959), locates Mencken's instincts and accomplishments as an editor within the beginnings of literary modernism in the United States. For perspective on the Scopes trial and Mencken's role in it, readers should consult Edward J. Larson, *Summer for the Gods: The Scopes Trial and America's Continuing Debate over Science and Religion* (New York: Basic Books, 2006).

Mencken's own achievement as a writer took shape primarily in his essays. His own assessment of his writings undergirds the pieces he chose to reprint in these anthologies, the most important of which were his *Prejudices* series, recently installed in the Library of America series: *H. L. Mencken: Prejudices, First, Second, and Third Series*, ed. Marion Elizabeth Rodgers (New York: Library Classics of the United States, 2010); *H. L. Mencken: Prejudices, Fourth, Fifth, and Sixth Series*, ed. Marion Elizabeth Rodgers (New York: Library Classics of the United States, 2010). Other anthologies that Mencken assembled were H. L. Mencken, *A Mencken Chrestomathy* (New York: Knopf, 1949), and H. L. Mencken, *A Second Mencken Chrestomathy*, ed. Terry Teachout (New York: Knopf/Doubleday, 2013). Again, a number of editors have collected Mencken's essays around specific themes. Of great help for this book was S. T. Joshi's *H. L. Mencken on Religion* (Amherst, NY: Prometheus Books, 2002). Another collection that shows the range of Mencken's energetic mind is Marion Elizabeth Rodgers's *The Impossible H. L. Mencken: A Selection of His Best Newspaper Stories* (New York: Doubleday, 1991). A tribute to the force of Mencken's prose and argument is that he sustained an audience for occasional pieces that remained fresh even after several decades.

To classify some of Mencken's writing as serious as opposed to ephemeral does not do justice to the craft that all his work shows. But in a special class go his trilogy on serious topics along with his study of the American language and a collection of quotations. These include: H. L. Mencken, *Notes on Democracy* (New York: Knopf, 1926); H. L. Mencken, *Treatise on the Gods* (New York: Knopf, 1930); H. L. Mencken, *Treatise on Right and Wrong* (New York: Knopf, 1934); H. L. Mencken, *The American Language: A Preliminary Inquiry into the Development of English in the United States* (New York: Knopf, 1919); H. L. Mencken, *The Ameri-*

can Language: A Preliminary Inquiry into the Development of English in the United States, Supplement I (New York: Knopf, 1945); H. L. Mencken, *The American Language: A Preliminary Inquiry into the Development of English in the United States, Supplement II* (New York: Knopf, 1948); and H. L. Mencken, *A New Dictionary of Quotations on Historical Principles from Ancient and Modern Sources* (New York: Knopf, 1942).

Mencken's rehabilitation in the 1940s, after his sardonic observations looked out of place in Depression-era America, owed much to his memoirs trilogy, *Happy Days* (1939), *Newspaper Days* (1940), and *Heathen Days* (1941), cited above. His autobiographical reflections hit a nerve and prompted him to tally up other recollections that were only published, according to his intentions, posthumously: H. L. Mencken, *My Life as Author and Editor*, ed. Jonathan Yardley (New York: Vintage Books, 1992); and H. L. Mencken, *Thirty-Five Years of Newspaper Work: A Memoir*, ed. Fred Hobson, Vincent Fitzpatrick, and Bradford Jacobs (Baltimore: Johns Hopkins University Press, 1996). Mencken did not wish for his diaries, written in the same era, to be published, but those responsible for adjudicating his wishes thought otherwise, and *The Diary of H. L. Mencken*, ed. Charles A. Fecher (New York: Knopf, 1989) is the result. Editors have also brought into print a number of collections of Mencken's private papers, such as his correspondence: Guy J. Forgue, ed., *Letters of H. L. Mencken* (New York: Knopf, 1961); Carl Bode, ed., *The New Mencken Letters* (New York: Doubleday, 1977); Thomas P. Riggio, ed., *Dreiser-Mencken Letters: The Correspondence of Theodore Dreiser & H. L. Mencken, 1907–1945*, 2 vols. (Philadelphia: University of Pennsylvania Press, 1986, 1996); Marion Elizabeth Rodgers, ed., *Mencken and Sara: A Life in Letters; The Correspondence of H. L. Mencken and Sara Haardt* (New York: Anchor Books, 1992); Edward Alexander Martin, ed., *In Defense of Marion: The Love of Marion Bloom & H. L. Mencken* (Athens: University of Georgia Press, 1996); S. T. Joshi, ed., *From Baltimore to Bohemia: The Letters of H. L. Mencken and George Sterling* (Madison, NJ: Farleigh Dickinson University Press, 2001); and Peter Dowell, ed., *Ich Kuss die Hand: The Letters of H. L. Mencken to Gretchen Hood* (Tuscaloosa: University of Alabama Press, 2003). Betty Adler's *Man of Letters: A Census of the Correspondence of H. L. Mencken* (Baltimore: Enoch Pratt Free Library, 1969) remains the best guide to the scope of Mencken's letters and is an indication of the important and impressive efforts that Baltimore's city library, Enoch Pratt Free Library, has conducted for years in preserving and promoting the writings and related activities of Mencken.

Mencken was by no means the most important thinker of his generation. Some might argue that he does not measure up as an intellectual because he was undisciplined and untrained in his most serious reflection. But Mencken's relationship to the canon of American letters and ideas raises a host of poignant questions about who gets in and what it takes. Is Mencken any less of an intellectual or any less prolific than Ralph Waldo Emerson? Neither figure was a scholar, and neither writer identified with a school of systematic thought. Yet the connections that Emerson had to the most important university in the United States, Harvard, and his location in New England give him credentials that writers like Mencken, living in out-of-the-way places and unaffiliated with the professoriate, lack. That a definitive, academically approved biography of Mencken does not exist is just one indication of his odd position in the ranks of American intellectuals and writers. Mencken continues to receive attention from a host of editors and authors, from amateurs to literary scholars. But without a standard, academically certified account (from the historical profession and worthy university press) of Mencken's life and work, he remains a figure on the margins. If he had moved to New York, his reputation may have turned out differently, which is an indication that he is responsible in large measure for his relative isolation. Even so, his life provides a poignant window on the hierarchy of American intellectuals that persists in a nation that relishes equality. The aristocrat in Mencken might appreciate the irony.

Index